CONTEMPORARY AMERICAN WOMEN WRITERS

Longman Critical Readers

General Editor

Stan Smith, Professor of English, University of Dundee

Published Titles

CONTEMPORARY AMERICAN WOMEN WRITERS: GENDER, CLASS, ETHNICITY

Edited and Introduced by

LOIS PARKINSON ZAMORA

LONGMAN
LONDON AND NEW YORK

Addison Wesley Longman Limited
Edinburgh Gate
Harlow, Essex CM20 2JE
England
and Associated Companies throughout the world

Published in the United States of America
by Addison Wesley Longman Inc., New York

First published 1998

ISBN 0 582 22620-1 Paper
ISBN 0 582 22621-X Cased

Visit Addison Wesley Longman on the world wide web at
http://www.awl-he.com

British Library Cataloguing-in-Publication Data

A catalogue record for this book is available
from the British Library

Library of Congress Cataloging-in-Publication Data

Contemporary American women writers : gender, class, ethnicity /
  edited and introduced by Lois Parkinson Zamora.
    p. cm. — (Longman critical readers)
  Includes bibliographical references and index.
  ISBN 0–582–22621–X. — ISBN 0–582–22620–1 (pbk.)
    1. American literature—Women authors—History and criticism.
  2. Women and literature—United States—History—20th century.
  3. American literature—20th century—History and criticism.
  4. Gender identity in literature.   5. Social classes in literature.
  6. Ethnic groups in literature.   7. Sex role in literature.
  I. Zamora, Lois Parkinson.   II. Series.
  PS151.C667   1998
  810.9'9287'0904—dc21   98–16598
                                                        CIP

Set by 35 in 9/11½ pt Palatino
Produced by Addison Wesley Longman Singapore (Pte) Ltd.,
Printed in Singapore

Contents

General Editors' Preface

The outlines of contemporary critical theory are now often taught as a standard feature of a degree in literary studies. The development of particular theories has been a thorough transformation of literary criticism. For example, Marxist and Foucauldian theories have revolutionised Shakespeare studies, and 'deconstruction' has led to a complete reassessment of Romantic poetry. Feminist criticism has left scarcely any period of literature unaffected by its searching critiques. Teachers of literary studies can no longer fall back on a standardised, received methodology.

Lecturers and teachers are now urgently looking for guidance in a rapidly changing critical environment. They need help in understanding the latest revisions in literary theory, and especially in grasping the practical effects of the new theories in the form of theoretically sensitised new readings. A number of volumes in the series anthologise important essays on particular theories. However, in order to grasp the full implications and possible uses of particular theories it is essential to see them put to work. This series provides substantial volumes of new readings, presented in an accessible form and with a significant amount of editorial guidance.

Each volume includes a substantial introduction which explores the theoretical issues and conflicts embodied in the essays selected and locates areas of disagreement between positions. The pluralism of theories has to be put on the agenda of literary studies. We can no longer pretend that we all tacitly accept the same practices in literary studies. Neither is a *laissez-faire* attitude any longer tenable. Literature departments need to go beyond the mere toleration of theoretical differences: it is not enough merely to agree to differ; they need actually to 'stage' the differences openly. The volumes in this series all attempt to dramatise the differences, not necessarily with a view to resolving them but in order to foreground the choices presented by different theories or to argue for a particular route through the impasses the differences present.

The theory 'revolution' has had real effects. It has loosened the grip of traditional empiricist and romantic assumptions about language and literature. It is not always clear what is being proposed as the new agenda for literary studies, and indeed the very notion of 'literature' is questioned by the poststructuralist strain in theory. However, the uncertainties and obscurities of contemporary theories appear much less worrying when we see what the best critics have been able to do with them in practice. This series aims to disseminate the best of recent criticism and to show that it is possible to re-read the canonical texts of literature in new and challenging ways.

RAMAN SELDEN AND STAN SMITH

The Publishers and fellow Series Editor regret to record that Raman Selden died after a short illness in May 1991 at the age of fifty-three. Ray Selden was a fine scholar and a lovely man. All those he has worked with will remember him with much affection and respect.

Publisher's acknowledgements

We are grateful to the following for permission to reproduce copyright material:

the author, Norma Alarcon for 'Making *Familia* from Scratch: Split Subjectivities in the World of Helena Maria Viramontes and Cherrie Moraga' in *Chicana Creativity and Criticism: Charting New Frontiers in American Literature* Ed. Maria Herrera-Sobek and Helena M. Viramontes (Houston: Arte Publico Press, 1988); Frontiers Editorial Collective for the essay 'Claiming and Making: Ethnicity, Gender and the Common Sense in Leslie Marmon Silko's *Ceremony* and Zora Neale Hurston's *Their Eyes Were Watching God*' by Toni Flores in *Frontiers: A Journal of Women's Studies* 10, 3 (1989). Copyright © 1980 Frontiers Editorial Collective; Henry Holt & Co for extracts from *Tracks* by Louise Erdich in the article 'History, Postmodernism, and Louise Erdrich's *Tracks*' by Nancy J. Peterson in *Proceedings of the Modern Language Association* Vol. 109, v. (Oct. 1994) pp. 982–994; International Book Distributors Ltd (Prentice Hall)/University of Toronto Press for the essay 'History Memory and Language in Toni Morrison's *Beloved*' by Rebecca Ferguson in *Feminist Criticism: Theory and Practice* Toronto: University of Toronto Press 1991, pp. 109–127; the editor MELUS for the essay 'Native American Aesthetics: An Attitude of Relationship' by Sidner Larson in *Melus* 17, 3 (Fall 1991–2) pp. 53–67, and an extract from the essay 'Literary Foremothers and Writers' Silences: Tillie Olsen's Autobiographical Fiction' by Rose Kamel in *Melus* 12, 3 (Fall 1985) pp. 55–72; Modern Language Association of America for the article by Nancy J. Peterson 'History, Postmodernism, and Louise Erdrich's *Tracks*' in *Proceedings of the Modern Language Association* Vol. 109, v. (Oct. 1994) pp. 982–994; Oxford University Press and the author, Yvonne Yarbro-Bejarano for the article 'Gloria Anzaldua's Borderlands/La Frontera: Cultural Studies, "Difference," and the Non-Unitary Subject' from *Cultural Critique* 28 (Fall 1994) pp. 5–28; the author, Donna Perry her essay 'Initiation in Jamaica Kincaid's *Annie John*' in *Carribbean Women Writers: Essays from the First*

Publisher's acknowledgements

International Conference Ed. Cudjoe (Calaloux, 1990); State University of New York Press for the article 'Subject, Voice, and Women in Some Contemporary Black Women's Writing' by Mary O'Connor in *Feminism, Bakhtin and the Dialogic* Ed. Bauer & McKinstry (SUNY Press, 1991) pp. 199–217; the editor, Studies in Short Fiction for the article 'A Perfect Marginality: Public and Private Telling in the Stories of Grace Paley' by Victoria Aarons in *Studies in Short Fiction* 27, 1, 1990, pp. 35–43. Copyright 1990 by Newberry College; University of Chicago Press and the author, Thomas Foster for a shortened version of the essay 'History, Critical Theory, and Women's Social Practices: "Women's Time" and *Housekeeping*' in *Signs* 14: 1 (1988) Univ. Chicago Press; University of Toronto Press Inc and the author, Susan Koshy for the article 'The Geography of Female Subjectivity: Ethnicity, Gender and Diaspora' in *Diaspora* 3, 1 (1994) pp. 69–83; Wayne State University Press and the author, Malini Schueller for the article 'Questioning Race and Gender Definitions: Dialogic Subversions in *The Woman Warrior*' in *Criticism* 31, 4 (1989) pp. 421–437.

Author's acknowledgements

I am grateful to Veronica Toombs, Mousami Chowdhury Roy, and Melanie Malinowski for their intelligence and diligence in helping me to select and prepare this collection. Thanks also go to Stan Smith, and the staff at Addison Wesley Longman for their good advice, and their patience.

Lois Parkinson Zamora
May 1998

Introduction: Moveable Boundaries –
Public Definitions and Private Lives

This collection brings together critical essays that examine questions
of identity and community in the fiction of contemporary American
women writers. These critics consider how selves and societies are
dramatized in particular works of fiction and how they reflect cultural
communities outside the fictional frame – often the communities in
which their authors live and work. They ask how/whether definitions
of gender, race, ethnicity, and class have been constituted within these
communities or imposed from outside; how these definitions impel
or impede meaningful communities; and how/whether they may be
challenged, refused, revised. This fiction charts the moveable boundaries
of public definitions and private lives in a transitional period in the
United States – transition that has sometimes been gradual, sometimes
volatile, often painful and productive. The American writers under
discussion question the nature of community as such: its dangers and
desires, its necessary impositions upon individual lives and its equally
necessary accommodation of individual differences.

The increasing awareness in the United States of cultural diversity
– what Christopher Hitchens calls 'the hyphenate principle'[1] – has
encouraged (and been encouraged by) writers who foreground
multiple and co-existing cultural forms. The United States now
generally understands itself as an 'ethnocultural nation', and
contemporary women writers often engage the cultural dynamics of
this fact.[2] The essays included here concern fictional representations
of African American, Latino, Asian American, Native American, Anglo
and Euroamerican communities and their interactions in the multicultural
United States. Each critic asks, in his or her own way, how a particular
writer (or group of writers) transforms aspects of her (or their) social
grounding into language and works of literature. And each confronts the
'conceptual difficulty of theorizing difference', to use Yvonne Yarbro-
Bejarano's phrase from the first essay of the collection.

My own strategy for theorizing difference begins by gathering essays
on women writers from various racial, ethnic, and socio-economic

communities. In so doing, I aim to complicate the notion of 'minority' as it has been used historically in the United States, with its implication of marginalization and isolation from some vaguely defined 'mainstream'. Since the 1960s, the growing cultural and political awareness of minority groups has impelled a radical redefinition of 'mainstream' US culture, and recent literature has been both an agent and a beneficiary of this process. What I have found in this criticism, and in the literature it treats, is a longing for communal coherence in the face of failed or fragmented or emergent communities – a longing that exceeds simple notions of nostalgia (a projection backwards to some lost past) or utopianism (a projection forwards to some imagined future). A certain social idealism is inherent in this longing, but literary fictions must tie ideals to actual behaviours, social and personal. This literature does so, and its best critics are concerned to trace the process.

This collection, then, is interested in what it means to be an 'American' writer now, in the late twentieth century and the early twenty-first. We will see that 'American' is no longer defined by geographical or national borders but by cultural contact: several of the writers discussed here dramatize the ways in which cultures outside US territory impinge upon and enrich American communities. Nor is the historical context of this fiction limited to what is usually considered American history. African, Mexican, Caribbean, European Jewish, Moslem, Chinese, Native American are among the cultural diasporas that are recuperated and included in this amplified American cultural territory, as is the experience of displacement as such – the experience of immigrant communities longing at once to remember and forget. These multiple cultural perspectives are inseparable from feminist perspectives, as the following essays demonstrate. In contemporary fiction by American women, gender overarches and underpins questions of culture, class, and history.

By collecting essays on women writers from a variety of American cultural contexts, I hope to create an inclusive critical context. While recognizing the specific conditions and pressures operating in different racial, ethnic, and class contexts, the essays, when placed together, reveal affinities among these writers – affinities that are thematic, formal, and ideological. As a group, the essays have the effect of foregrounding the shared experiences of women in stressed or embattled communities, their shared possibilities of solidarity and autonomy, and their shared impulse to create a community of writers and readers. The need to overcome silence and share stories in a common speech community is an issue upon which all of these essays dwell. Individual identity is possible only after an acceptable communal identity has been established. The boundaries of society and self are moveable, but the territories remain stubbornly interdependent.

This process is discussed not only in the essays collected here but by virtually all critics of contemporary American women's fiction. They consider how individual identity, as it is dramatized in the work of fiction, depends upon the recuperation (or creation) of a usable communal past. Mary O'Connor epitomizes the relation of African American women writers to their unrepresented history by citing a statement from Alice Walker's *The Color Purple*: 'You black, you pore, you ugly, you a woman. Goddam, he say, you nothing at all.'[3] O'Connor argues that 'This nothingness – constituted by all that is the negative of society's values in race, class, and gender – may be seen as a place of origin for not only Alice Walker's *The Color Purple* but for much black feminist writing. It is a nothingness imposed from without, an entity defined by the patriarchal and white world of power and wealth' (32). Contemporary American women writers contest this 'nothingness' by dramatizing the painful process of constituting a cultural history and identity. Their characters create shared histories in order to confer significance upon the single self.

The problem, as O'Connor indicates, is not just the absence of history ('you nothing at all') but the presence of long histories distorted by negative stereotypes and oppressive cultural prescriptions. The historical past must be revised and reconstituted by turning oppressive images inside out, a process facilitated by the use of images from the mythic or legendary past. Yarbro-Bejarano analyses Gloria Anzaldúa's engagement of the Aztec goddess Coatlicue to create a 'mestiza consciousness' that bridges cultures and centuries. Nancy J. Peterson, in her discussion of Louise Erdrich's *Tracks*, foregrounds the process of 'forging a new historicity'[4] from Native American oral sources, as well as written ('official') records. Sidner Larson precedes Peterson in lamenting the imposition upon Native Americans of 'the logic of literacy, of the historical archive, rather than of changing collective memory'.[5] And Malini Schueller celebrates Maxine Hong Kingston's use of Chinese myths and ancient cultural practices to fill in the blanks of her family's history and her own.

This process takes literary form in metaphors, as these critics note: Rebecca Ferguson writes about 'rememory' in Toni Morrison's *Beloved*; Rose Kamel about Tillie Olsen's 'literary foremothers'; Thomas Foster about 'women's time' in Marilynne Robinson's *Housekeeping*; Victoria Aarons about the 'community of memory' in the short stories of Grace Paley; Toni Flores about 'common sense' in Leslie Marmon Silko's *Ceremony* and Zora Neale Hurston's *Their Eyes Were Watching God*. Such historicizing strategies would seem to be related to the poststructuralist displacement of history by textuality, but they are not. In fact, these narrative (re)constructions are impelled by very different motives than those assumed by poststructuralist theory. As Nancy J. Peterson points out in her essay on Louise Erdrich's *Tracks*, to dismiss history is the luxury of those who have written it. For those who have not, creating a usable past is the necessary first step.

The convergence of critical attention on this point foregrounds a basic experience that cuts across cultural lines in the United States: community is often a matter of recuperating what has been overshadowed or destroyed by official (*un*moveable) public definitions. Women writers are especially good at challenging such fixity because women have been constrained by public definitions even as we are asked to maintain and perpetuate them. Women are, therefore, likely to depict their cultural communities as unjustly treated in relation to institutions *outside* the community (legal, economic, educational structures) and themselves – as women – unjustly treated *within* their community. Here, the moveable boundaries of public definition and private life require that characters (and writers) negotiate multiple cultural contexts. 'Split subjectivity' and 'mestiza' or 'border consciousness' are Yarbro-Bejarano's metaphors for this negotiation; she also uses 'non-unitary subject' and 'migratory subjectivity' to discuss Gloria Anzaldúa's bicultural 'Coatlicue state'. Mikhail Bakhtin's 'dialogism' allows Mary O'Connor, Thomas Foster, and Malini Schueller to theorize a plural self, as do the concepts of 'diaspora' and 'dislocation' in Susan Koshy's essay.

In short, these critics may not agree on what the self is, but they agree on what it is *not*: it is not singular but several, not fixed but fluid, shifting, dialogic, intersubjective, communicative, communal. Identity is itself mobile, moveable. In her essay on Maxine Hong Kingston's *The Woman Warrior*, Malini Schueller writes: 'What is politically important for women and racial minorities is not to frame correct definitions of female and ethnic identity but to question all such definitions. Above all it means to reject the concept of a stable and autonomous self upon which such definitions depend' (52). Rebecca Ferguson, analysing a passage from Toni Morrison's *Beloved*, writes that 'the self exists both subjectively and objectively, but never integrally . . .' (162). Both *The Woman Warrior* and *Beloved* include ghosts that epitomize the instability and unknowability of the self, as well as the impossibility of drawing any boundary at all between past and present. Ghosts or not, in the fiction under consideration in these essays, characters are valorized not as isolated or autonomous individuals but as parts of the larger frameworks of family, neighbourhood, nation, culture, the mythic past. In fiction by contemporary American women writers, individual psychology is now linked to what we might call a collective communal psyche.

Subjectivity is several, social, and it is embodied. In their different ways, these essays theorize female sexuality and the gendered body. Yarbro-Bejarano writes of 'the lived experience of the ways is which race, class and gender converge' (12), and she uses Cherríe Moraga's concept of a 'theory in the flesh' to elaborate her own theory of 'gendered racial identities' or 'racialized gender identities'. Lesbian sexuality is theorized by Norma Alarcón in terms of Gloria Anzaldúa's 'neither/nor' in Helena M. Viramontes's story 'Growing' and Cherríe Moraga's *Giving Up the Ghost*. In these latter works, Alarcón engages Julia Kristeva's theory of the 'symbolic contract' and Luce Irigaray's discussion of 'irreconcilable bodies' to discuss dramas of self-division in which female characters' bodies are split into a physical body and a socially determined (commodified) body. Here, the boundaries between public definitions and private, physical realities are not moveable but set in cement, and separated by an unbreachable gap. This gap leads Alarcón to conclude, along with Toril Moi, that 'woman' is 'that which cannot be represented, that which is not spoken, that which remains outside naming and ideologies'.[6]

Perhaps. But it is a telling irony that speech (and, more specifically, storytelling) is frequently viewed as an antidote to displacement and isolation in contemporary American women's fiction. This idea flies in the face of poststructuralist discussions of language, including Moi's, that focus on what is *deferred* by signs: what is repressed, mediated, or otherwise compromised by oppressive cultural narratives. American women writers may thematize language as sedimented layers of occluded or contaminated or erased meanings, but they are potentially meaningful layers nonetheless. In their telling, language may serve to *construct* narratives, as well as be deconstructed by them. Stories may *reveal* cultural meanings, as well as defer them. Historical recuperation and narrative creation are inseparable activities, a situation that gives rise to action rather than philosophical disengagement. This action – this 'discursive production of consciousness', to use Yarbro-Bejarano's descriptive phrase – is very different from the plot projected by poststructualist theory, in which the poststructuralist speaker is no longer agent but acted upon. The contrary is true in this fiction. The characters' potential mastery is usually dramatized as oral rather than written – another departure from poststructuralist theory, which privileges written language over spoken speech.[7] In fact, discursive self-formation is *the* central drama of this fiction, and it is a drama that actively engages 'the revolutionary potential of language', to cite Donna Perry's essay on Jamaica Kincaid.[8] So we see what Thomas Foster means, in his essay on Marilynne Robinson, when he speaks of the 'feminist expropriation of deconstruction' by both the writers and the critics of this fiction.

Strands of speech and silence are interwoven in these texts, and they condition the possibility of selfhood for both writers and characters. If silence is the prescription of the patriarchal mainstream for women, 'voice' is a manifestation of resistance to that mainstream – a manifestation of psychic energy in the service of self-formation.[9] In her essay on Tillie Olsen, Rose Kamel discusses the thematics of silence in gendered terms, citing Olsen's dramatized dialectic between a woman writer 'in need of a voice, and a silence societally imposed, psychically internalized' (202). Inverting Harold Bloom's concept of the anxiety of influence, Kamel argues that for women, locating 'literary foremothers' is empowering rather than anxiety-producing. If, in Bloom's account, male writers eschew (or 'misread') their literary predecessors, women writers seek them out and struggle to (re)connect. They value origins over originality, for a tradition of one's own allows women's voices to be heard.

Speech is, then, an antidote to isolation, and its metaphoric instantiation, 'voice', runs throughout this fiction and its criticism. As a critical concept, 'voice' responds to specific ideological and psychological imperatives as 'language' does not. Characters become intersections of dialogue, shifting composites of 'voices' in particularized cultural contexts. Maxine Hong Kingston's persona in *The Woman Warrior* is perhaps the most explicit example of this 'multivocal' self, as Malini Schueller demonstrates, but other examples abound. Mary O'Connor illustrates the positive charge given to this process in her essay on African American writers: 'The more voices that are ferreted out, the more discourses that a woman can find herself an intersection of, the freer she is from one dominating voice . . .' (35). O'Connor engages Bakhtin's discussion of the novel's dialogic form in order to address the ways in which characters (and their authors) constitute multivocal discourses of their own design.

Not surprisingly, the narrative forms created to contain these designs transgress the expected conventions of literary genres. If characters seek selfhood along the moveable boundaries of public and private realms, their authors operate along the moveable boundaries of genres. Poetry is interspersed with prose, and history, legend, and myth go hand in hand. As I have already suggested, the writers discussed here con/fuse the complementary impulses to record and to imagine, creating brilliant mixtures of myth, history, and the remembered past. In such mixtures, autobiography and fiction naturally overlap and invade each other's usual territory. Because 'ethnicity is something reinvented and reinterpreted in each generation', the anthropologist Michael Fischer argues that autobiographical writing is as necessary as it is inevitable.[10] Referring implicitly to Kingston's *The Woman Warrior*, Fischer comments that being Chinese in America is not the same thing as being Chinese-American: 'there is no role model for becoming Chinese-American. It is a matter of finding a voice or style that does not violate one's several components of identity' (196). Even women writers who do not explicitly engage issues of ethnicity or race are likely to write autobiographically, as Tillie Olsen illustrates. Thus, critics correctly suppose a proximity between women's fiction and their lived experience and, more than critics of male writers, they depend upon personal interviews for critical insight.[11]

This con/fusion of generic conventions is addressed in several of the following essays. Yarbro-Bejarano cites Gloria Anzaldúa's characterizations of *Borderlands* as a 'crazy dance', a 'mosaic' that 'spills over the boundaries', offering a 'hybridization of metaphor' that refuses the neat dichotomy of 'deep structure' and 'smooth surfaces' (22). Metaphors proliferate, but whatever she labels it, Yarbro-Berjarano is correct: *Borderlands* does not conform to recognizable rules of the novel, autobiography or the personal essay. Con/fusion of temporal strata also challenges usual generic structures. Rebecca Ferguson shows how, in Morrison's *Beloved*, official history and women's 'rememory' operate simultaneously and also oppositionally: 'While those parts of the narrative that deal with the Reconstruction era set up a linear, progressive chronology, the text is fragmented – shattered, one might say – by what is termed "rememory": the continual entry and re-entry of past into present. . . . This deeper memory is expressed above all in a constant emphasis on recurrence and synchrony; the text dwells on images, sensory impressions, phrases and metaphors which connect and repeat themselves so often that it has the force of an obsession, a highly poetic haunting' (158).

Quoting Julia Kristeva, Thomas Foster, too, links generic innovation to the multiple and contradictory histories that operate simultaneously in women's lives and literary works. 'Women's time', as Kristeva calls this complex historical positioning, requires 'the insertion into history and the radical *refusal* of the subjective limitations imposed by this history's time on an experiment carried out in the name of the irreducible difference'.[12] Following Kristeva, Foster argues that the confrontation among temporal orders opens up a space in which to revise the very premises of historical interpretation. The generic structures that accommodate such revision will 'restore conflict, ambiguity, and tragedy to the centre of historical process'.[13] Add to this feminist revision the cultural and racial diversity of the writers discussed in these essays: the result is that their narratives generally defy the linear causality and chronology of conventional novelistic structure.

In a relatively short period of time, the canon of American literature has been challenged and enlarged by these writers. In American universities, their fiction is read in 'women's courses' as well as in ethnically and racially based curricula – Mexican American literature, Asian American literature, African American literature, Native American studies. Such courses and curricula have revitalized the ways in which American literature is taught. Twenty-five years ago, the canonized greats of American literature – Poe, Hawthorne, Melville, Whitman,

James, Adams, Fitzgerald, Faulkner, Hemingway – were rarely
interrupted by women's voices, much less by writers from communities
defined by race or ethnicity. Now, American students will certainly have
read works by Morrison, Hurston, Kingston, Erdrich, Cisneros, and often
in more classes than one. This development is, I think, a grass roots one.
The presence of feminist and multicultural perspectives has been
impelled not so much by professors as by readers who are asking
questions about the nature of communal identity in America, and finding
brilliant responses in the work of contemporary women writers.

And it hardly needs stating that this canonical revolution is not
limited to American readers. The current interest in 'postcolonial'
writing worldwide obviously encompasses the literature written by
American women: Toni Morrison's Nobel Prize confirms the point, if
confirmation were necessary. The critical essays included here conform
to postcolonialist positions in their treatment of subjectivity and identity,
place and displacement. They react to dominant discourses imposed
upon colonized subjects (usually female) and propose alternative ways
to constitute and convey the experiences of those subjects.

The accessibility of contemporary American women's writing has been
enhanced by numerous anthologies of critical essays. This collaborative
approach departs notably from other areas of contemporary literary
theory. Take, for example, the poststructuralists – Barthes, Bhabha,
Bloom, Derrida, Foucault, Jameson, Lyotard – who remain singular
authorities presiding over their own staked territory, even as they
contest the hierarchies and hegemonies of such territorialism. To the
contrary, the prevalence of critical anthologies (including this one) on
American women's writing suggests that, at least for now, critics prefer
choruses to solos. When these critics do refer to poststructuralist theory,
it is to question its applicability to the experiences of women and
oppressed peoples. So, Rebecca Ferguson quotes Toni Morrison as
saying that 'black women had to deal with "post-modern" problems
in the nineteenth century and earlier. . . . Certain kinds of dissolution,
the loss of and the need to reconstruct certain kinds of stability . . .'
(156). While poststructuralist theory may have been useful to critics
of contemporary American women's writing in foregrounding
the institutional operations of power, the following essays use
poststructuralism largely for the purpose of distinguishing more
relevant paradigms.

What are these more relevant paradigms? I have mentioned a number
of them: the repeated reference to literary theorists who stress
intersubjective contexts and relational knowing – Bakhtin, Kristeva,
Irigaray, Cixous, Moi – as well as to cultural critics working to define
multicultural American histories and collectivities – Spillers, hooks,
Anzaldúa, Hutcheon. You will find that the authors of these essays are

phenomenologists in their concern for the lived experience of embodied subjects, Marxian in their concern for the material bases of that lived experience, and anthropologists and folklorists in their concern for culturally legitimated narratives of race, gender, class, and ethnicity. In short, they are eclectic opportunists, as they must be to negotiate the moveable/moving boundaries in contemporary fiction by American women writers. And as we must be, to read their work with sensitivity and pleasure.

Notes

1. Hitchens defines this principle as the preference of old and new minorities 'to emphasize their micro-diversities, while many among the majority regard that very stress as un-American . . .'. *New York Times Book Review*, 25 June 1995, p. 7.

2. The quoted term is MICHAEL LIND's in *The Next American Nation: The New Nationalism and the Fourth American Revolution* (New York: The Free Press, 1995). Lind's distinctions among the stages of US demographic structures and ideological attitudes towards difference are useful: he proposes Anglo-America (1789–1861), Euro-America (1875–1957), and Multicultural America (1972–present).

3. ALICE WALKER, *The Color Purple* (New York: Pocket Books, 1982), p. 187.

4. Peterson quotes this phrase from DIANA FUSS's essay, 'Getting into History', *Arizona Quarterly* 45, 4 (1989): 95.

5. Larson cites JAMES CLIFFORD's *The Predicament of Culture* (Cambridge, MA: Harvard University Press, 1988), p. 329.

6. TORIL MOI, *Sexual/Textual Politics: Feminist Literary Theory* (New York: Methuen, 1986), p. 163.

7. In *Of Grammatology* and *Writing and Difference*, both originally published in 1967, Jacques Derrida argues for the primacy of the written or printed word. Spoken speech is relegated to an inferior status by Derrida because it supposedly reinforces an illusory 'metaphysics of presence' – the mistaken sense that the world can be known: '. . . the thought of the thing as *what* it *is* has already been confused with the experience of pure speech; and this experience has been confused with experience *itself*. Now, does not pure speech require inscription somewhat in the manner that the Leibnizian essence requires existence and pushes on toward the world, like power toward the act?' Virtually all poststructuralists have followed Derrida on this point. JACQUES DERRIDA, 'Force and Signification', in *Writing and Difference*, trans. Alan Bass (Chicago: University of Chicago Press, 1978), p. 9 (Derrida's emphasis).

8. In this context, Perry also refers to Paule Marshall, the daughter of Barbadian immigrants, who repeatedly equates talking with empowerment. See the 1982 interview of Marshall by SABINE BRÖCK, 'Talk as a Form of Action', in

History and Tradition in Afro-American Culture, ed. Gunter H. Lenz (Frankfurt: University of Frankfurt Press, 1989), pp. 194–206.

9. TONI MORRISON complicates this binary in her essay 'Unspeakable Things Unspoken: The Afro-American Presence in American Literature', *Michigan Quarterly Review* 28, 1 (1989): 1–34. Morrison argues that there are many kinds of silence, some of them as eloquent as speech.

10. MICHAEL FISCHER, 'Ethnicity and the Post-modern Arts of Memory', in *Writing Culture: The Poetics and Politics of Ethnography*, ed. James Clifford and George E. Marcus (Berkeley: University of California Press, 1990), p. 198.

11. I have listed a number of collected interviews with contemporary American women writers in my bibliography, but the most helpful interviews are still to be found separately in literary critical journals.

12. JULIA KRISTEVA, 'Women's Time', trans. Alice Jardine and Harry Blake, in *Feminist Theory: A Critique of Ideology*, ed. Nannerl O. Keohane, Michelle Z. Rosaldo, and Barbara C. Gelpi (Chicago: University of Chicago Press, 1982), p. 38.

13. Thomas Foster quotes this phrase from ELIZABETH FOX-GENOVESE, 'Placing Women's History in History', *New Left Review* 133 (1982): 29.

1 Gloria Anzaldúa's *Borderlands/La frontera*: Cultural Studies, 'Difference', and the Non-Unitary Subject*

YVONNE YARBRO-BEJARANO

Yvonne Yarbro-Bejarano is a leading example of the creative eclecticism characteristic of critics working in this area. Her discussion of Gloria Anzaldúa's *Borderlands/La Frontera: The New Mestiza* concerns 'identity politics', which she approaches by means of a variety of Anzaldúa's 'new paradigms': 'mestiza consciousness', 'border consciousness', 'Coatlicue state', etc. These terms call attention to the multicultural contexts they address: hispanic and anglo cultures in the United States, as well as the indigenous Mexican heritage and the gender crossings symbolically encoded in the Aztec goddess Coatlicue.

Beginning with an array of theories of difference and adding an anthropological element of her own, Yarbro-Bejarano constructs a polemical response to imposed structures of gender and cultural identity, in which feminist and postcolonialist critiques overlap. The unstated premise of Yarbro-Bejarano's argument is that if inherited boundaries among cultures, languages, gender scripts and class divisions can be 'transgressed', autonomy *and* solidarity, selfhood *and* community can be achieved. Such transgressive tactics as Yarbro-Bejarano finds in Anzaldúa's text are aimed at enabling Chicanas to become 'self-writing', self-determining subjects. This essay, like Anzaldúa's text, is impelled by an implied idealism: the 'neither/nor' of Anzaldúa's 'boundary state' contains the potential 'either/or' of 'the new mestiza'.

In 1979, Audre Lorde denounced the pernicious practice of the 'Special Third World Women's Issue' (100). Ten years later, the title of one of the chapters in Trinh T. Minh-ha's *Woman, Native, Other* – 'Difference: A Special Third World Women's Issue' – alludes to the lingering practice of acknowledging the subject of race and ethnicity but placing it on the margins conceptually through 'special issues' of journals or 'special

* Reprinted from *Cultural Critique* 28 (Fall 1994): 5–28.

panels' at conferences. In her 'Feminism and Racism: A Report on the 1981 National Women's Studies Association Conference', Chela Sandoval critiqued the conference's structure, which designated one consciousness-raising group for women of color yet offered proliferating choices for white women (60). Nine years later, a conference at UCLA on 'Feminist Theory and the Question of the Subject' replicated this scenario, presenting a plenitude of panels on different aspects of the question of the subject, while marking off a space for 'minority discourse' that simultaneously revealed the unmarked status of the generic (white) subject of the other panels. Isaac Julien and Kobena Mercer, the guest editors of a special issue of *Screen*, formulate its title as an ironic question: 'The Last Special Issue on Race?' They point out that the logic of the 'special' issue or panel 'reinforces the perceived otherness and marginality of the subject itself'. In their critique, they invite us to identify the relations of power/knowledge that determine which cultural issues are intellectually prioritized in the first place ... to examine the force of a binary relationship that produces the marginal as a consequence of the authority invested in the center.

The persistence into the 1990s of discourses and practices that reinscribe the margin and the center indicates the problems inherent in theorizing 'difference'. In 'The Politics of Difference', Hazel Carby suggests that discourses on difference and diversity in the 1980s functioned to obscure structures of dominance. Linda Gordon offers a 'white-woman's narrative and perspective about the appropriation of the notion of differences among women by a white-dominated women-studies discourse' in her article 'On Difference' (100). The reinscription of the politics of domination within the discourse on difference inheres in part in the practice of theorizing difference within a paradigm that implies a norm and the tolerance of deviance from it (Gordon 100 and Spelman). The 'additive' model, in which heretofore excluded categories are 'included' in an attempt at correction, works against understanding the relations among the elements of identity and the effect each has on the other (Spelman 115 and Uttal).

This critique has been accompanied by an awareness that the failure to produce a relational theory of difference (Lippard 21) is not just a sin of omission, a result of 'laziness or racism', but points to a profound 'conceptual and theoretical difficulty' (Gordon 101–2). What is needed is a new paradigm that permits the expansion of categories of analysis in such a way as to give expression to the lived experience of the ways race, class, and gender converge (Childers and hooks). The writing of women of color is crucial in this project of categorical expansion, producing what Cherríe Moraga calls 'theory in the flesh' (Moraga and Anzaldúa, *Bridge* 23). This embodied theory emerges from the material reality of multiple oppression and in turn conceptualizes that materiality. The embodied subjectivities produced in the texts of women of color allow for an understanding of 'gendered racial identities' or 'racialized gender identities' (Gordon 105).

Cultural studies would appear to provide ideal terrain for the mapping of this new paradigm, with its 'commitment to examining cultural practices from the point of view of relations of power' and its understanding of culture as both 'object of study and site of political critique and intervention' (Grossberg et al. 5). However, it is important to keep in mind that the current attention to the intersections of race, nation, sexuality, class, and gender within cultural studies is the result of struggles initiated by people of color within the British movement to construct 'new political alliances based on non-essential awareness of racial difference' (Grossberg et al. 5). Lata Mani and bell hooks, among others, express concern at cultural studies' potential failure to articulate a new politics of difference – 'appropriating issues of race, gender and sexual practice, and then continuing to hurt and wound in that politics of domination' (hooks, Discussion 294).

In what follows, I will examine Gloria Anzaldúa's theory of *mestiza* or border consciousness and its contribution to paradigmatic shifts in theorizing difference, as well as contentious issues in the *reception* of this text: on one hand, the enthusiastic embrace of *Borderlands/La frontera: The New Mestiza* by many white feminists and area scholars and, on the other, the critiques voiced by some critics, particularly Chicana/o academicians.

Given the above discussion on the conceptual difficulty in theorizing difference, it is understandable that a text like *Borderlands* would be warmly received. But, as Chandra Talpade Mohanty points out, the proliferation of texts by women of color is not necessarily evidence of the decentering of the hegemonic subject (34). Of crucial importance is the *way* the texts are read, understood, and located. Two potentially problematic areas in the reception of *Borderlands* are the isolation of this text from its conceptual community and the pitfalls in universalizing the theory of *mestiza* or border consciousness, which the text painstakingly grounds in specific historical and cultural experiences.[1]

Unlike Sandoval's use of the adjectives 'oppositional' or 'differential' in her theory of consciousness,[2] Anzaldúa's choice of the terms 'border' and particularly '*mestiza*' problematizes the way her theory travels. Clearly, non-Chicana readers and critics may relate to the 'miscegenation' and 'border crossing' in their own lives and critical practices. For example, in her discussion of David Henry Hwang's play *M. Butterfly*, Marjorie Garber uses the term 'border crossings' in a way similar to Anzaldúa to describe the activity of presenting binarisms (West/East, male/female) in order to put them into question (130). The point is not to deny the explanatory power of Anzaldúa's model, but to consider the expense of

13

generalizing moves that deracinate the psychic 'borderlands' and *'mestiza'* consciousness from the United States/Mexican border and the racial miscegenation accompanying the colonization of the Americas that serve as the material reality for Anzaldúa's 'theory in the flesh'. If every reader who identifies with the border-crossing experience described by Anzaldúa's text sees her/himself as a 'New *mestiza*', what is lost in terms of the erasure of difference and specificity?

Other readings are possible that resist the impulse to read the text as one looks in a mirror. Elizabeth Spelman cautions against what she calls 'boomerang perception: I look at you and come right back to myself' (12). Appropriative readings are precluded by the constant interrogation of the conditions and locations of reading. It is one thing to choose to recognize the ways one inhabits the 'borderlands' and quite another to theorize a consciousness in the name of survival, to transform 'living in the Borderlands from a nightmare into a numinous experience' (Anzaldúa, *Borderlands* 73).

A useful strategy in teaching or reading *Borderlands* is to locate both reader *and* text: the reader, *vis-à-vis* plural centers and margins, and the text, within traditions of theorizing multiply embodied subjectivities by women of color[3] and living in the borderlands by Chicanas and Chicanos. Contextualizing the book in this manner, rather than reading it in a vacuum, helps avoid the temptation to pedestalize or even fetishize *Borderlands* as the invention of one unique individual. Given the text's careful charting of *mestiza* consciousness in the political geography of one particular border, reading it as part of a collective Chicano negotiation around the meanings of historical and cultural hybridity would further illuminate the process of 'theorizing in the flesh', of producing theory through one's own lived realities. Angie Chabram-Dernersesian documents Chicana texts dating from the early 1970s that represent 'shifting positionality, variously enlisting competing interests and alliances throughout time and space' and 'multiple evocations of a female speaking subject who affirms various racial identities' (85–9). Women of color thinkers such as the writers in *Bridge* and Sandoval were developing notions of multiple subjectivity in a context of political resistance in the early 1980s. In the mid-80s, Chicano artists such as David Avalos and the Border Arts Workshop attempted to expose, or even to celebrate, the political and economic contradictions of the border that sustain the officially illegal but unofficially sanctioned market in undocumented workers from Mexico. In Chicana/o criticism, the border constitutes a powerful organizing category in such works as Sonia Saldívar-Hull's 'Feminism on the Border: From Gender Politics to Geopolitics' and the collection *Criticism in the Borderlands: Studies in Chicano Literature, Culture, and Ideology*, edited by Héctor Calderón and José David Saldívar.

In her discussion of 'deterritorializations', the displacement of
identities, persons, and meanings endemic to the postmodern world
system, Caren Kaplan examines the process of 'reterritorialization' in
the movement between centers and margins and how that process of
reterritorialization is different for First World and Third World peoples.
For Kaplan, the challenge of the First World feminist critic is to avoid
'theoretical tourism' (or in the case of Anzaldúa's text, becoming
'boarders in the borderlands'), to avoid 'appropriating . . . through
romanticization, envy, or guilt' (194) by examining her simultaneous
occupation of both centers and margins: 'Any other strategy merely
consolidates the illusion of marginality while glossing over or refusing
to acknowledge centralities' (189).[4] Rather than assuming Anzaldúa's
metaphors as overarching constructs for like-minded theoretical
endeavors, it might be more helpful to set them alongside the metaphors
garnered from the rigorous examination of one's own lived personal and
collective history. Kaplan argues that recognizing one's own processes
of displacement 'is not a process of emulation' (194); Minnie Bruce Pratt
states: 'I am compelled *by my own life* to strive for a different place than
the one we have lived in' (48–9; quoted in Kaplan 364).

Universalizing readings of *Borderlands* occur in the larger 'postmodern'
context of increasing demarginalization of the cultural practices of people
of color as well as the simultaneous destabilizing of certain 'centered'
discourses of cultural authority and legitimation (Julien and Mercer).
Although many critics of the postmodern proclaim, either nostalgically
or celebratorily, the end of this and that, very few focus the crisis of
meaning, representation, and history in terms of the 'possibility of the
end of [Euro-] *ethnocentrism*' (Julien and Mercer 2). Stuart Hall, former
director of Birmingham's Centre for Contemporary Cultural Studies
(CCCS) and a black Jamaican who migrated to England, savored the
irony of the centering of marginality at a conference entitled 'The Real
Me: Post-modernism and the Question of Identity':

Thinking about my own sense of identity, I realise that it has always
depended on the fact of being a *migrant*, on the *difference* from the
rest of you. So one of the fascinating things about this discussion is to
find myself centred at last. Now that, in the postmodern age, you all
feel so dispersed, I become centred. What I've thought of as dispersed
and fragmented comes, paradoxically, to be *the* representative modern
experience! This is 'coming home' with a vengeance! Most of it I much
enjoy – welcome to migranthood. (44)

Hall sees it as an important gain that 'more and more people now
recognize . . . that all identity is constructed across difference', but he also
insists that narratives of displacement have 'certain conditions of

existence, real histories in the contemporary world, which are not only or exclusively psychical, not simply "journeys of the mind"' (44). Whereas Jean Baudrillard and other Eurocentric postmodernists explain the fragmentation of identity in relation to the end of the Real, Hall refers here to what some have called the Real that one cannot not know, the 'jagged edges' of poverty and racism.[5]

For this reason, Hall proposes the possibility of another kind of 'politics of difference'. New political identities can be formed by insisting on difference that is concretely conceived as 'the fact that every identity is placed, positioned, in a culture, a language, a history'. This conception of the self allows for a politics that constitutes ' "unities"-in-difference' (45), a *politics of articulation*, in which the connections between individuals and groups do not arise from 'natural' identity but must be articulated, in the dual sense of 'expressed in speech' and 'united by forming a joint'.[6]

Anzaldúa's *Borderlands* exemplifies the articulation between the contemporary awareness that *all* identity is constructed across difference and the necessity of a new *politics* of difference to accompany this new sense of self. Dorinne Kondo points out the difference between deconstructions of fixed identity that 'open out' the self to a 'free play of signifiers' and Anzaldúa's representation of multiple identity in the 'play of historically and culturally specific power relations' (23). While Anzaldúa's writing recognizes the importance of narratives of displacement in the formation of her subjectivity, she is also aware of the material conditions of existence, the real histories of these narratives. Hers is a 'power-sensitive analysis that would examine the construction of complex, shifting "selves" in the plural, in all their cultural, historical, and situational specificity' (Kondo 26).[7]

Borderlands maps a sense of 'the plurality of self' (Alarcón, 'Theoretical' 366), which Anzaldúa calls *mestiza* or border consciousness. This consciousness emerges from a subjectivity structured by multiple determinants – gender, class, sexuality, and contradictory membership in competing cultures and racial identities. Sandoval has theorized this sense of political identity that allows no *single* conceptualization of our position in society as a skill developed by those marginalized in the categories of race, sex, or class for reading the shifting of the webs of power ('Report' 66–7). She sees the term 'women of color' not as a single unity but as a conscious strategy, a new kind of community based on the strength of diversities as the source of a new kind of political movement. Her theory legitimates the multiplicity of tactical responses to the mobile circulation of power and meaning and posits a new, shifting subjectivity capable of reconfiguring and recentering itself, depending on the forms of oppression to be confronted. Anzaldúa enacts this consciousness in *Borderlands* as a constantly shifting process or activity of breaking down binary dualisms and creating the third space, the in-between, border, or interstice that allows contradictions to co-exist in the production of the new element (*mestizaje*, or hybridity). Crucial in her project are the ways 'race' works in the complex 'interdefining' and 'interacting' among the various aspects of her identity.[8] Her essay 'La Prieta' (the dark-skinned girl or woman), published in *Bridge*, already introduced the concerns she will explore in *Borderlands*: her relationship to her dark Indian self and the denial of the indigenous in Chicano/Mexicano culture. It is the representation of the indigenous in the text that has evoked the most critical response from Chicana/o and non-Chicana/o readers alike.

Primary among these concerns are what are seen as the text's essentializing tendencies, most notably in the reference to 'the Indian woman' and the privileging of the pre-Columbian deity Coatlicue, which obscures the plight of present day Native women in the Americas.[9] This wariness toward the invocation of 'Indianness' and the pre-Columbian pantheon must be contextualized in the contemporary critique of the cultural nationalism of the Chicano Movement, which engineered a romanticized linking between Chicanos and indigenous cultures as part of the process of constructing a Chicano identity. Many of us are engaged in an ongoing interrogation of the singular Chicano cultural identity posited by dominant masculinist and heterosexist discourses of the Chicano Movement and the role *indigenismo* played in this exclusionary process.[10]

This seems to me to be the crucial distinction between the project of such Chicano Movement artists as Luis Valdez or Alurista and Anzaldúa's project in *Borderlands*: whereas the first invoked *indigenismo* in the construction of an exclusionary, singular Chicano identity, the latter invokes it in the construction of an inclusive, multiple one. The theory of *mestiza* consciousness depends on an awareness of subject positions – a concept which Diana Fuss maintains represents the *essence* of social constructionism (29) – working against the solidifying concept of a unitary or essential 'I'. Fuss suggests that the seeming impasse between 'essentialism' and 'social constructionism' is actually a false dichotomy, and she calls attention to the ways they are deeply and inextricably co-implicated (xii). Perhaps more productive (and more interesting) than firing off the label 'essentialist' as a 'term of infallible critique' is to ask what *motivates* the deployment of essentialism (xi), which carries in itself the potential for both progressive and reactionary uses. In her discussion of subaltern studies, Gayatri Spivak speaks of the '*Strategic* use of positivist essentialism in a scrupulously visible political interest' (205), an analysis that would focus 'essentialist' moves in *Borderlands* in terms of 'who', 'how', and 'where': the lack of privilege of the writing subject, the specific deployment of essentialism and 'where its effects are concentrated' (Fuss 20).

On more than one occasion in the text, Anzaldúa,[11] who as a Chicana lesbian of working-class origins enjoys no privilege in the categories of race, culture, gender, class, or sexuality, explicitly articulates her project: 'belonging' nowhere, since some aspect of her multiple identity always prohibits her from feeling completely 'at home' in any one of the many communities in which she holds membership, she will create her own 'home' through writing.

> I want the freedom to carve and chisel my own face, . . . to fashion my own gods out of my entrails. And if going home is denied me then I will have to stand and claim my space, making a new culture – *una cultura mestiza* – with my own lumber, my own bricks and mortar and my own feminist architecture. (22)

Mestiza consciousness is not a given but must be *produced*, or 'built' ('lumber', 'bricks and mortar', 'architecture'). It is spatialized ('A piece of ground to stand on', 23), racialized ('*mestiza*'), and presented as a new mythology, a new culture, a nondualistic perception and practice:

> the future depends on the straddling of two or more cultures. By creating a new mythos – that is, a change in the way we perceive reality, the way we see ourselves, and the ways we behave – *la mestiza* creates a new consciousness. (80)

In *Borderlands*, this new consciousness is created through *writing*; Anzaldúa's project is one of discursive self-formation. Through writing she constructs a *consciousness* of difference, not in adversary relation to the Same but as what Alarcón calls the 'site of multiple voicings' ('Theoretical' 365) or what Trinh calls 'critical difference from myself' (*Woman* 89). The evocation of essentialism in the text is in the service of a constructionist project, the production of a border or *mestiza* consciousness that gives voice and substance to subjects rendered mute and invisible by hegemonic practices and discourses, and is understood as the necessary prelude to *political* change (87).

Borderlands' emphasis on the elaboration of a *consciousness* that emerges from an awareness of multiple *subjectivity* not only contributes to the development of a new paradigm for theorizing difference but also addresses aspects of identity formation for which theories of subjectivity alone are unable to account. Only theories of consciousness, such as Alzaldúa's or Sandoval's, can elucidate what Richard Johnson calls 'structural shifts or major re-arrangements of a sense of self, especially in adult life' (68). In his article 'What Is Cultural Studies Anyway?', Johnson, who followed Hall as director of the CCCS, distinguishes between subjectivity and consciousness:

Subjectivity includes the possibility . . . that some elements or impulses are subjectively active . . . without being consciously known. . . . It focuses on the 'who I am' or, as important, the 'who we are' of culture. . . . Consciousness embraces the notion of a consciousness of self and an *active mental and moral self-production*. (44)

Anzaldúa's construction of *mestiza* consciousness helps us begin to explain what Johnson calls the

subjective aspects of struggle . . . [that] moment in subjective flux when social subjects . . . produce accounts of who they are, as conscious political agents, that is, constitute themselves, politically. . . . subjects *are* contradictory, 'in process', fragmented, produced. But human beings and social movements also strive to produce some coherence and continuity, and through this, exercise some control over feelings, conditions and destinies. (69)

One axis for the enactment of *mestiza* consciousness in Anzaldúa's text is the use of personal histories and private memories that necessarily entail a context of political struggle.[12] Another privileged site for the construction of border consciousness is Coatlicue, Lady of the Serpent Skirt, a pre-Columbian deity similar to India's Kali in her nondualistic fusion of opposites – both destruction and creation, male and female, light and dark. The text's emphasis on Coatlicue has sparked the criticism that Anzaldúa compresses and distorts Mexican history. While Mexicanists and historians may have good reason to be disgruntled at Anzaldúa's free handling of pre-Columbian history, it appears to me that the text's investment is less in historical accuracy than in the imaginative appropriation and redefinition of Coatlicue in the service of creating a new mythos, textually defined as 'a change in the way we perceive reality, the way we see ourselves, and the ways we behave' (80).

In her article 'Chicana Feminism: In the Tracks of the Native Woman', Alarcón stresses a two-pronged process in Chicana writers' treatment of the Indian woman: invocation and recodification (252). Chicana writers reappropriate the Native woman on their own feminist terms because of the multiple ways the Chicana body has been racialized in discourses on both sides of the border (251). Their purpose is not to 'recover a lost "utopia" nor the "true" essence of our being', but rather to bring into focus, by invoking 'the maligned and abused indigenous woman', 'the cultural and psychic dismemberment that is linked to imperialist racist and sexist practices' (251). Alarcón cites Anzaldúa's 'Coatlicue state', the continuous effort of consciousness to 'make sense' of it all, as an example of this invocation and recodification of the Native woman in the exploration of racial and sexual experience (251). For me, criticisms of essentialism or elitism in Anzaldúa's use of Coatlicue are shortsighted in light of her function in Anzaldúa's project of pluralizing the unitary subject and dealing with difference in a nonhierarchical fashion (*Borderlands* 46).

Yet another area of contention is that *Borderlands* offers a spectacle of the painful splits that constitute Chicanas' multiple positioning for the voyeuristic delectation of European American readers. In the foreword to the second edition of *Bridge*, Anzaldúa herself seems to be aware of the backfiring potential of feeding non-Chicana readers' perception that being a person of color is an exclusively negative experience: 'Perhaps like me you are tired of suffering and talking about suffering. . . . Like me you may be tired of making a tragedy of our lives. . . . *[L]et's abandon this auto-cannibalism: rage, sadness, fear*' (iv; emphasis in original).[13] Other artists who use the border as a sign of multiplicity have been criticized for the opposite, for an excessive or inappropriate celebratoriness. Some artists and writers in Tijuana question what they see as the 'euphemized vision' of the contradictions and uprootedness of the border in the work of Guillermo Gómez Pena and others in the Border Arts Workshop and their bilingual publication *La Línea Quebrada/The Broken Line* (García Canclini). These other cultural workers on the border reject what they see as the celebration of migrations often caused by poverty in the place of origin, a poverty repeated in the new destination.

It seems to me that different readings of Anzaldúa's text, for different reasons, could emphasize either the positivity or negativity of 'living in the Borderlands'. What strikes me is the emphasis she places on the work involved in transforming the pain and isolation of 'in-between-ness' into an empowering experience through the construction of *mestiza* consciousness in writing.[14] Anzaldúa does describe the paralyzing tensions of her multiple positionings:

> Alienated from her mother culture, 'alien' in the dominant culture, the woman of color does not feel safe within the inner life of her Self. Petrified, she can't respond, her face caught between *los intersticios*, the spaces between the different worlds she inhabits. (20)

But she also figures the 'Coatlicue state', the effort to 'make sense' of contradictory experience, in the language of undocumented border crossings: 'to cross over, to make a hole in the fence and walk across, to cross the river . . . kicking a hole out of the old boundaries of the self and slipping under and over' (49). While she turns the pain of living in the psychic and material borderlands into a strength, she never loses sight of the concrete processes of displacement.

Borderlands is marked by such contradictory movements: the pain *and* strength of living in the borderlands, a preoccupation with the 'deep . . .

underlying structure' *and* the affirmation that 'the bones often do not exist prior to the flesh' (66), *la facultad* as both a dormant 'sixth sense' *and* a 'survival tactic' developed by the marginalized (38–9). Since, as Mohanty points out, the 'uprooting of dualistic thinking . . . is fundamentally based on knowledges which are often contradictory' (37), *mestiza* consciousness involves 'negotiating these knowledges, not just taking a simple counterstance' (Mohanty 36).[15] Adopting the 'new *mestiza*' subject position requires

> developing a tolerance for contradictions, a tolerance for ambiguity. . . . Not only does she sustain contradictions, she turns the ambivalence into something else. . . . That third element is a new consciousness . . . and though it is a source of intense pain, its energy comes from *continual creative motion that keeps breaking down the unitary aspect of each new paradigm.* (79–80; my emphasis)

This articulation of Anzaldúa's project challenges the Western philosophical tradition based on binary oppositions and its own textual workings, given the tension between *mestiza* consciousness as an activity or process of the non-unitary subject and the crystallized production of the 'name' *mestiza* consciousness in *Borderlands*. 'Naming', 'the active tense of identity' (Lippard 19), both extends the possibilities of 'crossings and mixings' and 'inevitably sets up boundaries' (Lippard 245). For Trinh, 'moments when things take on a proper name can only be positional, hence transitional' (*Moon* 2), but 'access to proper names as moments of transition . . . requires that "the imagination also [be] a political weapon."'[16] For, there is no space really untouched by the vicissitudes of history, and emancipatory projects never begin nor end *properly*' (*Moon* 7–8). Neither writer nor critic can inhabit a pure place of resistance or contestation (Kondo).[17] Although neither reader nor writer, like Trinh's 'impure subject' (*Moon* 104) or the 'new *mestiza*', can ever 'merely point at the sources of repression from a safe articulatory position' (*Moon* 93), *mestiza* consciousness provides a model for knowing that the 'only constant is the emphasis on the irrestible to-and-fro movement across (sexual and political) boundaries' (*Moon* 105).

The first six essays of the book inscribe a serpentine movement through different kinds of *mestizaje* that produce a third thing that is neither this nor that but something else: the blending of Spanish, Indian, and African to produce the *mestiza*, of Spanish and English to produce Chicano language, of male and female to produce the queer, of mind and body to produce the animal soul, the writing that 'makes face'. The final essay, '*La conciencia de la mestiza*/Towards a New Consciousness', reveals this serpentine movement that structures both the text itself and *mestiza* consciousness.

Borderlands juxtaposes essays and poetry, political theory and cultural practice, not separating one from the other but producing a fusion of the two, a 'theory in the flesh'. The writing of both Anzaldúa and, in *Loving in the War Years*, Moraga gives theory a new 'face'. They struggle to make sense of what it means to be working-class Chicana lesbians in essays that are collages of dreams, journal entries, poems, and autobiographical reflection. King characterizes this kind of writing as 'mixed genres emerging from and theorizing mixed complex identities' (88). As Trinh points out, in this kind of writing,

> the borderline between the theoretical and the non-theoretical is blurred and questioned, so that theory and poetry necessarily mesh, both determined by an awareness of the sign and the destabilization of the meaning and writing subject. (*Woman* 42)

The Vietnamese writer's reflections on writing as a 'gendered' kind of theory also describe Anzaldúa's and Moraga's texts:

> From jagged transitions between the analytical and the poetical to the disruptive, always shifting fluidity of a headless and bottomless storytelling, what is exposed in [these texts] is the inscription and de-scription of a non-unitary female subject of color through her engagement, therefore also disengagement with master discourses. (*Woman* 43)

Anzaldúa herself characterizes *Borderlands'* 'mosaic' or 'weaving pattern' as writing that threatens to 'spill over the boundaries', that offers a 'hybridization of metaphor . . . full of variations and seeming contradictions', that refuses the neat dichotomy of 'deep structure' and 'smooth surfaces' in its 'central core, now appearing, now disappearing in a crazy dance' (66).

In the first essay, entitled 'Homeland', Anzaldúa addresses the history of the border between the United States and Mexico. 'Homeland' establishes the originary presence of the Indians on the land ('This land was Mexican once,/was Indian always/and is./And will be again,' 3), and introduces the notion of *mestizaje* in racial terms – the product of the sexual union of Spaniard and Indian. This essay traces the successive waves of conquest and domination of the land and its peoples by Spain, Mexico, and the United States, including the systematic lynching of Mexicans by Anglo settlers, and ends with the contemporary situation of the undocumented worker. Anzaldúa refers to the border as a '1,950 mile-long open wound/dividing a *pueblo*, a culture,/running down the length of my body,/staking rods in my flesh,/splits me splits me' (2). This initial image figures the border as the writing subject's own body, exemplifying Anzaldúa's embodied theory and subjectivity.

After having established the border and racial and cultural *mestizaje* as 'homeland', Anzaldúa problematizes the concept of 'home' in the second essay, 'Movimientos de rebeldía y las culturas que traicionan' ('Movements of Rebellion and Cultures That Betray'). Paradoxically, she must leave home to find home (16). In this essay, she records her rebellion against her culture's betrayal of women. She demands an accounting from all three cultures (white, Mexican, and Indian) of what has been oppressed in each. In their analysis of Pratt's personal history as white, Southern, Christian, and lesbian, Biddy Martin and Mohanty focus on a similar tension between 'being home' and 'not being home':

'Being home' refers to the place where one lives within familiar, safe, protected boundaries; 'not being home' is a matter of realizing that home was an illusion of coherence and safety based on the exclusion of specific histories of oppression and resistance, the repression of differences even within oneself. (196)

In Anzaldúa's case, 'being home' depends on the exclusion of women and specifically the dark-skinned Indian self she had to repress to remain within the safe boundaries of 'home'. It is in this second essay that Anzaldúa constructs lesbian identity as that which keeps her from 'being home': 'Being lesbian and raised Catholic, indoctrinated as straight, I *made the choice to be queer*. . . . It is a way of balancing, of mitigating duality' (19). In a textual move privileging lesbianism often overlooked in the critical reception of the text, Anzaldúa makes 'being queer', like the Coatlicue state, signify a 'path to something else'. Identifying with the woman in the town that people gossiped about as being half male and half female, Anzaldúa rewrites lesbian identity as 'neither/nor,' introducing, with this move, a new notion of *mestizaje* that produces the queer as a third gender.[18]

In this second essay, Anzaldúa recounts a student's mistaken conception that homophobia meant fear of going home. Anzaldúa affirms this semantic slippage as an eloquent articulation of her predicament as a Chicana lesbian. Again, the parallel with Pratt's text, as analyzed by Martin and Mohanty, is striking:

Her lesbianism is what she experiences most immediately as the limitation imposed on her by the family, culture, race, and class that afforded her both privilege and comfort, at a price. Learning at what price privilege, comfort, home, and secure notions of self are purchased, the price to herself and ultimately to others is what makes lesbianism a political motivation as well as a personal experience. (203)

Although Anzaldúa's consciousness is not enacted in relation to an identity of class and skin privilege, her lesbianism, like Pratt's, is neither centered nor essentialized, but represents 'that which makes "home" impossible, which makes her self non-identical' (202).

For the Chicana lesbian, both her Indianness (as *mestiza*) and her sexual identity form part of the 'unacceptable aspect of the self' that is repressed to avoid rejection by 'mother/culture/race' (20). Anzaldúa calls this multifaceted internalized oppression the 'Shadow-Beast', which not only must be confronted but empowered: 'How does one put feathers on this particular serpent?' (20). The serpentine imagery describing the Shadow-Beast ('her lidless serpent eyes . . . fangs bared and hissing') links it with the representation of the Coatlicue state, embracing both positive and negative poles.[19]

It is at this moment in the text, when she is confronted with her paradoxical belonging and not belonging, her 'difference' – both externally and internally imposed as Indian, female, and queer – that Anzaldúa formulates her project as the self-writing subject referred to above.

In the next two essays, 'Entering into the Serpent' and 'La herencia de Coatlicue/The Coatlicue State', Anzaldúa uses the serpentine imagery she associates with Coatlicue in all her contradictory manifestations to describe the nondualistic movement necessary to keep from being caught in the multiple borders that shape her subjectivity. In these essays, she draws on pre-Columbian culture to refigure the opposition of mind and body as the 'animal soul' (26). These essays also develop two crucial components of *mestiza* consciousness: *la facultad* and the Coatlicue state. In her discussion of 'el mundo zurdo' (the left-handed world) in *Bridge*, Anzaldúa privileges the disenfranchised as spearheading movements for visionary social change. Here it is the 'females, the homosexuals of all races, the darkskinned, the outcast, the persecuted, the marginalized, the foreign' who are 'more apt to develop' *la facultad*, defined as 'an instant "sensing", a quick perception arrived at without conscious reasoning' (38). While on one level *la facultad* is a kind of survival skill honed by the nonprivileged, it is also linked to the Coatlicue state and *mestiza* consciousness as facilitating a re-grounding of consciousness, or 'shift in perception' (39).

Coatlicue, identified with 'the underground aspects of the psyche' (46) and the contradictory fusion of opposites (47), also represents the activity of producing consciousness. Internalized oppression causes the self to perceive its differences as monstrous: 'the secret sin I tried to conceal – *la seña*, the mark of the Beast' (42). The mark of the Beast, earlier associated with internalized racism and homophobia, is here linked with physical abnormality[20] and multiplicity: 'She has this fear/ that she has no names/that she has many names' (43).[21] The immobility caused by the perception of the monstrosity of difference is shattered by the process of 'seeing' or 'making connections': 'My resistance, my refusal to know some truth about myself brings on that paralysis, depression – brings on the Coatlicue state' (48). Whether the blockage is the result of complacency or paralysis, the Coatlicue state triggers the 'crossing', the 'rupture in our everyday world' necessary for the construction of the 'third perspective' (46), the *mestiza* consciousness.

The next two sections, 'How to Tame a Wild Tongue' and 'Tlilli Tlapalli: The Path of the Red and Black Ink', deal with language and writing, the tools for the discursive production of *mestiza* consciousness. In 'How to Tame a Wild Tongue', Anzaldúa records both her refusal to remain silent (the wild tongue cannot be tamed, only cut out) and the ways in which her language is not 'appropriate' according to dominant norms (54). Like Trinh's 'inappropriate/d other' ('She'), Anzaldúa is both inappropriate according to the dominant norm and 'inappropriated' by it. She writes of the 'linguistic terrorism' experienced by Chicanos whose language inhabits the border between Mexico and the United States. The tradition of silence has been imposed not just by the dominant English speaking culture (punished for speaking Spanish at school, criticized by Mexican relatives for speaking English with an accent) but also by 'standard' Spanish speakers of Spain and Latin America.

These two essays confect yet another kind of *mestizaje* informing the border consciousness: linguistic *mestizaje*, the language of the border that trangresses the boundaries between Spanish and English, high and low decorum, insider and outsider speech. Anzaldúa claims her language as another kind of homeland (55) and as part of the serpentine movement that mediates the binary split to construct the third element.

In 'The Path of the Red and Black Ink', writing for Anzaldúa is not so much an analytical activity as a shamanistic process of transformation (66). Anzaldúa uses the nahual notion of writing as creating face, heart, and soul to elaborate the idea that it is only through the body that the soul can be transformed. Trinh makes the distinction between writing yourself, i.e., writing the body, and writing about yourself. The second reinscribes the Priest/God standpoint of the all-knowing subject; 'the first refers to a scriptive act – the emergence of a writing self' (*Woman* 28). Although the two overlap in *Borderlands*, it is the first that Anzaldúa describes as crucial to her new mythology and to her project of rupturing the dualism opposing body and soul, writing and the body.

Here, Anzaldúa contextualizes the Coatlicue state in the activity of writing: 'Blocks (Coatlicue states) are related to my cultural identity. . . . The stress of living with cultural ambiguity both compels me to write and blocks me' (74). To the signifiers of '*mestiza*' and 'queer' as border crossers Anzaldúa adds that of 'writer': 'Being a writer feels very much like being a Chicana, or being queer' (72). All, through 'shifts' – cultural, racial, gender, and linguistic shifts – 'reprogram consciousness', the writer 'through words, images, and body sensations' (70).

The final essay constructs the 'new *mestiza*' as the point of confluence of conflicting subject positions:

> This assembly is not one where severed or separated pieces merely come together. Nor is it a balancing of opposing powers. In attempting to work out a synthesis, the self has added a third element which is greater than the sum of its severed parts. (79–80)

The cultural practice that proceeds from and in turn constitutes the new *mestiza* shows 'in the flesh and through the images in her work how duality is transcended' (80). In the preface to the book, Anzaldúa refers to border or *mestiza* consciousness as an 'alien' element that nevertheless constitutes a new home: 'Living on borders and in margins, keeping intact one's shifting and multiple identity and integrity, is like trying to swim in a new element, an "alien" element. . . . No, not comfortable, but home' (vii). With this textual gesture, she expropriates the term 'alien' from the rhetorical mythology of the border, used to demonize undocumented workers. Other examples of images in Anzaldúa's writing that embody *mestiza* consciousness are the female subject – part fish, part woman – produced through the transgression of the body's borders in the poem 'Letting Go'; the *mestiza* survivors of the new age whose newly evolved double eyelids give them the power to 'look at the sun with naked eyes' in 'Don't Give Up, Chicanita'; and the interspecies lesbian sex between the alien and the human subject in 'Interface'.

The cultural practice of the new *mestiza* is also a *political practice* made possible by the achievement of awareness and acceptance of the plural self (87). In its emphasis on the *inner* struggle, this essay provokes thought on the relationship between individual transformation and social change (87). As Hall suggests, the new conception of the non-unitary self, or *mestiza* consciousness, allows for a politics of articulation, not of essential unity or correspondence, but of 'unities-in-difference'. In this spirit, Anzaldúa proposes coalitions with men, particularly Mexican/Chicano men, who are willing to become anti-sexist – to unlearn the Virgin/Malinche duality and to put Coatlicue back in Guadalupe – and with white people of both sexes who are willing to become anti-racist – to learn all peoples' histories of oppression and resistance.

This last essay ends with 'el retorno' (the return), bringing the reader back to where Part One began: on the border, in the homeland. But the image describing the river that marks the border as a 'curving, twisting serpent' (89) suggests that there is no return without transformation. Only after the writing/*mestiza*/queer subject has created a new 'home' through discursive self-production, can she return to the land that awakens all the historical and cultural memories inscribed on her senses: 'This land was Mexican once/was Indian always/and is./And will be again' (91).

The six sections of poems that follow the essays map out a movement similar to that of Part One. Space limitations do not permit a detailed analysis of these parallels, but further study could show how Part Two replicates the serpentine path of the essays, both establishing the border as 'home' and unsettling this stability through differences of gender and sexuality. Like the essays, the poems also explore writing as the medium for the eruption of the unknown allowing new consciousness to be formed. The title of the last section of poems is 'El retorno' (return). As in the final essay, which ends with the return to a present filled with the past and pointing to a future political project, these poems presage the arrival of 'the left-handed world' ('Arriba mi gente') and envision a future belonging to cultural, racial, and gender *mestizos* (194, 203).

It is my hope that the kind of contextualized readings I propose of both Parts One and Two might alleviate problematic areas in the reception of *Borderlands* that have to do with reading out of context, either deracinating the text from its various communal traditions or seizing on textual moments without taking the whole into account. A contextualized reading of both Parts One and Two locates *mestiza* consciousness and the indigenous, particularly Coatlicue, within a textual movement that replicates the movement of border consciousness itself. This process, constantly 'breaking down the unitary aspect' of each previous textual moment, leaves no home but the discursive production of consciousness itself, a consciousness linked with political activity.

Notes

1. See Sonia Saldívar-Hull for an analysis of the text's grounding in history.

2. The term 'differential' appears in her recent article in *Genders*.

3. Is it stylistic or conceptual restriction that leads the editors of *Nationalisms and Sexualities* to write: 'Elaborated over the past twenty years in socialist-feminist, psychoanalytic and deconstructive thought and in the writings of women of color, this insight . . .' (Parker et al., Introduction 4)?

4. Trinh T. Minh-ha calls on the reader to 'assert her difference (not individualizing her perception) but setting into relief the type of individualization that links her (whether centrally or marginally) as an individual to the systems of dominant values' (*Moon* 113).

5. See the interview with Cornel West in *Universal Abandon?* (Ross, ed.).

6. This new conception of politics 'requires us to begin, not only to speak the language of dispersal, but also the language of, as it were, contingent closures of articulation' (45). Hall discusses his use of the theory of 'articulation', as developed by Ernesto Laclau in *Politics and Ideology in Marxist Theory*, in the interview with Lawrence Grossberg ('On Postmodernism and Articulation').

7. See also Mohanty on Anzaldúa's *mestiza* consciousness: 'Thus, unlike a Western, postmodernist notion of agency and consciousness which often announces the splintering of the subject, and privileges multiplicity in the abstract, this is a notion of agency born of history and geography. It is a theorization of the materiality and politics of the everyday struggles of Chicanas' (37).

8. Katie King uses these terms to counteract the reductive notion of *simultaneous* oppressions or occupation of the subject positions, in favor of a model of 'overlapping necessities' (86).

9. See, for example, Rosaura Sánchez's critique.

10. See, for example, Fregoso and Chabram's introduction to *Cultural Studies*.

11. I use both 'Anzaldúa' and 'the writing subject' to refer to the mediated 'I' of the text.

12. See Mohanty on the relationship among memory, writing, and the production of consciousness and political resistance (32–5); Johnson for a discussion of the importance of personal histories and private memories in discursive self-production (69); and Fregoso's work – a conference presentation and an essay – on Chicano film for the role of 'counter-memory' in the formation of a political or cultural identity.

13. For Spelman, the denial of the positive aspects of racial identities is linked to seeing racism as a product of sexism (124).

14. It is in the context of writing (in 'Tlilli, Tlapalli: The Path of the Red and Black Ink' from *Borderlands*) that Anzaldúa articulates (in Hall's dual sense) the passage from negativity to positivity quoted above: 'When I write it feels like I'm carving bone. It feels like I'm creating my own face, my own heart – a Nahuatl concept. . . . It is this learning to live with *la Coatlicue* that transforms living in the Borderlands from a nightmare into a numinous experience. It is always a path/state to something else' (73).

15. For the repudiation of the counterstance, see *Borderlands*, 78.

16. The quote within the quote is from Elizam Escobar.

17. For Trinh, there can be no essential inside (*Moon* 75), never a pure elsewhere (104).

18. De Lauretis elaborates a theory of the 'third gender' in 'Sexual Indifference and Lesbian Representation'.

19. Earlier in the essay, Anzaldúa defines the Shadow-Beast as the rebel in her that 'refuses to take orders . . . that hates constraints of any kind' (16).

20. For Ana Castillo, 'Anzaldúa's spiritual affinity for Coatlicue serves as a resonant reflection of this particular writer's desire for a disembodiment that would free her of tremendous physical and emotional anguish' (172).

21. See Alarcón for an analysis of this passage ('Chicana Feminism' 249–50).

Works cited

ALARCÓN, NORMA. 'Chicana Feminism: In the Tracks of the Native Woman'. *Cultural Studies* 4.3 (1990): 248–55.

———. 'The Theoretical Subject(s) of *This Bridge Called My Back* and Anglo-American Feminism'. Anzaldúa, *Making Face* 356–69.

ANZALDÚA, GLORIA. *Borderlands/La frontera: The New Mestiza*. San Francisco: Spinsters/Aunt Lute, 1987.

———, ed. *Making Face, Making Soul/Haciendo Caras: Creative and Critical Perspectives by Women of Color*. San Francisco: Aunt Lute, 1990.

CALDERÓN, HÉCTOR, and JOSÉ DAVID SALDÍVAR, eds. *Criticism in the Borderlands: Studies in Chicano Literature, Culture, and Ideology*. Durham: Duke UP, 1991.

CARBY, HAZEL. 'The Politics of Difference'. *Ms.* (Sept.–Oct. 1990): 84–5.

CASTILLO, ANA. 'Massacre of the Dreamer: Reflection on Mexican-Indian Women in the U.S.: 500 Years After the Conquest'. *Critical Fictions: The Politics of Imaginative Writing*. Ed. Philomena Mariani. Seattle: Bay Press, 1991, 161–76.

CHABRAM-DERNERSESIAN, ANGIE. ' "I Throw Punches for My Race *but* I Don't Want to Be a Man" Writing Us: Chica-nos (Girl/Us)/Chicanas into the Movement Script'. Grossberg et al. 81–95.

CHILDERS, MARY, and BELL HOOKS. 'A Conversation about Race and Class'. Hirsch and Fox-Keller 60–81.

DE LAURETIS, TERESA. 'Sexual Indifference and Lesbian Representation'. *Performing Feminisms: Feminist Critical Theory and Theatre*. Ed. Sue-Ellen Case. Baltimore: Johns Hopkins UP, 1990, 17–39.

FREGOSO, ROSA LINDA. 'Re-membering the Border through Chicano Cinema'. Conference on 'Chicano Cultural Studies: New Critical Directions'. 25–26 May 1990. Santa Barbara: University of California, 1990.

———. '*Zoot Suit* (1981): The "Return to the Beginning" '. *Mediating Two Worlds: Cinematic Encounters in the Americas*. Ed. Manuel Alvarado, John King, and Ana M. Lopez. London: British Film Institute, 1993, 269–78.

FREGOSO, ROSA LINDA, and ANGIE CHABRAM, eds. 'Chicano/a Cultural Representations: Reframing Alternative Critical Discourses'. *Cultural Studies* 4.3 (1990): 203–12.

FUSS, DIANA. *Essentially Speaking: Feminism, Nature and Difference*. New York: Routledge, 1989.

GARBER, MARJORIE. 'The Occidental Tourist: *M. Butterfly* and the Scandal of Transvestism'. Parker et al. 121–46.

GARCÍA CANCLINI, Nestor. *Culturas híbridas*. Mexico City: Grijalbo, 1989.

GORDON, LINDA. 'On Difference'. *Genders* 10 (Spring 1991): 91–111.

GROSSBERG, LAWRENCE. 'On Postmodernism and Articulation: An Interview with Stuart Hall'. *Journal of Communication Inquiry* 10.2 (1986): 45–60.

GROSSBERG, LAWRENCE, CARY NELSON, and PAULA TREICHLER, eds. *Cultural Studies*. New York: Routledge, 1992.

HALL, STUART. 'Minimal Selves'. *Identity*. Ed. Lisa Appignanesi. London: ICA Document 6, 1987, 44–6.

HIRSCH, MARIANNE, and EVELYN FOX-KELLER, eds. *Conflicts in Feminism*. New York: Routledge, 1990.

HOOKS, BELL, et al. Discussion of Stuart Hall's 'Cultural Studies and its Theoretical Legacies'. Grossberg et al. 286–94.

JOHNSON, RICHARD. 'What Is Cultural Studies Anyway?' *Social Text* 16 (Winter 1986/87): 38–80.

JULIEN, ISAAC, and KOBENA MERCER. 'Introduction: De Margin and De Centre'. *Screen* 29.4 (1988): 28–40.

KAPLAN, CAREN. 'Deterritorializations: The Rewriting of Home and Exile in Western Feminist Discourse'. *The Nature and Context of Minority Discourse*. Ed. Abdul R. JanMohamed and David Lloyd. New York: Oxford UP, 1990, 357–68.

KING, KATIE. 'Producing Sex, Theory, and Culture: Gay/Straight Remappings in Contemporary Feminism'. Hirsch and Fox-Keller 82–101.

KONDO, DORINNE. '*M. Butterfly*: Orientalism, Gender, and a Critique of Essentialist Identity'. *Cultural Critique* 16 (1990): 5–29.

LACLAU, ERNESTO. *Politics and Ideology in Marxist Theory: Capitalism, Fascism, Populism*. London: New Left, 1977.

LIPPARD, LUCY R. *Mixed Blessings: New Art in a Multicultural America*. New York: Pantheon, 1990.

LORDE, AUDRE. 'The Master's Tools Will Never Dismantle the Master's House'. Moraga and Anzaldúa 98–101.

MANI, LATA. 'Cultural Theory, Colonial Texts: Reading Eyewitness Accounts of Widow Burning'. Grossberg et al. 392–405.

MARTIN, BIDDY, and CHANDRA TALPADE MOHANTY. 'Feminist Politics: What's Home Got to Do with It?' *Feminist Studies/Critical Studies*. Ed. Teresa de Lauretis. Bloomington: Indiana UP, 1986, 191–212.

MOHANTY, CHANDRA TALPADE. 'Introduction: Cartographies of Struggle'. *Third World Women and the Politics of Feminism*. Ed. Chandra Mohanty, Ann Russo, and Lourdes Torres. Bloomington: Indiana UP, 1991, 1–47.

MORAGA, CHERRÍE. *Loving in the War Years. Lo que nunca paso por sus labios*. Boston: South End, 1983.

MORAGA, CHERRÍE, and GLORIA ANZALDÚA, eds. *This Bridge Called My Back: Writings by Radical Women of Color*. Watertown: Persephone, 1981. 2nd edn, New York: Kitchen Table, 1983.

PARKER, ANDREW, MARY RUSSO, DORIS SOMMER, and PATRICIA YAEGER. Introduction. Parker et al., *Nationalisms and Sexualities* 1–18.

PARKER, ANDREW, MARY RUSSO, DORIS SOMMER, and PATRICIA YAEGER, eds. *Nationalisms and Sexualities*. New York: Routledge, 1992.

ROSS, ANDREW, ed. *Universal Abandon?: The Politics of Postmodernism*. Minneapolis: U of Minnesota P, 1988.

SALDÍVAR-HULL, SONIA. 'Feminism on the Border: From Gender Politics to Geopolitics'. Calderón and Saldívar 203–20.

SÁNCHEZ, ROSAURA. 'The Politics of Representation in Chicano Literature'. Conference on 'Chicano Cultural Studies: New Critical Directions'. 25–26 May 1990. Santa Barbara: University of California, 1990.

SANDOVAL, CHELA. 'Feminism and Racism: A Report on the 1981 National Women's Studies Association Conference'. Anzaldúa, *Making Face* 55–71.

——. 'U.S. Third World Feminism: The Theory and Method of Oppositional Consciousness in the Postmodern World'. *Genders* 10 (Spring 1991): 1–24.

SPELMAN, ELIZABETH V. *Inessential Woman: Problems of Exclusion in Feminist Thought*. Boston: Beacon, 1988.

SPIVAK, GAYATRI. 'Subaltern Studies: Deconstructing Historiography'. *In Other Worlds: Essays in Cultural Politics*. New York: Methuen, 1987.

TRINH T. MINH-HA. Introduction to special issue. 'She, the Inappropriate/d Other'. *Discourse* 8 (Fall–Winter 1986–87): 3–10.

——. *When the Moon Waxes Red: Representation, Gender and Cultural Politics*. New York: Routledge, 1991.

——. *Woman, Native, Other: Writing, Postcoloniality and Feminism*. Bloomington: Indiana UP, 1989.

UTTAL, LYNNE. 'Inclusion without Influence: The Continuing Tokenism of Women of Color'. Anzaldúa, *Making Face* 42–5.

Relevant to this discussion is MARY LOUISE PRATT, ' "Yo soy La Malinche": Chicana Writers and the Poetics of Ethnonationalism', *Callaloo* 16, 4 (1993): 859–73. GLORIA ANZALDÚA has co-edited *This Bridge Called My Back: Writings by Radical Women of Color* (San Francisco: Spinster/Aunt Lutz Press, 1981) with Cherríe Moraga. See also DONNA PERRY's interview with Anzaldúa in *Backtalk: Women Writers Speak Out* (New Brunswick, NJ: Rutgers University Press, 1991), pp. 19–42.

2 Subject, Voice, and Women in Some Contemporary Black American Women's Writing*

MARY O'CONNOR

In her discussion of three works by contemporary African American women writers, Mary O'Connor engages Mikhail Bakhtin's conception of the novel as a dialogue among competing 'voices'. Bakhtin's 'dialogism' has proven particularly useful to critics writing in this area, for it asks how difference may enter and unsettle the structure of a literary work, and how this process is conditioned by particular historical and cultural circumstances. Bakhtin emphasizes the social exchange inherent in all utterance, and the changing cultural significance of utterance over time. 'Voice', then, is historical and cultural: the literary work consists of 'voices' containing the multiple echoes of past speakers and present ideologies.

O'Connor amplifies Bakhtin's conception of 'voice' to include the psychological realm of literary character and, by extension, the constitution of subjectivity as a relational (i.e., 'dialogic') process. Indeed, O'Connor's essay creates a kind of Bakhtinian dialogue of its own among the works she discusses: Alice Walker's *The Color Purple*, Gloria Naylor's *The Women of Brewster Place*, and Ntozake Shange's *for colored girls who have considered suicide/when the rainbow is enuf.*

You black, you pore, you ugly, you a woman. Goddam, he say, you nothing at all.

(Walker, 187)

This nothingness – constituted by all that is the negative of society's values in race, class, and gender – may be seen as a place of origin for

* Reprinted from *Feminism, Bakhtin and the Dialogic*. Ed. DALE M. BAUER and S. JARET MCKINSTRY (New York: SUNY Press, 1991), pp. 199–217. An original version of this paper, entitled 'Feminist Dialogics and Contemporary Black American Women Writers', was read at the International Bakhtin Conference, Hebrew University of Jerusalem, 15 June 1987.

not only Alice Walker's *The Color Purple* but for much black feminist
writing. It is a nothingness imposed from without, an entity defined by
the patriarchal and white world of power and wealth. Many feminist
books begin with male voices embedded in the words of whatever
women narrators, characters, or authors are speaking, but this male
language is also the condition against which the books fight. If all plot
entails conflict, some rupture in a more-or-less stable structure, then that
conflict in these books is the fight against the domination of male voices
in an attempt to inundate them with viable alternatives.

I do not use the term 'voices' loosely here, but as a technical term
to refer to language as it exists in a historical context. The linguistic
theories of Mikhail Bakhtin are helpful for a feminist analysis of
literature precisely because they insist on the historical nature of
utterances rather than the mechanical definitions of the structuralist's
langue. Despite Bakhtin's own limitations in considering gender or
race in his discussion of voices, his statements such as 'I hear *voices* in
everything and the dialogic relationships between them' stand against
any formalist a-historical analysis of literature (Shukman, 4). The works
of the Bakhtin circle – Vološinov's *Marxism and the Philosophy of
Language*, Bakhtin and Medvedev's *The Formal Method in Literary
Scholarship*, Bakhtin's *Problems of Dostoevsky's Poetics* and the essays in
The Dialogic Imagination – have consistenly argued for an understanding
of the social context of discourse in any linguistic or literary analysis.
Feminist critics have turned to the Bakhtin circle for just this reason: 'the
dialogic, because of its asystemic nature and its insistence on the social
significance of discourse, is a term that embraces both a comparative and
an ideological interrogation of literary practices' (Herrmann, 4).[1]

An argument might be made that many contemporary books written
by black women are so compelling to women readers because they
return us to the bourgeois illusion that art can be a place of truth, some
metaphysical space of visions and retreat. This feeling of solidarity
eases the pain, offering some compensatory world of connectedness.
Many of the writers even believe in the ultimate truth of a spiritual life,
if not filled with a traditional male God, at least with the spirits of
their grandmothers. Both connectedness and spiritual life can be seen as
modes of revolution when placed in the context of a life of isolation and
physical brutality. Books such as Alice Walker's *The Color Purple*, Gloria
Naylor's *The Women of Brewster Place*, and Ntozake Shange's *for colored
girls who have considered suicide/when the rainbow is enuf*, work through
and towards moments of connectedness, of love between women, but
they do so not as some utopian world of escape. I would rather argue,
as Susan Willis has done, that utopian space can offer revolutionary
possibilities for change ('Eruptions', 263–83). Walker's, Naylor's, and
Shange's texts figure women whose 'stories' are 'ferret[ed] out', to use

Shange's expression, from the silence of their burrows until the many voices that have been producing these women are sung and debated. There is always a composite voice, whether it is the seven women in Shange who gather their 'half-notes scattered/without rhythm', or Naylor's sequence of women living in the tenements of Brewster Place telling their stories. In every case the voices struggle with names and stereotyping, with silence and screams.[2]

Women's literature has been motivated by the imperative to know who we are and how to act on that knowledge, but our liberation comes belatedly as we discover that the 'wholeness' of men is indeed a fabrication, constructed by the ideologies or superstructure of a certain economic base. Freedom in this poststructuralist world must come from analyzing and subverting all constructed identities, especially those which place us in an exploited position. Women must still deconstruct the patriarchal image of ourselves as silent, submissive, and an object of pleasure or possession, but problems arise when we start to construct our own identity.

These issues have been debated in feminist literary theory – whether it is our job to establish a new identity, unified and strong, based on personal experience that is not dependent on male dominance, or to forego this Romantic illusion and look for an identity that is based on the fluid process of history. Cora Kaplan

> would rather see subjectivity as always in process and contradiction, even female subjectivity, structured, divided and denigrated through the matrices of sexual difference. I see this understanding as part of a more optimistic political scenario than the ones I have been part of, one that can and ought to lead to a politics which will no longer over value control, rationality and individual power, and which, instead, tries to understand human desire, struggle and agency as they are mobilized through a more complicated, less finished and less heroic psychic schema. (181)

With this premise in mind I have turned, in part, to the theories of Bakhtin for a methodological context. His position, it may be argued, is a critique of the transcendental subject, offering in its place a theory of co-existent subject positions which we take up in relation to the various discourses that are active in our world. His *dialogism*, which is 'a struggle among socio-linguistic points of view, not an intra-language struggle between individual will or logical contradictions' (*DI*, 273), takes into account the various determining and producing historical factors in our lives and at the same time allows for the idea of an active response on the part of the subject to these various discourses and other subject positions. Thus, his theories do away with the need for the cogito or

unified self which we have come to see as an illusory construct.
They allow for a model of intersecting ideologies, in other words, a
connection with history in society, as well as a model of connecting
with others. Finally, they allow for process and change. This last
category is supported by his theory of the carnivalesque where cultural
productions, whether a festival in the street or a literary text, can
present us with an image of the overthrow of authority.

It might be fruitful to compare, for instance, Gloria Naylor's resolution
in *The Women of Brewster Place* to what Susan Willis sees as the 'eruptions
of funk' in the work of Toni Morrison, eruptions that produce alternative
social worlds, often a household of three women (278). Naylor is in no
way sentimental about the reality of communities, male or female. In many
ways Willis's arguments are similar to those of Bakhtin, as the lower
bodily stratum or the grotesque in Bakhtin's terms may be translated into
eruptions of funk. In his theory as well as in that of Willis's analyses of
Morrison, the evocations of the grotesque, the portrayal of otherness, can
produce a moment of utopian vision which relativizes the authoritative
norm and thus produces the possibility of change.

The more voices that are ferreted out, the more discourses that a
woman can find herself an intersection of, the freer she is from one
dominating voice, from one stereotypical and sexist position. The male
voices are heard, but contended, in these books. Although consciousness
may seem to be the ultimate goal – one single definition of self by which
to live – this self must be one in constant transition because it is always
in dialogue with other personalities who represent other social forces.
The self produced for the moment must necessarily redo itself in its next
encounter. In the moment of so-called knowing itself in language, it must
revise that knowledge because one's language is always handed down
and always addressed to another. 'The word in written discourse', as
Díaz-Diocaretz has argued, 'is part of an ideological argument, in a
constant process of transferral, since the word does not forget where it
has been and can never wholly free itself from the context of which it has
been a part' ('Sieving', 120, on Bakhtin, *Dostoevsky*, 167). Depending on
the structure and ethos of the text, the conclusion or closure will be more
or less ironic, more or less utopian. Even if, as in *The Color Purple*, the
fairy-tale structure (Lupton, 409) risks the bathos of a happy-ever-after
ending, we are made aware of the struggle throughout the novel by the
battle of words with words.[3]

The struggle may be seen in relation to what Showalter and
others have called the 'poetics of the Other' (Showalter, 184) or what
Wayne Booth has called the double-voiced discourse of feminist texts
(Booth, 45–76). But it must also be seen in relation to the sense of
double-voicedness in black culture theorized as early as 1903 in
W.E.B. DuBois's *Souls of Black Folk*:

After the Egyptian and Indian, the Greek and Roman, the Teuton and Mongolian, the Negro is a sort of seventh son, born with a veil, and gifted with second-sight in this American world, – a world which yields him no true self-consciousness, but only lets him see himself through the revelation of the other world. It is a peculiar sensation, this double-consciousness, this sense of always looking at one's self through the eyes of others, of measuring one's soul by the tape of a world that looks on in amused contempt and pity. One ever feels his two-ness, – an American, a Negro; two souls, two thoughts, two unreconciled strivings; two warring ideals in one dark body, whose dogged strength alone keeps it from being torn asunder. (3)

With variations, this 'double-consciousness' appears again in Ralph Ellison's 'double-vision' (132) and, significantly, in Henry Louis Gates, Jr.'s 'two-toned discourse', inspired in part by Bakhtinian theory ('Criticism', 4; *Signifying*, 51).

My use of Bakhtin's dialogism might best be illustrated by an example he gives in 'Discourse in the Novel' of one whose language is for the most part not dialogized: the peasant. In speaking of the process by which a peasant might develop a dialogic awareness of language (with apologies for a simplification of the real peasant's life), he emphasizes the process of confrontation and relativization of any given set of languages. His theory of dialogism and the example of the peasant offer possibilities for a feminist analysis of literary texts:

Thus an illiterate peasant, miles away from any urban center, naively immersed in an unmoving and for him unshakable everyday world, nevertheless lived in several language systems: he prayed to God in one language (Church Slavonic), sang songs in another, spoke to his family in a third and, when he began to dictate petitions to the local authorities through a scribe, he tried speaking yet a fourth language (the official-literate language, 'paper' language). All these are *different languages*, even from the point of view of abstract socio-dialectological markers. But these languages were not dialogically coordinated in the linguistic consciousness of the peasant; he passed from one to the other without thinking, automatically: each was indisputably in its own place, and the place of each was indisputable. He was not yet able to regard one language (and the verbal world corresponding to it) through the eyes of another language (that is, the language of everyday life and the everyday world with the language of prayer or song, or vice versa).

As soon as a critical interanimation of languages began to occur in the consciousness of our peasant, as soon as it became clear that these were not only various different languages but even internally variegated languages, that the ideological systems and approaches to the world that were indissolubly connected with these languages contradicted each other and in no way could live in peace and quiet with one another – then the inviolability and predetermined quality of these languages came to an end, and the necessity of actively choosing one's orientation among them began. (*DI*, 295–6)

Walker's *The Color Purple* could well be plotted by the heroine's growing awareness of the languages that surround her. My feminist analysis is interested in the voices that are thereby made relative and thus changeable and those that help to initiate change and in what direction. Walker is able to convey this juxtaposition and evaluation of languages in an early scene where Celie's stepfather is trying to marry her off. Celie recounts the scene, since the book is made up of a series of letters written by her to God or to her sister Nettie, and letters from Nettie to Celie.

Well, He say, real slow, I can't let you have Nettie . . . But I can let you have Celie . . . She ain't fresh tho, but I spect you know that. She spoiled. Twice. But you don't need a fresh woman no how. I got a fresh one in there myself and she sick all the time. He spit, over the railing. The children git on her nerve, she not much of a cook. And she big already.

Mr. – he don't say nothing. I stop crying I'm so surprise.

She ugly. He say. But she ain't no stranger to hard work. And she clean. And God done fixed her. You can do everything just like you want to and she ain't gonna make you feed it or clothe it.

Mr. – still don't say nothing. I take out the picture of Shug Avery. I look into her eyes. Her eyes say Yeah, it *bees* that way sometime.

Fact is, he say, I got to git rid of her. She too old to be living here at home. And she a bad influence on my other girls. She'd come with her own linen. She can take that cow she raise down there back of the crib. But Nettie you flat out can't have. Not now. Not never.

Mr. – finally speak. Clearing his throat. I ain't never really look at that one, he say.

Well, next time you come you can look at her. She ugly. Don't even look like she kin to Nettie. But she'll make the better wife. She ain't smart either, and I'll just be fair, you have to watch her or she'll give away everything you own. But she can work like a man.

    Mr. – say How old she is?

    He say, She near twenty. And another thing – she tell lies. (17–18)

Celie's voice would seem to be absent from this account of the male voices around her. But at two points we find an intersection of other positions: Celie's 'I stop crying. I'm so surprise' and Shug Avery's 'Yeah, it *bees* that way sometime'. On the one hand, Celie's surprise signals the reader to shift perspective, to stand outside what is being said. On the other hand, Shug's 'it *bees* that way', a quotation that Celie imagines the face on a photograph to be saying, stands with Celie, both enlightening her as to the ways to the world – the world that she is still learning about and experiencing in all its horrors – and at the same time standing with her as some form of reassurance: this is the way the world is and I'm still here to talk about it. The voice is both specifically Shug Avery's – the woman who will provide Celie with an emancipatory discourse – and, more generally, the discourse of a popular tradition – a communal voice of black women.[4] As readers, we are meant to choose and assess with Celie.

    Henry Louis Gates, in his revealing analysis of *The Color Purple*, points out that, in fact, the only voice we hear is Celie's own, since all is written in the epistolary form: 'There is no true mimesis . . . , only diegesis . . . the opposition between them has collapsed' (*Signifying*, 249). I want to argue that even within the diegetic mode of letter writing, the other person's voice is heard either as reported speech or as dialogized borrowed speech. What is remarkable in *The Color Purple* is this movement from a juxtaposition of languages to a dialogized evaluation of them.

    The at-first seemingly monological appropriation of the male discourse about women is thus slowly undermined by the text so that when Albert (the Mr. –, of this quotation, who does eventually marry Celie) later tells her she is nothing but 'pore, black and a woman', she is able to respond, taking his word and supplementing them, transforming them into her own affirmation:

    I'm pore, I'm black, I may be ugly and can't cook, a voice say to everything listening. *But I'm here.*

    Amen, say Shug. Amen, amen. (187, my emphasis)

The nothing, then, is transformed and defeated by existence, by *I'm here*, and by her saying, '*I'm here*'.[5] I am, therefore I am not nothing, or *not* an object to be bartered, possessed, exploited, and abused. The fact of her presence resists formulations and implies a reality beyond the labels of one man's discourse. A further discourse, that of Shug's 'amen' repeated three times, echoes Celie's claim, but not entirely in a monological way. The fact of another's speech affirms the existence of two subjects. As Herrmann argues, Bakhtin's dialogic allows for 'the recognition of the other not as object but as "an/other" subject' (6). Furthermore, the fact of Celie's *saying* 'I'm here' confirms her position as a subject in discourse, fully acknowledged and active in dialogic relation to others. I am, therefore I speak, and you better listen, listen to all my voices, all the other voices I've found to contradict you with. In fact, Albert has tried to reduce her to nothing because she has used language against him by cursing him: 'You can't curse nobody . . . you nothing at all' (187).

The beginning of the novel establishes the link between existence, speech, and freedom. The novel opens with Alphonso (the stepfather)'s exhortation to Celie – his prohibition quoted in italics which stands on its own before Celie's first letter. It is the only sentence in this epistolary novel outside the letter form:

You better not tell nobody but God. It'd kill your mammy. (11)

Once again male speech is at the origins of Celie's speech – the origin of the novel. Her body, her actions, the existence of the child inside her, are at this point to be denied. If spoken, they are a threat to the existence of someone Celie loves, her mammy. Speaking would be an act of murder, a matricide. But ironically enough, Alphonso gives her one way out: 'don't tell nobody *but God*' (my italics) – perhaps the result of some dialogical residue of his Christian culture. Celie picks up the idea, and although she is too ashamed of her life to talk to God, to face that person, she can, through the mediation of pen and paper, write to God. And so her words begin with 'Dear God'.

Celie has more than a trace of her white Christian heritage in her speech. Her first letter continues, 'I am fourteen years old. I am I have always been a good girl. Maybe you can give me a sign letting me know what is happening to me' (11). She presents her qualifications – her age and the fact that she has always been a 'good girl', suggesting she is talking to an ideal authority by whose rules she has lived her life: in other words, to the white male God. But the 'I am' is ironically crossed out, and instead we get a story: 'Last spring after little Lucious come . . .' So, with existence denied, she can still turn to writing, to her letters, and through them she will eventually reclaim her 'I am'. Narrative, thus, is produced by the displaced, repressed, or absent being. As Gates has argued, Celie from 'an erased presence . . . writes herself into being' (*Signifying*, 243).

The male voices that forbid her to speak and demand that she be a good girl will be overthrown. The ideal male authority – the white God himself – will be transformed through counter-voices into a multiplicity

39

of voices. Once Celie has worked her way toward some awareness of her exploitation, she is able to say to her friend Shug:

> What God do for me? I ast.
>
> She say, Celie! Like she shock. He gave you life, good health, and a good woman that loves you to death.
>
> Yeah, I say, and he give me a lynched daddy, a crazy mama, a lowdown dog of a step pa and a sister I probably won't ever see again. Anyhow, I say, the God I been praying and writing to is a man. And act just like all the other mens I know. Trifling, forgitful and lowdown.
>
> She say, Miss Celie, You better hush. God might hear you.
>
> Let 'im hear me, I say. If he ever listened to poor colored women the world would be a different place, I can tell you. . . . [He] just sit up there glorying in being deef, I reckon. (175–6)

Here God himself is monological – deaf to the languages of 'poor colored women'. Ultimately the other voices will drown out the monological male voice of God until God is transformed into 'everything that is or ever was or will be'. Celie writes:

> Still, it is like Shug say, You have to git man off your eyeball, before you can see anything a'tall.
>
> Man corrupt everything, say Shug. He on you box of grits, in you head, and all over the radio. He try to make you think he everywhere. Soon as you think he everywhere, you think he god. But he ain't. Whenever you trying to pray, and man plop himself on the other end of it, tell him to git lost, say Shug. Conjure up flowers, wind, water, a big rock. (179)

Celie's sister Nettie on the other side of the Atlantic, in her highly ambiguous role as a black Christian missionary doing the work of white people among the black tribes of Africa, has to work through a similar displacement especially of a white European God. When she tries to mix the two discourses – black and white, European and African – she inevitably is forced to give up one, or both, be it the photographs of Livingston, Stanley or Christ, or the African tribe's scarification of faces, or the Olinka men who begin to sound like 'Pa back home'.

If Celie starts her letters in silence, in silent confessions to a white male God because he's the only one she, at this point in time, has to take 'along' (26), she eventually shifts her addressee to Nettie, her lost sister, and it might be argued that the lost sister, the other woman, is the only true receiver of Celie's tale. 'I don't even look at mens' writes Celie. 'I look at women, tho, cause I'm not scared of them' (15). She escapes the patriarchal voice dominating her by means of the voices of other women and the connection she feels with these women. An alternative to her exploitation by men does show up within the first few pages of the novel – the photograph of Shug Avery, the beautiful cabaret singer and Albert's lover. The photograph introduces Celie to another world of wealth (furs and motorcars) and triumph (Shug stands with her foot on someone else's car), while still maintaining an element of Celie's own experience (Shug's eyes are sad). Celie is immediately riveted into silent action:

An now when I dream, I dream of Shug Avery. She be dress to kill, whirling and laughing. (16)

The dream eventually turns into reality as Shug becomes her mentor and her lover. From Shug, Celie learns to stand up and fight, to enjoy her body, to be economically self-sufficient, and to create her gender-free God.

The connection with women, even to the extent of sexual love between them, has a privileged place in the novel. It weaves through the book in ascending power as the domination of men over Celie diminishes, and as Celie's own self-awareness and sense of identity grow. One climactic moment occurs when Celie tells Albert she's leaving him:

What will people say, you running off to Memphis like you don't have a house to look after?

Shug say, Albert. Try to think like you got some sense. Why any woman give a shit what people think is a mystery to me.

Well, say Grady, trying to bring light. A woman can't git a man if peoples talk.

Shug look at me and us giggle. Then us laugh sure nuff. Then Squeak start to laugh. Then Sofia. All us laugh and laugh.

Shug say, Ain't they something? Us say um *hum*, and slap the table, wipe the water from our eyes. (182)

The carnivalesque joke here is that Celie has found emotional and sexual satisfaction beyond the world of men. The last thing she wants is to 'git a man'.

Celie will also achieve economic self-sufficiency. Her designing and sewing lead her into both the world of the artist and the world of economic production. It has been argued that Walker risks 'mimicking the values of the dominant [capitalist] culture' (Lupton, 414); rather, she

is trying to produce a combination of artist creation and cottage industry.
The extent of her enterprise so far includes two women who work and
talk with her. One of the most moving passages in the book describes
Celie's designing of pants for various characters – she designs each pair
of pants for a specific individual to serve her or his work in life:

> I start to make pants for Jack. They have to be camel. And soft and
> strong. And they have to have big pockets so he can keep a lot of
> children's things. Marbles and string and pennies and rocks. And
> they have to be washable and they have to fit closer round the leg
> than Shug's so he can run if he need to snatch a child out of the way
> of something. And they have to be something he can lay back in
> when he hold Odessa in front of the fire. (191–2)

The pleasure the reader derives here is from Celie's success, but also her
inventiveness, her clear unchecked creativity which is not self-centered
but directed outward.

Celie's last letter is addressed to 'Dear God. Dear stars, dear trees, dear
sky, dear peoples. Dear Everything. Dear God' (249). With Nettie's
return, no more letters are necessary. It is implied that speech will
replace writing as the two sisters will be able to commune, to share
their 'stories' face to face as they live them. The ending finally defeats
narration because it solves the problem of silence, the 'Don't tell nobody'
of the opening. There is an attempt to establish a de-gendered
community centered around Celie and her sister. The villain step-pa is
killed off (although he only dies in his sleep); Albert is 'converted' and
can be seen sitting on the porch sewing with Celie, the two of them
smoking their pipes and Albert listening to Celie's tales, finding her
such good company; Adam, Celie's son, has scarred his face to match his
Olinka bride's; some of the women wear pants; and some of the men
wear dresses (even though these are called robes); the family structure,
which up till now had proven disastrous for all the characters, is now
reconstituted in this new household of husband and wife, lesbian lovers,
adulterous lovers, and grown children who now have birth mother,
adoptive father, aunt and stepmother all under the same roof. The book
ends with a Fourth of July party, not celebrating the birth of a Nation,
but the freedom of its slaves:

> White people busy celebrating they independence from England
> July 4th . . . so most black folks don't have to work. Us can spend
> the day celebrating each other. (250)

The racist problems are not solved in this book, although there is a
suggestion that Sophia has established something with her former white

ward. The socio-economic world outside this small black community of friends and relatives has not changed except that a few black women now have a house, work, love, and an income. But within the community all differences have been dispersed in a fairy-tale ending. We have indeed moved beyond Bakhtin's world of dialogism into his world of the community, an ideal social state where 'aggressive intercutting of discourses' is no longer necessary (Godzich, Oct. 1).

At the end of *The Women of Brewster Place*, Naylor brings women together cooking and partying, but her resolution comes within the very real confines of a racist, sexist, and class-conscious society. The question here is how to survive. The party is a block party, a first step towards establishing this tenement community and pressuring the landlord for better living conditions. Nevertheless, the narrator's conclusion retains some irony: the tenements deteriorate and the inhabitants move on to yet another Brewster Place – even if it is not called that – to encounter more of the same. Again the economic world of production and exploitation is not changed. The novel at its end only claims to have given us the existence and persistence of these women, the 'I'm here' of *The Color Purple*. However, empowerment has come to the novel's characters through solidarity and the telling of their tales. The author stands behind the 'colored daughters' who will dream on, who survive, now and with the addition of this book, not always in silence. Once again, the key to persistence comes from a kind of narrative, this time figured in the novel as dreaming. The dreams, however, are not intimations of a transcendent presence as much as they are modes of producing a self that is not oppressed.

The women are framed by the street itself, its history of corruption and decay. Within this context they struggle to survive as human entities, as something more than biological specimens of a decaying world. When, in Mattie Michael's last dream, the women tear the brick wall down at the end of Brewster Place, that is, demolish the deterministic structure that has entombed them in a naturalist's world of exploitation, poverty and brutality, we know this action is a metaphor for breaking out of that deterministic world. The women, working on an entirely unconscious and collective impulse, start to throw the bricks out into the avenue. The carnivalesque scene of chairs and barbecues, umbrellas and spiked high heels going at the wall and being hurled at the windows of the station wagons and Datsuns outside, expresses the violence and at the same time the confines of these women's experience. The violence that has been done to them by the 'normal' bourgeois world of Datsuns (those people who have profited by the exclusion, the blocking out of view, of Brewster Place from the main avenue) is now literally thrown back at them in this parody of a revolution. This is not a travesty; the women are in no way demeaned by their activity. Rather, their material conditions erupt out of silence and are made known. Their contrast with the norm allows for a momentary vision of change.

Nevertheless, despite the collectivity and the carnival spirit, the scene does not ultimately undo the memory of staring into these same bricks with Lorraine while she goes insane during her rape one story earlier. The violence lingers as both a violence done to these women and one that necessarily erupts in reaction. To claim their own, to define themselves as something other than the discourse imposed on them by patriarchy or capitalism, they must rally their high heels and their barbecues in violent combat. Their actions as actual political revolution must be seen on one level as impotent gestures – there is no takeover of municipal power. Like the medieval carnivals that inspired Bakhtin's theories, this revolutionary gesture is only temporary and the old order will be resumed – a new Brewster Place will be built and the women will continue to suffer. But the vision has taken place and indeed has threatened those outsiders, figured in the taxi driver who races away from the 'riot in this street' (187).

There is another moment earlier in the novel which does perhaps balance the horror of Lorraine's rape. Ciel, a young woman, has lost both her children, one through an abortion her husband forced her to have, the other through an accident while her husband tells her in another room that he is leaving her. Ciel goes dead; she cannot mourn and is killing herself by not eating:

> Mattie stood in the doorway, and an involuntary shudder went through her when she saw Ciel's eyes. Dear God, she thought, she's dying, and right in front of our faces.
>
> 'Merciful Father, no!' she bellowed. There was no prayer, no bended knee or sackcloth supplication in those words, but a blasphemous fireball that shot forth and went smashing against the gates of heaven, raging and kicking, demanding to be heard.
>
> 'No! No! No!' Like a black Brahman cow, desperate to protect her young, she surged into the room, pushing the neighbor woman and the others out of her way. She approached the bed with her lips clamped shut in such force that the muscles in her jaw and the back of her neck began to ache.
>
> She sat on the edge of the bed and enfolded the tissue-thin body in her huge ebony arms. And she rocked. Ciel's body was so hot it burned Mattie when she first touched her, but she held on and rocked. Back and forth, back and forth – she had Ciel so tightly she could feel her young breast flatten against the buttons of her dress. The black mammoth gripped so firmly that the slightest increase of pressure would have cracked the girl's spine. But she rocked.

And somewhere from the bowels of her being came a moan from Ciel, so high at first it couldn't be heard by anyone there, but the yard dogs began an unholy howling. And Mattie rocked. And then, agonizingly slow, it broke its way through the parched lips in a spaghetti-thin column of air that could be faintly heard in the frozen room.

Ciel moaned. Mattie rocked. Propelled by the sound, Mattie rocked her out of that bed, out of that room, into a blue vastness just underneath the sun and above time. She rocked her over Aegean seas so clean they shone like crystal, so clear the fresh blood of sacrificed babies torn from their mother's arms and given to Neptune could be seen like pink froth on the water. She rocked her on and on, past Dachau, where soul-gutted Jewish mothers swept their children's entrails off laboratory floors. They flew past the spilled brains of Senegalese infants whose mothers had dashed them on the wooden sides of slave ships. And she rocked on. (102–3)

The chapter continues on for two more pages until finally Ciel can cry and fall asleep. The love, bodily warmth, and blasphemous fireball of the older woman eventually exorcize the deadness and the silence. Mattie's 'No! No! No!', like Shug Avery's 'Amen, Amen, Amen', affirms existence rejecting in its repetitions the voices that stand against it. The 'blasphemous fireball' exorcises the silence until an inaudible moan is eeked out.

The book leaves us finally with these connected and now vocal colored daughters. The author can write that the street only 'dies when the odors of hope, despair, lust, and caring are wiped out by the seasonal winds . . .' (192). Instead of the death of the street, the last line of the book is 'So Brewster Place still waits to die'. The book ends with the ongoing life of the women despite the fact they have all been evicted:

But the colored daughters of Brewster, spread over the canvas of time, still wake up with their dreams misted on the edge of a yawn. They get up and pin those dreams to wet laundry hung out to dry, they're mixed with a pinch of salt and thrown into pots of soup, and they're diapered around babies. They ebb and flow, ebb and flow, but never disappear. (192)

As I have noted, these dreams play an important role in the novel. As figures of desire they embody all that is not defined by discourse directed against them and as such put that discourse into question. From the acknowledgements and the epigraph through each story a dream is figured right up to the final revolution in Mattie's dream. With the end of that chapter, Etta wakes up Mattie: 'Woman, you still in bed? Don't you know what day it is? We're gonna have a party' (189).

Ntozake Shange, in her preface to *for colored girls who have considered suicide*, also displaces her authority to speak of the play's origins in a women's group, in performance, and in dance workshops. She describes the evolution of the work in terms of an interplay between actors and audience, or between the different actors, between writers and environment. The thrust of the book was to clarify 'our lives – & the lives of our mothers, daughters, & grandmothers – as women' (xiv), but the process is achieved through a presentation and intersection of various different voices – a process, in other words, essentially dialogical, as the play presents us with seven different women and their stories. The goal is not to establish all women as equal or as identical, but to present the uniqueness and, as in *The Color Purple* and *Brewster Place*, the connectedness of women. The play opens with the women running in from separate exits, freezing in postures of distress. When one woman tries to call to the others there is no response: they are silent, separate, and in pain. The opening poem, 'dark phrases of womanhood', presents the problem to be solved by the play. As yet, woman is only 'half-notes scattered/without rhythm', and this is partly because she has the prohibition, as in *The Color Purple*, not to speak: 'don't tell nobody don't tell a soul/she's dancin on beer cans & shingles' (1–2). This separateness continues as some women reject others, parodying one dancing, or refusing to dance, but gradually as the stories unfold, as difference and similarity are established, they begin to dance together until the end when they can 'enter into a closed tight circle' (67).

The ending of *for colored girls* comes close to a utopian world of love and connectedness as the seven women sing their 'song of joy': 'i found god in myself/& i loved her', but the last line with its present progressive tense ('& this is for colored girls who have considered suicide/but *are movin* to the ends of their own rainbows' [my italics]) suggests that the struggle continues well after the dance. As the title implies, the play is made up of two impulses: one toward suicide and the other toward hope. By the end of the play women have sung the song of their body, dancing, poetry and love of women, but the various stories, including Beau Willie's story where a mad husband drops his two children from the fifth-story window, leave us with no doubt that the inevitable confrontation with despair will continue. The voices speak back to the numerable irresponsible lovers, rapists, or bearers of privilege and accepted morality, but we are reminded of fatal consequences of silence in the abortion poem or most dramatically when Crystal's lack of voice takes her children from her:

i stood by beau in the window/with naomi reachin for me/&
kwame screamin mommy mommy from the fifth story/but i cd
only whisper/& he dropped em. (63)

This story calls for a period of mourning, a process of soothing and
healing perhaps comparable to Mattie's rocking of Ciel, and indeed
the play ends with a communal song that takes the women up through
the pain.

In another context, the poem called 'toussaint', while being a story of a
young black girl who in 1955 was forced to attend integrated schools and
live in an integrated neighborhood, is also about history and the position
of the subject in it. The child's sense of reality is ironically first evoked
when she *reads* about Toussaint L'Ouverture. Her voice of rebellion must
pass through her imaginary historical friend, while her identity is only
fully articulated when she finds her voice and place in history. At each
stage the historical context is crucial: the time of the revolutionary in
Haiti and the time of the young girl in America. While Toussaint is one
who 'didnt low no white man to tell him nothin/no napolean/not
maximillien/not robespierre' (27), the young girl has to figure out 'how
to remove white girls from my hop-scotch games/& etc . . . 1955 was not
a good year for lil blk girls' (28–9).

Having found a young black boy called Toussaint Jones who 'waznt
too different/from' the slave hero, she moves into her own historical
moment fully conscious of her position and her desire to change it:

toussaint jones waz awright wit me
no tellin what all spirits we cd move
down by the river
st. louis 1955 (32)

The poem ends with this signature of place and date.

What I have been calling a play is actually a series of poems, which
in turn are stories, memoirs, or exhortations. Within these stories are
multiple voices heard and debated. Even the dances that punctuate the
stories offer other voices which have helped to constitute the subjects
of these poems, songs by Martha and the Vandellas or the Dells. Shange
is able to introduce the various voices without appropriating them all,
without making them all hers.

Without having ferreted out all the voices, male and female, for these
works, the project is remarkably clear. The Bakhtinian dialogism is not
a strict binary opposition between, for instance, the marginal woman's
voice and the central dominant male voice. It is rather, in these books,
the exploration and activating of the unvoiced exiled world of women
– that other place in all its variety. It defines and redefines the subject
with multiple heroines, multiple stories, themselves in constant struggle
to ferret out the voices of the past and present, be it Martha and the
Vandellas, Toussaint l'Ouverture, or the spirits of their grandmothers.
If there is any trace of idealism left, I would say it is in the persistent

call for love between women, a love seen as a healing of the wounds created in our patriarchal world. Perhaps this is the new ethos of our age – a carnivalesque one in as much as the fact that this love has been forbidden by the male authority and is seen as a premise for changing the world, for turning it upside down.

Notes

1. See also Bauer, Carby [*Reconstructing*], Díaz-Diocaretz, Finke, and Yaeger.

2. For a broader discussion of the struggle with naming, see Benston, 151–72.

3. In revising this paper, I have had the benefit of King-Kok Cheung's insights into *The Color Purple*: 'Despite the excruciating process of change [Celie has] endured', she argues, the 'text conveys a sense of triumph that is due ... less to the happy ending itself than to the way the final stage is negotiated, to the means by which a voice truly one's own is fostered' (172). Although I would take issue with the voice that 'is truly one's own'. Cheung's emphasis on the process of negotiating success is crucial.

4. See Hazel V. Carby's analysis of the lyrics of Afro-American women's blues.

5. Cheung makes a similar point (168).

Works cited

BAKHTIN, MIKHAIL. *The Dialogic Imagination: Four Essays*. Ed. Michael Holquist. Trans. Caryl Emerson and Michael Holquist. Austin: Texas University Press, 1981.

——. *Esthétique de la création verbale*. Trans. Alfreda Aucouturier. Paris: Gallimard, 1984.

——. *Rabelais and his World*. Trans. H. Iswolsky. Cambridge, MA: MIT Press, 1968.

BAKHTIN, MIKHAIL and P.N. MEDVEDEV. *The Formal Method in Literary Scholarship: A Critical Introduction to Sociological Poetics*. Trans. Albert J. Wehrle. 1978; Cambridge, MA: Harvard University Press, 1985.

BAUER, DALE. *Feminist Dialogics: A Theory of Failed Community*. Albany, NY: State University of New York Press, 1988.

BENSTON, KIMBERLY W. 'I Yam What I Am: The Topos of (Un)naming in Afro-American Literature'. In *Black Literature and Literary Theory*. Ed. Henry Louis Gates, Jr. New York: Methuen, 1984, 151–72.

BOOTH, WAYNE C. 'Freedom of Interpretation: Bakhtin and the Challenge of Feminist Criticism'. *Critical Inquiry* 9 (1982): 45–76.

CARBY, HAZEL V. 'It Jus Be's Dat Way Sometime: The Sexual Politics of Women's Blues'. *Radical America* 20 (1986): 9–22.

———. *Reconstructing Womanhood: The Emergence of the Afro-American Woman Novelist*. New York: Oxford University Press, 1987.

CHEUNG, KING-KOK. ' "Don't Tell": Imposed Silences in *The Color Purple* and *The Woman Warrior'*. *PMLA* 103 (1988): 162–74.

DÍAZ-DIOCARETZ, MYRIAM. 'Black North American Women Poets in the Semiotics of Culture'. In *Women, Feminist Identity and Society in the 1980s*. Ed. M. Díaz-Diocaretz and I.M. Zaval. Amsterdam: John Benjamins, 1985, 37–60.

———. 'Sieving the Matriheritage of the Sociotext'. In *The Difference Within: Feminism and Critical Theory*. Ed. Elizabeth Meese and Alice Parker. Amsterdam: John Benjamins, 1988.

DUBOIS, W.E.B. *The Souls of Black Folk: Essays and Sketches*. Chicago: A.C. McClurg, 1918.

ELLISON, RALPH. *Shadow and Act*. New York: Random House, 1964.

FINKE, LAURIE. 'The Rhetoric of Marginality: Why I Do Feminist Theory'. *Tulsa Studies in Women's Literature* 5 (1986): 251–72.

GATES, HENRY LOUIS, JR. 'Criticism in the Jungle'. In his *Black Literature and Literary Theory*. New York: Methuen, 1984, 1–24.

———. *The Signifying Monkey: A Theory of Afro-American Literary Criticism*. New York: Oxford University Press, 1988.

GODZICH, WLAD SEMINAR. Comparative Literature 1400L: The Critical Theory of Bakhtin and his Circle. 1987–88. University of Toronto.

HERRMANN, ANNE. *The Dialogic and Difference: 'An/Other Woman' in Virginia Woolf and Christa Wolf*. New York: Columbia University Press, 1989.

KAPLAN, CORA. 'Speaking/Writing/Feminism'. In *On Gender and Writing*. Ed. Michelene Wandor. London: Routledge and Kegan Paul, 1983. Rpt. in *Feminist Literary Theory: A Reader*. Ed. Mary Eagleton. Oxford: Basil Blackwell, 1986.

LUPTON, MARY JANE. 'Clothes and Closure in Three Novels by Black Women'. *Black American Literature Forum* 20 (1986): 409–21.

NAYLOR, GLORIA. *The Women of Brewster Place*. 1982; Harmondsworth: Penguin, 1983.

SHANGE, NTOZAKE. *for colored girls who have considered suicide/when the rainbow is enuf*. 1977; New York: Bantam, 1980.

SHOWALTER, ELAINE. 'The Other Bostonians: Gender and Literary Study'. *Yale Journal of Criticism* (1988): 179–87.

SHUKMAN, ANN, ed. *Bakhtin School Papers*. Somerton, Oxford: RPT Publications, 1983.

VOLOŠINOV, V.N. *Marxism and the Philosophy of Language*. Trans. L. Matejka and I.R. Titunik. New York: Seminar Press, 1973.

WALKER, ALICE. *The Color Purple*. New York: Pocket Books, 1982.

WILLIS, SUSAN. 'Eruptions of "Funk": Historicizing Toni Morrison'. In *Black Literature and Literary Theory*. Ed. Henry Louis Gates, Jr. New York: Methuen, 1984, 263–83.

———. *Specifying: Black Women Writing the American Experience*. Madison: University of Wisconsin Press, 1987.

YAEGER, PATRICIA. *Honey-Mad Women: Emancipatory Strategies in Women's Writing.* New York: Columbia University Press, 1988.

Complementary readings of these novels are by: WENDY WALL, 'Lettered Bodies and Corporeal Texts in *The Color Purple*', *Studies in American Fiction* 16, 1 (1988): 83–97; MICHAEL AWKWARD, *Inspiriting Influences: Tradition, Revision, and Afro-American Women's Novels* (New York: Columbia University Press, 1991), Chapter 3, 'Authorial Dreams of Wholeness: (Dis)Unity, (Literary) Parentage, and *The Women of Brewster Place*', pp. 97–133.

3 Questioning Race and Gender Definitions: Dialogic Subversions in *The Woman Warrior**

MALINI JOHAR SCHUELLER

Like the previous essay, this one engages Bakhtin's theory of dialogism. Like O'Connor, Malini Schueller notes Bakhtin's limited attention to race and gender and thus to her own purpose of uncovering structures of oppression. Schueller moves to revise this limitation by placing Bakhtin squarely in a feminist context. Noting Julia Kristeva's early appreciation of Bakhtin theories 'as sites of women's resistance and women's voicing', she also invokes Hélène Cixous and Monique Wittig to support her argument that dialogic thinking is necessarily subversive and, therefore, the goal for 'all marginal or oppressed groups'. In Schueller's account, Bakhtinian 'voices' are by definition voices from the margins, alternative, resistant voices that express otherness in an 'intersubjective' context that is always deeply political.

Schueller applies this politicized Bakhtin to issues of self and society in Maxine Hong Kingston's *The Woman Warrior*. In an absolute assertion that threatens to undercut the very dialogism that it proclaims, she insists that women and minorities must 'reject the concept of a stable and autonomous self' in favour of destabilized and destabilizing identities. Schueller finds *The Woman Warrior* to exemplify this process, both in its dramatization of unstable subjectivity and its multiple literary and cultural forms of expression.

Ever since its publication in 1976, Maxine Hong Kingston's *The Woman Warrior* has been praised as a feminist work. But while critics have written extensively about the articulation of female experience in *The Woman Warrior*, they have been unable to deal simultaneously with the questions of national and racial identity that the book so powerfully raises. However, if we approach women's writing as centrally concerned not strictly with gender but with oppression, we can fruitfully examine

* Reprinted from *Criticism* 31, 4 (1989): 421–37.

the conjuncture and relationship between female and ethnic identity, an important issue not only for this text but for feminist theory as well. I will briefly examine the politicization of female identity offered by some feminist critics and then examine *The Woman Warrior* as a dialogic text, one which subverts singular definitions of racial and ethnic identity and which valorizes intersubjectivity and communication.

In 'The Laugh of the Medusa' Helene Cixous proclaimed a manifesto for women's writing: 'A feminine text cannot fail to be/ more than subversive. It is volcanic;/ as it is written it brings about an/ upheaval of the old property crust,/ carrier of masculine investments.'[1] Feminist critics have long recognized that what constitutes female experience is not biological gender or a specific female psyche but the constraints and limitations felt by women as a result of the cultural constitution of gender and the phallocentric organization of society. To write socially and politically as a woman is therefore to question the truth status and ostensible ideological neutrality of cultural norms and institutions. The feminine text, Cixous continues, 'shatter[s] the framework of institutions'. Kristeva has similarly argued that women's writing should 'reject everything finite, definite, structured, loaded with meaning, in the existing state of society'.[2] Even though Marxist feminists like Monique Wittig have criticized the apparent lack of recognition by feminists of 'women' (as opposed to mythical 'woman') as an oppressed social class, it is obvious that Cixous and Kristeva are in fact very aware of this oppression. The subversions of institutions and cultural norms that Cixous and Kristeva call for in women's writing are goals for all marginal and oppressed groups. Marginal groups have little investment in concepts of unity, coherence, and universality because their own political efficacy depends upon forcing a recognition of the value of difference and diversity upon the dominant culture.[3] Third world feminists have in fact challenged the presupposition of feminists who speak in the name of a singular womanhood and whose own analyses are blind to racial difference.[4] The danger of theorizing about marginalized groups – women and racial minorities – is actually that of positing an essential blackness and feminity.[5] What is politically important for women and racial minorities is not to frame correct definitions of female and ethnic identity but to question all such definitions. Above all it means to reject the concept of a stable and autonomous self upon which such definitions depend.

Bakhtin's privileging if the dialogic rests upon a similar awareness of the dangers of unified thinking and the liberative potential of dialogic subversions. Dostoevsky, the examplar of dialogic thinking, succeeds not by creating a single consciousness at the center of the text but by presenting 'a whole formed by the interaction of several consciousnesses, none of which entirely becomes an object for the other'.[6] Dialogic

thinking is based on intersubjectivity. It celebrates the Otherness of
language, the potential of words to always carry echoes of other words.
That is why feminist critics are increasingly beginning to use Bakhtin's
theories as sites of women's resistance and women's voicing.[7] Kristeva
was the first to see the productive challenge of dialogic thinking.
'Bakhtinian dialogism', according to Kristeva, 'identifies writing as both
subjectivity and communication, or better, as intertextuality.'[8] Dialogic
forms such as the carnival challenge 'God, authority, and social law'.[9]
Dialogic subversions, as Patricia Yaeger has usefully demonstrated,
are emancipatory strategies in women's writing.[10] Few contemporary
American writers are as aware of the need to question and subvert
accepted cultural definitions as Maxine Hong Kingston. *The Woman
Warrior* is a sustained subversion of cultural, racial and gender
definitions and an affirmation of a radical intersubjectivity as the
basis of articulation.

The Woman Warrior is a collection of 'memoirs' of Kingston's
experiences of growing up in an immigrant family in Stockton,
California. Kingston reveals the squalor and poverty of Chinatowns, the
endemic racism, the traumas of acculturation in a hostile environment,
and her own attempt to subvert gender hierarchies by imaginative
identification with the woman warrior. But although Kingston writes
polemically against the subjugation of women and the racial hostility
experienced by Chinese Americans, she does not do so from a position
of stability or unity. Articulation itself is a complex issue in the text.
The very act of speaking involves breaking through the gender and race
barriers that suppress voicing from the margins. But the voice Kingston
speaks through is not isolated and autonomous. It refracts, echoes, and
is creatively conjoined with the numerous voices with which it interacts.
This undefined basis of narration dramatizes Kingston's determination
not to create singular definitions of ethnic identity in order to combat
the impoverishing stereotypes to which Chinese Americans are subject,
not to postulate the foundations of a new hierarchy.

It is clear at the very outset that the act of articulation itself will be a
major concern in the book. Kingston begins her memoirs with a secrecy
oath imposed on her by her indomitable mother: 'You must not tell
anyone', and a moral drawn from the story of the adulterous aunt
who has been banished from family memory. 'Don't humiliate us. You
wouldn't like to be forgotten as if you had never been born.'[11] Kingston
is aware of the temerity involved in the very act of her writing. To
articulate herself she must break through the numerous barriers that
condemn her to voicelessness. The unnamed narrator thus begins her
recollections with the act of listening rather than speaking. Sworn to
silence, she hears the tale of the unnamed aunt who gives 'silent birth'
to 'save her inseminator's name' (p. 13). This initial story establishes the

denial of expression women are condemned to in patriarchy and the cultural stranglehold the narrator must fight in order to express herself. The narrator here is a present-day prototype of the 'madwomen' of the Nineteenth Century, whispering their secrets from patriarchal attics.[12] 'Go away and work', her mother tells her. 'Whispering, whispering, making no sense. Madness. I don't feel like hearing your craziness. . . . I shut my mouth, but I felt something alive tearing at my throat' (p. 233).[13] She feels the agony of silence, the 'pain in [her] throat' that comes from holding back the two hundred things she has to tell her mother (p. 229).

But the anxiety of articulation is also peculiarly a racial one. Kingston is sensitive to the brutality and degradation experienced by Chinese immigrants. *China Men* records the heroism of Chinese railroad workers and sugarcane planters who survive hostility and violence. Living in a culture that had for long grouped Orientals with imbeciles and denied Chinese immigrants legal and naturalization rights, the present-day immigrants in *The Woman Warrior* still live in fear.[14] Immigrants thus 'guard their real names with silence' and even after years of living in America avoid signing innocuous permission slips for their children at school (pp. 6, 194). The narrator realizes that 'silence had to do with being a Chinese girl' (p. 193). In the American school she is overcome by dumbness, her voice reduced to a whisper. In the Chinese school she finds her voice but it is a strained one: 'You could hear splinters in my voice, bones rubbing jagged against one another' (p. 196).

These vivid accounts of being tortured by silence are metaphors for the particular limitations the marginal writer must overcome in order to be heard. African-Americans had to demonstrate their very humanity by being able to write when public strictures expressly forbade schooling for them.[15] Ralph Ellison felt compelled to 'prove' his artistry by emulating the modernists. His unnamed, invisible narrator of *Invisible Man* could only discover his identity underground, in a Manhattan city sewer. Alice Walker's heroine, Celie, finds herself unable to speak to anyone but an abstract God; Toni Morison's Pecola remains trapped within a racial silence that condemns her to look forever at her image in the mirror. Kingston's voicelessness is a symbolic expression of the culture's refusal to give her voice legitimacy. But the alternative to this disempowerment, Kingston knows, is not to create a 'true' Chinese woman's voice or to define a singular Chinese identity to celebrate, but to question the very political structures that make positions of power and powerlessness possible. Kingston deconstructs oppositions between American and Chinese male and female, and most importantly between Self and Other by articulating herself through a language in which opposed and diverse voices constantly coexist. By doing so, Kingston questions the values of the autonomous self and definitions of racial and sexual identity, and simultaneously presents dialogic intersubjectivity and community as the realm of hope and possibility.

The tale of Fa Mu Lan, the legendary swordswoman who took her father's place in battle, fought gloriously, returned victorious, and lived obediently thereafter with her parents, is a fascinating and complex narrative of multiple voicing and gender reconstruction. Like most of the stories in the book, this one is not an 'original'. But Kingston revels in retelling tales, deriving her inspiration from the community of tellers before her rather than from defining her own singular voice. The tales of swordswomen become part of the imagination of children as they listen to the adults 'talk-story'. Brave Orchid, the narrator's mother, recreates for her, in turn, the most adventuresome of the swordswomen tales. 'Night after night my mother would talk-story until we fell asleep. I couldn't tell where the stories left off and the dreams began, her voice, the voice of the heroines in my sleep' (p. 24). The narrator remembers her own participation in the continuation of folklore. '. . . As a child I had followed my mother about the house, the two of us singing about Fa Mu Lan. . . . I had forgotten this chant that was once mine, given me by my mother, who may not have known its power to remind' (p. 24). The origins of the tale are communal and familial and the narrator's continuation of it attests to the relatedness of her voice to other voices. It is obvious that the intents of Brave Orchid's and the narrator's tales vary greatly; but the fascinating aspect of the tale is the narrator's ability to tell her own tale both in opposition to, and in harmony with Brave Orchid's tale.

The folkloric intent of the tale is the strengthening of the institution of the family. Girls are reminded that growing up as wives or slaves is a mark of mediocrity, failure. They have the potential to be 'heroines, swordswomen'. But the task of the swordswoman is similar to that of a wife: maintaining the family honor. The swordswoman 'got even with anybody who hurt her family' (p. 23).[16] Brave Orchid's version emphasizes filiality and obedience to the patriarchal order. Fa Mu Lan is 'the girl who took her father's place in battle . . . and returned alive from the war to settle in the village' (p. 24). The narrator will both dialogically challenge certain familial values and retain others. The conflictual role of the narrator within the institution of the family is evident from the beginning. The girl (with whom the narrator identifies) decides to begin her tutelage under the old man and woman of the mountains after hearing their arguments. The old man challenges her: 'You can go pull sweet potatoes, or you can stay with us and learn how to fight barbarians and bandits.' The old woman continues: 'You can avenge your village. . . . You can be remembered by the Han people for your dutifulness' (p. 27). A complex structure of oppositions is built up here. The girl leaves her family to seek her future alone but finds solace in a substitute household; the new family invites her to transgress her traditional role as a female and become a fighter, but the purpose of this transgression is to fight barbarians (read: outsiders); and she must always maintain strict filiality.

But soon within the tale, gender oppositions and family structures become less clear. The old man and woman become, for instance, an embodiment of perennial, natural forces, always changing but always in harmony. They are the dancers of the earth everywhere, two angels, perhaps an infinite number of angels. 'They were light; they were molten, changing gold – Chinese lion dancers, African lion dancers in midstep. . . . Before my eyes, gold bells shredded into gold tassles that fanned into two royal capes that softened into lions' fur' (p. 32). Kingston here seems to attempt a move beyond gender difference to a higher 'unity' beyond gender. But this vision is only an initial move in the attempt to question traditional definitions of gender and deny gender hierarchies.[17] The couple often appear like young lovers. He appears as a 'handsome young man' and she as a 'beautiful young woman' who in spring 'dressed like a bride' (pp. 33–4). But to the girl the manner of the couple suggests that 'the old woman was to the old man a sister or friend rather than a wife' (p. 34) because they do not reduplicate patriarchy. Having problematized traditional gender roles, Kingston presents the complex figure of the swordswoman ready for battle. As the swordswoman leaves her village she is at once the knight in shining armor who rides on her talismanic white horse and the departing bride who receives gifts like wedding presents (p. 42). She wears men's clothes and ties her hair back in manly fashion and is complimented on her beauty. 'How beautiful she looks' (p. 43). Her husband appears before her during battle not as a titular head of the family, but as the lost part of the androgyne, 'the childhood friend found at last' (p. 46). With her pregnancy, the swordswoman's gendering is finally most complicated. She looks like a powerful man, carries the inscription of her family's revenge on her back and her baby in the front.

Through her retelling of the tale, Kingston, in addition to questioning gender roles, also recreates the role of avenger for her purposes. She needs to be the female avenger *and* the avenger of the family. Thus the woman warrior out in battle avenges not only the wrongs to her village but the hierarchical genderizing she has been subject to. In a scene of ironic misspeak, the swordswoman alights at the house of a rich baron and announces herself as a 'female avenger'. The baron, misunderstanding the appellation tries to appeal to her 'man to man'. Oh come now. Everyone takes the girls when he can. . . . "Girls are maggots in the rice." "It is more profitable to raise geese than daughters." He quoted to me the sayings I hated' (p. 51). The legend of the swordswoman becomes the personal story of the Chinese-American girl enraged at the misogynist proverbs she constantly hears in the immigrant community. But Kingston does not separate herself from the community. She also wishes to avenge the hardships of her family, their loss of their laundry in the process of urban renewal, and the pervasive racism to which the Chinese are subjected. 'The swordswoman and I are not so dissimilar', the narrator realizes. 'What we have in common are the words at our backs. . . . And I have so many words – "chink" words and "gook" words too' (p. 63).

Kingston deals with the necessity of maintaining and creating multiple ideological positions, of always letting the numerous voices echo in her own articulations. For Kingston this refraction of other voices is an affirmation of community and diversity. Thus it is appropriate that the final story of the book emphasizes differences and communicative interaction. 'Here is a story my mother told me . . . recently, when I told her I also talk story. The beginning is hers, the ending, mine' (p. 240). As opposed to the beginning of the book where the mother silences her, here the narrator emphasizes how their voices are inextricably and dialogically linked, even if they are different.[18] This relationship of mutuality becomes even more interesting in view of the fact that what the narrator presents as a single story is, compositionally, two stories. The first, in all probability the mother's story, is about the indomitable grandmother whose word is inevitably proven right, and therefore obeyed by the community. She fearlessly commands the household to accompany her to the theater, and true to her prediction, the bandits attack the theater that night, leaving the house safe. Brave Orchid and the grandmother, we guess, are spiritual as well as physical kin. Kingston's story, based on the songs of Ts'ai Yen, is about the importance of achieving mutually creative understanding of the Other. Ts'ai Yen, the embodiment of marginality, perseveres, even in an alien environment to understand and be understood by her captors. 'Her words seemed to be Chinese, but the barbarians understood their sadness and anger' (p. 243). But Ts'ai Yen also seems remarkably similar to the mother that has so vigorously been fleshed out in the book – captive in a strange land, who fights when needed, and whose children do not speak her language. 'She spoke it to them when their father was out of the tent, but they imitated her with senseless singsong words and laughed' (p. 242). These strong resemblances suggest that the two stories are integrally related to each other. Brave Orchid is both an indomitable matriarch, protector of the family, and a captive in a strange land, straining to be heard.

The narrating voice as it emerges in *The Woman Warrior* is thus highly provisional, always full of echoes of other voices, and never autonomous. Kingston does not merely wish to appropriate power and write an authoritative 'marginal' text. She wishes to celebrate marginality as a position of writing and not to postulate a new source of authority or a new hierarchy. Estelle Jelinek has suggested that personal narratives of men and women are fundamentally different. The emphasis by women is on 'the personal, especially on other people, rather than . . . their professional success, of their connectedness to current political or intellectual history'. Men, on the other hand, 'tend to idealize their lives or to cast them into heroic molds to project their universal import'.[19] Reviewing the history of women's autobiography, Carolyn Heilbrun has noted that till recently in women's narratives, the 'public and private life [could] not be linked, as in male narratives'.[20] Jelinek and Heilbrun's points are well taken although one could argue that the refusal of women to cast their lives into heroic molds or to universalize their experiences is in fact a radical form of resistance to patriarchal values. Virginia Woolf, certainly the progenitor of modern women's writing consciously tried to avoid the traditional stable and authoritative 'I'. In *A Room of One's Own* which Kingston echoes, Virginia Woolf said: ' "I" is only a convenient term for somebody who has no real being . . . call me Mary Beton, Mary Seton, Mary Carmichael or by any name you please.'[21] Denying universality, absolute values, and an autonomous self are crucial to writings of all marginal groups.[22]

Just as it is important for Kingston to treat gender as a site of difference, it is vtial for her to treat race too as a play of differences. Indeed to view *The Woman Warrior* as a book about an essential, abstract female self beyond culture and society is to miss the point entirely.[23] The immigrant experience is an integral part of the book. Kingston is sensitive to the dehumanizing definitions Chinese Americans are subject to and is determined not to perpetuate the same by merely inverting the hierarchies. At the base of such definitions is the destructive binary logic which hierarchically divides male and female, self and other, white and non white. Edward Said has compellingly demonstrated how such hierarchies have operated in depictions of the 'Oriental' as the passive and denatured Other.[24] In *The Woman Warrior* Kingston questions and undoes oppositions that make such sterile racial definitions possible.

The narrator of *The Woman Warrior* is uniquely positioned to dialogically question racial oppositions. She is the daughter of Chinese immigrants for whom America is temporary exile, and China home but who nevertheless will stay in America. Her only reality is America, but it is the America of the margins (Kingston makes no bones about Stockton being a racial and economic ghetto). She goes to Chinese school and to American school. Her own undefinable position is a metaphor for the way in which ethnicity will operate: 'I learned to make my mind large, as the universe is large, so that there is room for paradoxes. . . . The dragon lives in the sky, ocean, marshes, and mountains; and the mountains are also its cranium. . . . It breathes fire and water; and sometimes the dragon is one, sometimes many' (p. 35).

Reed Dasenbrock describes *The Woman Warrior* as a 'multicultural' text, one that is not only explicitly about a multicultural society, but one which is implicitly multicultural in 'inscribing readers from other cultures inside [its] own textual dynamics'.[25] Kingston's questioning of racial and cultural oppositions is multicultural in the latter sense – implicitly so, and highly fraught with political significance. On an obvious level Kingston obviously creates clear cultural oppositions, indeed as if she were speaking in the voice of the monocultural reader. American life is logical, concrete, free, and guarantees individual happiness; Chinese life is illogical, superstition-ridden, constricted by social roles, and weighted down by community pressures. The American school teaches that an eclipse is 'just a shadow the earth makes when it comes between the moon and the sun'; the Chinese mother prepares the children to 'slam pots and lids together to scare the frog from swallowing the moon' (p. 197) during the next eclipse. American culture promises the young girl opportunity for excellence if she gets straight 'A's. She can go to college. But she also has the freedom to be a lumberjack in Oregon. In China the girl fears she will be sold as a slave; or within the immigrant community she will be married off to a Fresh Off the Boat Chinese. Indeed the structure of hierarchical oppositions is so cleverly set up that the narrator's growth might be equated with being fully 'American'.[26]

But Kingston sets up these hierarchies only to subvert and make undecidable these singular oppositions. 'To make my waking life American-normal, I turn on the lights before anything untoward makes an appearance. I push the deformed into my dreams, which are in Chinese, the language of impossible dreams' (p. 102). But just as the conventional American reader might begin to feel at ease with the comfortable hierarchy (American-normal, Chinese-deformed), Kingston challenges it. 'When the thermometer in our laundry reached one hundred and eleven degrees on summer afternoons, either my mother or my father would say that it was time to tell another ghost story so that we could get some good chills up our backs' (p. 102). American-normal reality gets so nightmarish that Chinese ghost stories are needed to chase it away into imaginary chills. Not only is the cultural hierarchy subverted but the traditional associations of logicality and dreams are suspended. Similarly, Kingston questions other oppositions. If revolutionary China is a nightmare of ruthless disciplinary violence, Stockton, California has its own gratuitous slum violence. 'The corpses I've seen had been rolled and dumped, sad little dirty bodies covered with a police khaki blanket' (p. 61). The No Name aunt, who is punished for transgressing her social role as wife and daughter-in-law, has her American counterpart in another aunt. Moon Orchid comes to America at the behest of her sister Brave Orchid to claim the Americanized husband who has abandoned her. Her fate: insanity.

In fact the very subtitle of the book, 'Memoirs of a Girlhood Among Ghosts', is designed to question cultural oppositions. Reed Dasenbrock sees the use of the term 'ghost' in the book as a 'Shlovskian defamiliarization not so much of the word as of our self-concept' because as non-Chinese readers we are forced to question our perceptions of ourselves.[27] Ghosts is perhaps the most dialogically used term in the book because it describes the experience of living within both Chinese and American cultures. Kingston has said that ghosts are '"shadowy figures from the past" or unanswered questions about unexplained actions of Chinese, whites, and Chinese in America'.[28] Ghost is an appelation used for any concept that defies clear interpretation. The narrator lives in a double ghost world – that of the China of legends, rumor, history, ancestors she does not know and that of an American world full of its own ritual ghosts. Thus we have Brave Orchid, at once conjurer and Shaman, the exorciser of ghosts; the No Name aunt whose wandering ghost the narrator is drawn to; and the numerous American ghosts – Taxi Ghosts, Bus Ghosts, Police Ghosts, Fire Ghosts, Garbage Ghosts. The continued use of the term across cultures does not deny the idea of difference but that of hierarchical separation and thus definition.

Kingston's questioning of oppositions and her resistance to definition are intensely political strategies. For the marginal writer who is often the subject of singular definition, such a dialogic stance is often a strategy of survival.[29] Kingston thus problematizes and subverts racial definitions in order to reveal the dangers of maintaining them. Ironically, many of the early reviews of the book reflected the very essentialized definitions Kingston was fighting. The appraisals reflected a familiar 'Orientalism'. A *Publisher's Weekly* critic praised the book for its 'myths rich and varied as Chinese brocade' and prose that 'achiev[ed] the delicacy and precision of porcelain'.[30] Another critic claimed to be confused by the depiction of some Chinese women as aggressive and others as docile, suggesting that Chinese women have a singular identity.[31] Suzanne Juhasz, writing for a scholarly journal, saw Kingston's retention of a 'traditional literary style' a result of her need, as a daughter of immigrants, to prove her English language skills.[32] As these reviews suggest, Kingston's position in the literary world is more clearly implicated in her marginality, more political than are the positions of many other women writers.

Kingston operates out of this position to insert indeterminacy into cultural definitions. She presents Chinese culture as a conglomeration of diverse, multiple, often contradictory values that she does not attempt to unify into an easy explanation. Such unities, for Kingston, are the hallmarks of tourist propaganda, not lived culture. Kingston does not believe in the possibility of representing Chinese culture because that assumes that there is a simple 'Chinese' reality and culture easily available for representation. As Kingston puts it, 'There are

Chinese American writers who seek to represent the rest of us; they end up with tourist manuals or chamber of commerce public relations whitewash'.[33] In *The Woman Warrior* every aspect of Chinese culture and Chinese immigrant life is so diverse that it resists generalization. The striking contrast between the strength of the narrator's mother, Brave Orchid, who becomes a doctor in China and fights for her rights in America and Moon Orchid who accepts the role of abandoned wife, is only one of several. Immigrant Chinese range from the wealthy, Americanized husband of Moon Orchid, to the Stockton Chinese who maintain their native village affiliations, to refugees from the revolution. And the difference between the immigrant Chinese and the Chinese from the narrator's village is so vast that to the untutored eyes of Moon Orchid, the former appear like foreigners. 'I'm glad to see the Americans talk like us' says Moon Orchid to her sister. 'Brave Orchid was . . . again startled at her sister's denseness. "These aren't the Americans. These are the overseas Chinese"' (p. 157).

In addition to presenting a diverse variety of Chinese characters, Kingston uses traditional cultural material to question the concept of a unified culture. Thus she uses well-known myths to write a narrative that is deliberately anti-mythic. Myths, as many of the modernists saw, could play the conservative function of creating and preserving cultural unity. In his essay on Joyce, T.S. Eliot explained the mythic method as 'a way of controlling, of ordering, of giving a shape and significance to the immense panorama of futility and anarchy that is contemporary history. . . . a step toward making the modern world possible for art, toward . . . order and form . . .'.[34] It is possible for the mythic method to create order, shape and form because myths conventionally serve a stabilizing function in society.[35] Kingston, well aware of the traditional function of myths, uses them in order to subvert this function.

Kingston begins with the story of No Name Woman to suggest that all myths and legends are contingent upon some cultural necessity. Brave Orchid relates this family myth as a warning to her daughter, but the narrator realizes its fictitious aspect. There is the logical improbability of her mother having witnessed the attack when she and the aunt were not living in the same household. But this ambiguity does not trouble Kingston. Such an uncertainty allows her the freedom to continue the process of recreating the myth. With this initial move Kingston questions the privileged access to truth that myths claim and sets the stage for further destabilization of the function of myths. The choice of the story is also significant: 'She observes the custom of ancestor worship in such a way as to destroy its fundamental principle, that of maintaining patriarchal descent intact.'[36] Similarly Kingston narrates the legend of Fa Mu Lan through her own identification with it and makes its patriarchal moral about filial piety incidental. The purpose of the tale in Kingston's text, is to create uncertainty. Fa Mu Lan can represent the female avenger but she can also represent a continuation of patriarchy as Brave Orchid, to an extent, does. Ts'ai Yen's tale about her captivity by barbarians and her return home becomes a tale of intercultural understanding rather than, as is traditionally received, an ethnocentric tale about Chinese cultural superiority.[37]

More importantly, in *The Woman Warrior* myths do not solve moral and cultural conflicts but create them. Chinese myths abound with misogynistic rituals – smearing bad daughters-in-law with honey and tying them on ant nests, keeping ash ready near a birthing bed in order to suffocate a potential female child and so on. Kingston deliberately presents historical facts and exaggerated legends as if both are equally true and thus questions the truth status of both myth and history. Thus she uses the occasion of describing her mother's adventures as a doctor in China to talk about the rope bridges used by Chinese laborers in Malaysia and about the ghosts her mother encounters while walking on similar bridges in China (pp. 102–3); she writes about Chinese myths about Japan – the Japanese having descended from an ape that raped a Chinese princess or from the first Chinese explorers of Japan – in the midst of describing the Japanese occupation of China and relating the story about the crazy village woman lynched by refugees because she wears a shiny hat, possibly visible to the Japanese pilots. Kingston keeps up the uncertainty by blurring the boundaries between myth and history and never settling on the validity of either. Like the cryptic appelation 'Ho Chi Kuei' which means anything from 'centipede', 'grain sieve' to 'good frying', all that the narrator can glean from her mother about the social validity of myths is that Chinese people 'like to say the opposite' (pp. 237–8).

The Woman Warrior thus subverts all forms that have the potential of providing cultural stability and unity. Myths here create contradictions and confusions. Kingston writes polemically as a Chinese-American woman confronting and battling with the patriarchal, white American culture but she does so from a position that is radically unstable. She writes as a woman, but destabilizes the concept of gender; she speaks as a Chinese-American, but questions racial definitions. Authorship therefore becomes a complicated question because Kingston refuses to give us a traditional position from which she articulates. This does not mean that the text is apolitical or socially meaningless. Gender and race are important to Kingston, but not as transcendent and true categories. Kingston does not dismiss or destroy these categories, but radically transvalues them by making them dialogically interactive. And because she subverts these categories only in relation to the singular definitions imposed by the dominant culture and does not attempt to lay the foundations of another (more pure or true) set of categories, she resists impoverishing the issues of gender and race.

Notes

1. HELENE CIXOUS, 'The Laugh of the Medusa' in Elaine Marks and Isabelle de Coutrivon (eds.), *New French Feminism* (New York: Schocken Books, 1981), p. 258.

2. JULIA KRISTEVA, 'Oscillation du "pouvoir" au "refus"', Interview with Xaviere Gauthier, *Tel Quel* (1974), excerpted in *New French Feminists*, p. 166.

3. The very concepts 'margin' and 'center' raise important theoretical issues, all of which cannot be addressed here. My use of them, however, does not signify definitive, unchanging, essences. Marginality, as I will argue is a position opposed to definition. But that does not mean that the terms margin and center can merely be collapsed, that marginality is only an aspiration toward the center. As Edward Said, taking issue with Michel Foucault's notion of the diffusion of power, points out, 'If power oppresses and controls and manipulates, then everything that resists it is not morally equal to power. . . . Resistance cannot equally be an adversarial alternative to power and a dependent function of it, except in some metaphysical, ultimately trivial sense' (*The World, The Text, and the Critic* [Cambridge: Harvard Univ. Press, 1983], p. 246). However, even Foucault is not neutral about power as Said takes him to be. Foucault's notion of power as 'something which circulates' is a brilliant demonstration of how power works in ways most of us are unaware of – horizontally, rather than vertically through overt repression. Power may work covertly and insiduously. Foucault does not give up the notion of oppression. His interest is in seeing how 'mechanisms of power have been . . . invested, colonised . . . by ever more general mechanisms and by *forms of global domination*' (*Power/Knowledge: Selected Interviews and Other Writings 1972–1977* [New York: Pantheon Books, 1980], pp. 98–9 emphasis mine). To take a rather crude example, one might question the marginality of a writer like Kingston whose works, after all, are published by mainstream presses, but one can hardly do so in relation to John Updike or even E.L. Doctorow.

4. Perhaps the most powerful challenge to feminists who inadvertently or otherwise proclaim a singular identity for women has come from Gayatri Chakravorty Spivak. See, for example, her reading of the relationship of subjugation between Jane and Bertha Mason in *Jane Eyre*, a text touted as feminist ('Three Women's Texts and a Critique of Imperialism', *Critical Inquiry* 12 [1985], 243–61).

5. Barbara Johnson has written extensively about the problems of essentializing race and gender. She writes: 'There is no point of view from which the universal characteristics of the human or the woman, or of the black woman . . . can be selected and totalized. Unification and simplification are fantasies of domination, not understanding' (*A World of Difference* [Baltimore: Johns Hopkins Univ. Press, 1987], p. 170).

6. MIKHAIL BAKHTIN, *Problems of Dostoevsky's Poetics*, trans. Caryl Emerson (Minneapolis: Univ. of Minnesota Press, 1984), p. 18.

7. Feminists have also raised legitimate concerns about Bakhtin's failure to criticize Rabelais' misogyny and the apparent value he places on struggle and conflict. See DALE M. BAUER, *Feminist Dialogics: A Theory of Failed Community* (New York: State Univ. of New York Press, 1988), p. 5.

8. JULIA KRISTEVA, 'Word Dialogue and Novel' in Toril Moi (ed.), *The Kristeva Reader* (New York: Columbia Univ. Press, 1986), p. 39.

9. Kristeva, p. 49.

10. PATRICIA YAEGER, *Honey-Mad Women: Emancipatory Strategies in Women's Writing* (New York: Columbia Univ. Press, 1988), pp. 59–60.

11. MAXINE HONG KINGSTON, *The Woman Warrior: Memoirs of a Girlhood Among Ghosts* (New York: Random House, 1976), pp. 3, 5 (hereafter cited parenthetically in the body of the text).

12. SANDRA GILBERT and SUSAN GUBAR, *The Madwoman in the Attic: The Woman Writer and the Nineteenth Century Literary Imagination* (New Haven: Yale Univ. Press, 1979), p. 3.

13. Although it is her mother who admonishes her throughout the book, it is obvious that (in this role) the mother is the bearer of patriarchal values.

14. Till World War I, unrestricted and unlimited immigration was the policy of the government except for 'Orientals, paupers, imbeciles, and prostitutes' (in SAMUEL ELIOT MORISON, *The Oxford History of American Literature* (New York: Oxford Univ. Press, 1965), p. 897.

15. See HENRY LOUIS GATES, *Figures in Black: Words, Signs, and the 'Racial' Self* (New York: Oxford Univ. Press, 1988), p. 4.

16. Carol Mitchell points out that Fa Mu Lan becomes a warrior 'in order to save her elderly father from conscription and in order to right the wrongs that had been done in her village. Because she did her deeds out of filial respect, not just for personal glorification, she is an acceptable role model for a woman' ('"Talking Story" in *The Woman Warrior*: An Analysis of the Use of Folklore', *Kentucky Folklore Record*, 27 [1981], 8).

17. For an excellent analysis of the questioning of gender oppositions see LESLIE W. RABINE, 'No Lost Paradise: Social and Symbolic Gender in the Writings of Maxine Hong Kingston', *Signs*, 12 (1987), 471–92. Of this vision, Rabine says, 'This couple is reminiscent of the Tao in the I Ching where Yin, the masculine, and Yang, the feminine, are constantly in the process of changing into each other and where their changes engender chains of transformations similar to those Kingston expresses here in a poetic mode' (p. 476).

18. Lynn Z. Bloom also sees the mother–daughter relationship as a productive one. The narrator 'realizes that she and her mother are much alike as mature women – intelligent, energetic, determined, courageous, analysts and conveyors of a complex culture in an alien land' ('Heritages: Dimensions of Mother–Daughter Relationships in Women's Autobiographies' in CATHY N. DAVIDSON and E.M. BRONER (eds.), *The Lost Tradition: Mothers and Daughters in Literature* [New York: Frederick Ungar, 1980], p. 301).

19. Estelle Jelinek in ESTELLE JELINEK (ed.), *Women's Autobiography: Essays in Criticism* (Bloomington: Indiana Univ. Press, 1980), pp. 10, 14.

20. CAROLYN HEILBRUN, 'Women's Autobiographical Writings: New Forms' in Philip Dodd (ed.), *Modern Selves: Essays in Modern British and American Autobiography* (London: Frank Cass, 1986), p. 17.

21. VIRGINIA WOOLF, *A Room of One's Own* (New York: Harcourt, 1929), p. 103. Kingston echoes Woolf while musing about the realities and myths of

revolutionary China: Kingston writes, 'I've seen Communist pictures showing a contented woman sitting on a bunk sewing. . . . The woman looks very pleased. The Revolution put an end to prostitution by giving women what they wanted: a job and a room of their own' (p. 73).

22. Henry Louis Gates uses the figure of the signifying monkey who 'dwells in the margins of discourse' and whose speech is always double voiced, to explain the features of African American writing ('The "Blackness of Blackness": A Critique of the Sign and the Signifying Monkey', *Critical Inquiry* [1983], 685–723). In *The Signifying Monkey* he finds the basis of the radical multiplicity of black writing and the denial of a singular self in the Yoruba god, Esu.

23. The problem with this approach becomes painfully obvious when critics deny the very material Kingston works with. Suzanne Juhasz, for example, suggests that *The Woman Warrior* is a particularly female form of autobiography in that 'fantasy, the life of the imagination, creates female identity' ('Toward a Theory of Form in Feminist Autobiography: Kate Miller's *Flying and Sita*; Maxine Hong Kingston's *The Woman Warrior*', *International Journal of Women's Studies*, 2 [1979], 63). Juhasz makes no mention of the fact that Kingston is in fact working with folklore, and gives little importance to the constant concern with the lives of Chinese immigrants.

24. EDWARD SAID, *Orientalism* (New York: Random House, 1978), pp. 308–10.

25. REED WAY DASENBROCK, 'Intelligibility and Meaningfulness in Multicultural Literature in English', *PMLA*, 102 (1987), 10.

26. Linda Morante accepts this division and equates the narrator's finding a voice with her becoming American. Morante says that 'From childhood through adolescence, Kingston continues her quest for self-expression. As a teenager she is familiar with the English language and American culture, but her voice still squeals with ugly "duck" like insecurity' ('From Silence to Song: The Triumph of Maxine Hong Kingston', *Frontiers* 9.2 [1987], 79). She even interprets Chinese immigrants' secretiveness and changing of identities as a denial of (American) selfhood (p. 80). Such a reading completely ignores the very real fears to which Chinese immigrants were subject. Elaine H. Kim draws attention to some of these factors. From 1924–43, for example, any female American citizen who married a Chinese alien would automatically lose her citizenship. Only in 1952 Chinese were allowed to become naturalized U.S. citizens. And 'anti-miscegenation legislation remained on the books in California until 1967' (*Asian American Literature: An Introduction to the Writings and Their Social Context* [Philadelphia: Temple Press, 1982], pp. 96–7).

27. Dasenbrock, p. 14.

28. Quoted in Kim, p. 200.

29. I do not mean to suggest that all works by women and minority writers dialogically question oppositions and definitions. However, writers who write consciously from the margins and foreground this concern are likely to use such dialogic strategies.

30. Kim, p. xvi.

31. Kim, p. xvii.

32. Although Kingston has found critical acceptance in the last decade, popular reviews of her works still reflect a not-so-hidden Orientalism. A two-column

review of her most recent book, *Tripmaster Monkey* concentrated first on why Chinese writing was being taken seriously (Nixon's China visit and subsequent American diplomacy); after devoting two paragraphs to the book itself, it concluded by assessing Kingston's literary merits: 'Some of *Tripmaster* owes its atmosphere to Herman Hesse's overheated German Vaudeville Steppenwolf, and a few historical meditations are straight out of Saul Bellow . . . But Kingston's humor and idiom are her own, and so is the message . . .' (STEFAN KANFER, Review of *Tripmaster Monkey: His Fake Book* by Maxine Hong Kingston, *Time* May 1, 1989, pp. 70, 72).

33.   Quoted in MARILYN YALOM (ed.), *Women Writers of the West Coast: Speaking of Their Lives and Careers* (Santa Barbara: Capra Press, 1983), p. 71.

34.   T.S. ELIOT, *Selected Prose*, ed. Frank Kermode (London: Faber Press, 1975), pp. 177–8.

35.   Roland Barthes in *Mythologies* sees myths as traditional forms which oppose change and present themselves as complete (*Mythologies*, trans. Annette Lavers [New York: Hill & Wang], p. 117).

36.   Rabine, p. 484.

37.   According to Robert Rorex and Wen Fong the legend of Ts'ai Yen, with which the book ends, illustrates 'the superiority of Chinese civilization over cultures beyond her borders; the irreconciliability of the different ways of life' (Rabine, p. 485).

Other relevant critical essays on Kingston and the Asian American cultural context include SHIRLEY GEOK-LIN LIM, 'The Tradition of Chinese American Women's Life Stories: Thematics of Race and Gender in Jade Snow Won's *Fifth Chinese Daughter* and Maxine Hong Kingston's *The Woman Warrior*', in *American Women's Autobiography: Fea(s)ts of Memory*, ed. Margo Culley (Madison, WI: The University of Wisconsin Press, 1992), pp. 252–67; KING-KOK CHEUNG, '"Don't Tell": Imposed Silences in *The Color Purple* and *The Woman Warrior*', in *Reading the Literatures of Asian America*, ed. Shirley Geok-lin Lim and Amy Ling (Philadelphia: Temple University Press, 1992), pp. 163–89; MALINI JOHAR SCHUELLER, 'Theorizing Ethnicity and Subjectivity: Maxine Hong Kingston's *Tripmaster Monkey* and Amy Tan's *The Joy Luck Club*', *Genders* 15 (Winter 1992): 72–85.

4 History, Critical Theory, and Women's Social Practices: 'Women's Time' and *Housekeeping**

THOMAS FOSTER

Thomas Foster's essay is less eclectic than those preceding it. Foster bases his discussion of Marilynne Robinson's *Housekeeping* on a single theoretical model: Julia Kristeva's conception of 'women's time'. Foster traces Kristeva's stages of feminist historical awareness and finds that Robinson's novel coincides with the third generation: 'women who combine an entry into [official, linear] history with an affirmation of difference'. He cites a number of feminist theorists on Kristeva's conception of women's time and then enters into a detailed discussion of her dialectical and deconstructive strategies. He points to her 'expropriation of deconstruction' in her 'immanent critique of both materialist and deconstructive theories', even as she exploits these theories in the service of her own feminist critique.

Impelling Foster's analysis of *Housekeeping* is the assumption that (female) identities have been imposed by (male) power structures, and that it is the work of the novelist, critic, and reader to deconstruct these heretofore invisible (hence, insidious) structures. Happily, Foster complicates this binarism in his discussion of the novel's 'inverted separatism' and its related inversion of the public/private binary.

The value of the deconstructive critique to feminist theory and the form it should take within a political reading practice continue to be debated by feminist critics.[1] However, the relevance of Julia Kristeva's essay 'Women's Time' to this debate has not been generally acknowledged.[2] 'Women's Time' offers a historical model of recent developments in the women's movement, a model that presents feminist expropriation of deconstruction as a possibility generated by (at least) Western women's historical situation. Kristeva suggests that there is a material basis for feminist use of deconstructive strategies, but her model of the forms

---

* Reprinted from *Signs: Journal of Women in Culture and Society* 14, 1 (1988): 73–99.

feminist self-consciousness can take also implies that those forms stand in specific relation to historical materialism, including its use of dialectics in critical analysis. Feminist practices as Kristeva presents them function as an immanent critique of both materialist and deconstructive theories, while implying the need to retain as well as modify their analytic categories and procedures. Kristeva's essay presents itself as a commentary on the European women's movement, particularly in France and Italy, but the questions it raises find enough correspondence in the work of socialist feminists and critics engaged in politicizing deconstruction to interest Anglo-American readers.[3] As a literary representation of the lives of several generations of women, Marilynne Robinson's novel *Housekeeping* shows how an analysis like Kristeva's might organize a narrative of women's resistance to the historical limitations imposed on them.

Living (in) history

'Women's Time' (1979) begins with two examples of collectivities that cut across the linear history of the nation-state and unsettle the national identity founded on that shared history. Harking back to the student revolts of May 1968, women and young people are the examples Kristeva gives of groups causing this 'loss of identity' through their participation in what she calls 'monumental time' (*WT*, 32). In an early essay, Kristeva defines monumental history as 'a plurality of productions that cannot be reduced to one another', in contrast to the unitary narrative posited by 'the concept of *linear historicity*'.[4] In 'Women's Time', this heterogeneity results from the 'diagonal' relation established between European, North and South American, Indian, or Chinese women who retain their own particularity but also share a 'structural place in reproduction and its representations' (*WT*, 33). Kristeva's historical model distinguishes three 'generations' in the women's movement according to whether women seek to synchronize their time with the progress of linear history, affirm a cyclic or monumental time with archaic connotations, or establish a prefigurative practice that both exists in the 'Now' and belongs to a different future.[5]

The first two moments in this model correspond to the 'oscillation between power and denial' Kristeva described in an interview, five years before writing 'Women's Time'.[6] In the emergence of a third moment, Kristeva finds an alternative to those two extremes. Associated with suffrage movements and the impact of existential ideas on feminism, the first generation seeks 'to gain a place in linear time as the time of project and history' (*WT*, 36). This 'insertion into history' is structured by a 'logic

Thomas Foster

of identification' with the values of 'a rationality dominant in the nation-state', values which are also masculine; this generation rejects traditional feminine or maternal traits when they come into conflict with the goal of entering history (*WT*, 37). As the phallic rhetoric of insertion and entry indicates, for Kristeva this stage is marked by a desire for mastery, which seizes power without transforming or adequately questioning it.[7] Despite this criticism, she recognizes the political benefits of such activism, whose effects in her view exceed those of the industrial revolution (*WT*, 37). What this generation's efforts fail to exceed is the hegemonic culture's capacity to absorb and thrive on contradiction and challenge.

The second generation constitutes itself in reaction to the initial project of 'modernization' and the attempt to synchronize women's time with a history that has excluded women. This reaction is characterized by a reaffirmation of 'the specificity of female psychology and its symbolic realizations' (*WT*, 37). Women reject the linear time of historiography in favor of a cyclic and monumental temporality traditionally associated with female subjectivity and with ritual, marginalized religious practices, and mysticism. More importantly, women at this point reject a unitary image of self-identity, unmarked by internal contradictions such as differences between women: 'By demanding recognition of an irreducible identity, without equal in the other sex and as such exploded, plural, fluid, in a certain way nonidentical, this feminism situates itself outside the linear time of identities which communicate through projection and revindication' (*WT*, 37–8).

In this passage, Kristeva's use of 'identity' to name nonidentity or difference emphasizes that the second, separatist generation is constituting and reclaiming 'nonidentity' as a subject position from which to speak and act, an oppositional potential the third generation in her model will realize. But the same designation of difference as identity points to Kristeva's criticism of this second moment for a tendency to imagine itself as transcending differences of class, race, or sexuality and the tensions they create and instead thinking of itself as 'harmonious, without prohibitions, free and fulfilling' (*WT*, 45). Such a 'countersociety' recapitulates the sacrificial foundation of the social and symbolic contracts based on transactions between separate and equal individuals – that is, 'the expulsion of an excluded element, a scapegoat charged with the evil of which the community duly constituted can then purge itself' (*WT*, 45). In *Revolution in Poetic Language*, Kristeva describes the insight that sacrifice provides into the institution and functioning of the symbolic order of language and other semiotic systems: 'Sacrifice shows how representing . . . violence is enough to stop it and to concatenate an order. Conversely it indicates that all order is based on representation: what is violent is the irruption of the symbol, killing substance to make it signify.'[8] The idea is not to eradicate this violence, which is seen as the basis of language acquisition, but to transform it by intervening to prevent violence and the power it represents from being organized along the lines of social hierarchies. Kristeva's third generation raises the possibility of 'an ethics which, conscious of the fact that its order is sacrificial, reserves part of the burden for each of its adherents, therefore declaring them guilty while immediately affording them the possibility for *jouissance*, for various productions, for a life made up of both challenges and differences' (*WT*, 53). The current mode of social organization instead divides the social order into victims and executioners (*WT*, 52).

The third generation in Kristeva's model combines the responses of the first two: 'insertion into history and the radical *refusal* of the subjective limitations imposed by this history's time on an experiment carried out in the name of the irreducible difference' (*WT*, 38). The separatist moment is not abandoned, but neither do women refuse to engage with the dominant culture; rather they enter society and history to introduce into it the possibility of radical change and the fact of heterogenous social elements, the 'irreducible difference'. For Kristeva as for Luce Irigaray, 'It is in order to bring their difference to light that women are demanding their rights'.[9] In 'Women's Time' and other essays like 'Stabat Mater',[10] Kristeva treats mothering as a social practice with transformative cultural force when it comes into conflict with the dominant culture. I want to extend her analysis to the sexual division of labor, the exploitation of women's productive and reproductive work by an economic system that privileges exchange-value and the production of surplus-value over use-value, and the ideology of the home as a separate sphere, a private domestic space.

Kristeva's definition of a third generation of feminists who combine an entry into history with an affirmation of difference implies the possibility of radicalizing what Temma Kaplan calls 'female consciousness', the socially legitimated assumptions about qualities and activities required of women within specific cultures, assumptions women themselves internalize.[11] This third generation affirms the value and specificity of the consciousness produced by exclusion from an official history that uses women as a specular image to confirm masculine self-identity. But they reject the material and symbolic limitations, especially enclosure within a domestic space as well as the teleology of motherhood, that produced that consciousness.

Kristeva ends 'Women's Time' with the statement that her historical model does not describe a progression with a clear beginning and end; each generation is 'less a chronology than a signifying space, a both corporeal and desiring mental space' (*WT*, 51). Mary Jacobus's distinction between liberal and radical feminist attitudes toward language corresponds to the signifying spaces of Kristeva's first two generations.

For Jacobus, liberal feminists tend to treat dominant discourses as if they were neutral forms, to be filled with the content of female experience, while radical feminists insist on a separatist position, demanding a whole new language.[12] Margaret Homans aligns this distinction with Elaine Marks's definition of the different conceptions of women's situation within patriarchy used by Anglo-American and French feminists; the first group tends to treat women's oppression while the French focus on women's repression and difference. Kristeva's location of a third possibility suggests the emergence of productive conjunctions between the opposing positions these American critics have outlined.[13] Adrienne Rich's lesbian continuum represents one response to the need for retaining a perspective exceeding the hegemony's capacity to appropriate feminist activities, in order to *'change the social relations of the sexes'*.[14] A comparable statement is Luce Irigaray's description of 'non-integration' as both a necessity and a desire for women.[15]

Luce Irigaray's work exemplifies the emergence in France of Kristeva's third generation. When Irigaray tells an interviewer that for women it is not a question of 'installing' themselves within a masculine definition of woman as negativity, 'nor of reversing the economy of sameness by turning the feminine into *the standard for "sexual difference"* ', but instead it is 'a matter of trying to practice that difference', she defines a combination of entry into history and maintenance of difference.[16] Her comments on Freud's need to arrange differences into hierarchies pose the alternative that Kristeva locates in the third moment of her historical model:

> Let us imagine that man (Freud in the event) had discovered that the rarest thing – . . . the most faithful to factual materiality and the most historically curative – would be to articulate directly, *without catacombs* . . . these two syntaxes. Irreducible in their strangeness and eccentricity one to the other. . . . Had the man Freud preferred the play, or even the clash of those two economies rather than their disposition in hierarchical stages by means of one barrier (or two), one censorship (or two), then perhaps he would not finally have cracked his head against all that remains irreducibly 'obscure' to him in his speculations.[17]

For readers of Kristeva, this passage recalls her description of the preverbal negativity of the semiotic which always appears as a disruption within the symbolic order. Such disruptions call attention both to the contradictions on which that order is founded and to the subject's capacity to exceed and to transgress the preexisting social and linguistic structures in which we are inscribed.[18]

This thematics of heterogeneity and doubleness finds a parallel in recent socialist feminist theory that asserts the need to treat gender and class systems as neither separate nor reducible one to the other. In 'The Doubled Vision of Feminist Theory', Joan Kelly argues that the political goals of feminism 'are neither to participate as equals in man's world, nor to restore to woman's realm and values their dignity and worth. Conceptions such as these are superseded in the present will to extirpate gender and sex hierarchy altogether, and with them all forms of domination.'[19] Elizabeth Fox-Genovese extends this analysis while stressing the importance of retaining the separatist moment that restores 'to woman's realm and values their dignity and worth'. In 'Placing Women's History in History', Fox-Genovese implies that feminism confronts a masculine logic of identity: 'the expansion of capitalism and modern representative government has attempted to bind men of different classes, races, and ethnic groups together through the double promise of individualism in the public sphere and male dominance in the home'.[20] In what can be read as a variant of (or gloss on) Kristeva's critique of the second generation, Fox-Genovese believes that the rejection of 'all official history as irrelevant to female experience' only 'perpetuates the most pernicious myths' of that history, particularly its 'insistence upon the universal claims of female biology'.[21] For her, the 'confrontation between women's history . . . and mainstream history offers a special opportunity to rethink the basic premises that inform historical interpretation'.[22] The form that challenge takes is 'not to substitute the chronicle of the female subject for that of the male, but rather to restore conflict, ambiguity, and tragedy to the centre of historical process', elements excluded from 'the perspective of the authoritative male subject – the single, triumphant consciousness'.[23]

Both Kelly and Fox-Genovese are implicitly modifying the traditional Marxist analysis of capitalist class relations as the totalizing final instance to which all forms of oppression can be reduced. The privilege accorded to a unified working class as the vehicle of significant change, the motor of history, results from this reduction. Georg Lukacs refers to this status of the proletariat in Marxist theory when he calls it 'the identical subject-object of the historical process'.[24] The proletariat is unified as a class precisely through its function as the dialectic negation of an exploitation organized along class lines. In 'Women's Time', Kristeva comments on the problem with regarding the proletariat as 'the last oppressed class', to quote Lukacs again.[25] Because of an ideology that emphasizes productive labor in the marketplace, in most socialist countries (specifically Eastern Europe) feminist issues like birth control and more generally the role of domestic labor in the reproduction of capitalist social relations have appeared 'nonessential or even nonexistent' (*WT*, 38–9).

But Michèle Barrett stresses that, while forms of oppression involving ideologies of separate gender roles preceded the transition to capitalism and so would not automatically be eradicated by a socialist revolution,

the sexual division of labor has been appropriated by and become
functional for capitalism, to the extent that only radical changes in the
existing relations of production would have a significant impact on the
exploitation of women's work.[26] In Barrett's account, women have a dual
relationship to the class structure. The heterogeneity may result from
indirect dependence on the wage of a husband or father or, in the case
of many working women, combine direct involvement in wage-labor
with the obligation to perform domestic work traditionally defined as
unpaid.[27] For Kelly, socialist feminism's 'doubled vision' works against
attempts either 'to reduce sex oppression to class interests or to see the
relation of the sexes as always and ever the same, regardless of race,
class, or society'.[28] From this point of view, feminism complicates the
notion that a dialectical resolution can securely place diversity under
the sign of unity to transcend contradiction and conflict.

Dialectic (and) deconstruction

Kristeva's historical model participates in this critique of dialectics. Its
three-step design deliberately invites comparison to the movement of
the dialectic, which is a version of the linear time of the first generation
in her model. The contradiction inherent in an initial social formation
determines and generates its own negation. Women's attempts to enter
history by accepting the masculine values on which it is based (including
separation from the domestic space) lead to or are accompanied by
the return to female specificity, which Kristeva elsewhere calls the
'valorization of a silent underwater body'.[29] The third step, then, would
be the synthesis or *Aufhebung*, the negation of the second generation's
negation of the first, which should produce an affirmation of unity out
of seeming contradiction. But Kristeva asserts that the 'insertion into
history' is accompanied by an irruption of 'irreducible difference'
(*WT*, 38); her third moment is one of heterogeneous mixture, not
final unity. This departure from traditional dialectics focuses on the
category of contradiction as a permanent feature of historical process,
not merely a strategic moment within it.

However, Kristeva's model follows a deconstructive trajectory as much
as a dialectic one. The second generation in her model is responding
to the counter-productive results of declaring equality without, in
Derrida's terms, first overturning the structure of privilege that
marginalizes women:

> We must traverse a phase of *overturning*. To do justice to this necessity
> is to recognize that . . . we are not dealing with the peaceful coexistence

of a *vis-à-vis*, but rather with a violent hierarchy. One of the two terms governs the other . . . or has the upper hand. To deconstruct the opposition, first of all, is to overturn the hierarchy at a given moment. To overlook this phase of overturning is to forget the conflictual and subordinating structure of opposition. Therefore one might proceed too quickly to a *neutralization* that *in practice* would leave the previous field untouched, leaving one no hold on the previous opposition, thereby preventing any means of *intervening* in the field effectively. We know what always have been the practical (particularly political) effects of immediately jumping beyond oppositions.[30]

The separatist moment in Kristeva's model performs this inversion, giving priority to a privatized feminine subjectivity and field of action over a male-dominated history, but without necessarily challenging the opposition between public and private. The next step is the displacement of the power structure and the dominant term's claim to a privileged identity, by marking an interval, an irreducible and necessary alterity, that exists within both terms of the opposition and stands as a return of the repressed within self-identity. Recalling the title of Fox-Genovese's article, this interval locates the excluded and subordinated term of the opposition within the self-identity of the term governing the opposition.[31] Women claim historical agency as women, refusing to identify with the supposedly universal values that have supported masculine privilege. But women also reject a unitary notion of 'Woman', thus marking a difference operating within the social construction of both genders. Kristeva describes the logic of identity as a circular projection and revindication, a repetition of sameness. Her third generation's rejection of that logic corresponds to Derrida's moment of displacement. This rejection occurs both on a subjective and a collective level, and its goal is 'to avoid the centralization of power, . . . to detach women from it, and . . . to proceed through their critical, differential, and autonomous interventions, to render decision-making institutions more flexible' (*WT*, 45).

Kristeva's third generation retains the separatist moment of inversion, putting it into practice against the mystifications of official culture, with the aim of transforming social structures, including those that define the subject. The moment of inversion is 'not a question of a chronological phase'; rather the analyst interminably operates 'both an overturning deconstruction and a positively displacing, transgressive, deconstruction'.[32] This remark underscores the repetitive and cyclic character of deconstruction, in contrast to the dialectic model; the temporality of the deconstructive operation embraces the monumental time of Kristeva's second generation.

The combination of two kinds of temporality, linear dialectic and cyclic deconstruction, within Kristeva's historical model itself repeats the combination of linear, historical time and nonsynchronous women's time achieved by the third generation her model discusses. By implication, deconstruction *and* dialectic and modified. In *Revolution in Poetic Language*, Kristeva criticizes Derrida for carrying both his desire to 'think short' of the institution of hierarchies and his rejection of linear teleology to the point of ignoring or minimizing the possibility of deconstructive social practices: 'The grammatological deluge of meaning gives up on the subject and must remain ignorant not only of his [sic] functioning as social practice but also of his chances for experiencing jouissance or being put to death. . . . Demonstrating disinterestedness toward (symbolic and/or social) structure, grammatology remains silent when faced with its destruction or renewal.'[33] In Kristeva's model, the deconstructive moment of inversion is assimilated to the necessity of defining a counterhegemonic subject position whose full potential for resistance is realized in the third moment of the operation.

Kristeva's third generation offers a solution to the problem for Marxist theory posed by Stanley Aronowitz: 'It remains for us to find the bearers of a non-identical dialectic.'[34] Aronowitz's idea of the 'crisis in historical materialism' draws on his reading of Theodor Adorno's 'negative dialectics' and Ernst Bloch's 'polyphonous dialectics', both of which try to redefine a dialectic that avoids final unity, as Kristeva's historical model does in tracing the development of feminist practice.[35] 'Women's Time' also responds to Derrida's suggestion that feminism remains caught in the second moment of the deconstructive operation and only inverts traditional hierarchies without subverting the concept of hierarchy itself: 'Feminism is nothing but the operation of a woman who aspires to be like a man. And in order to resemble the masculine dogmatic philosopher this woman lays claim – just as much claim as he – to truth, science, and objectivity in all their castrated delusions of virility.'[36] Kristeva's historical model reveals this statement for the misreading of feminist possibilities that it is.[37]

The deconstructive strategy Kristeva sees as informing the development of the women's movement involves questioning material and symbolic boundaries between inside and outside, between the public space of political action and productive labor and the private, domestic space to which women's values and activities have historically been confined. The third generation of feminists in her model rejects the limitations placed on those values, both their spatial enclosure and the ideology that situates women's lives within a horizon of motherhood. The women's movement has begun to expose the contradictions inherent in representing home as a private space, when for women that space has functioned as the site of social responsibilities.[38] Marilynne Robinson's novel *Housekeeping* provides us with a literary representation of the (nonidentical) dialectic development Kristeva's model follows and of an alternative, prefigurative practice that comes into contradiction with dominant social forms precisely through the performance of deconstructive strategies.

Burning down the house

As Elizabeth Meese has pointed out, Marilynne Robinson's first novel performs a separatist inversion by offering a narrative of small-town American life in which men appear only marginally, as intruders.[39] The narrative follows two sisters, Ruth (the narrator) and Lucille, as they are cared for by a succession of relatives after their mother's suicide. After their grandmother's death, two of her sisters come to live with the children until they can arrange for the girls' aunt, Sylvie, to stay with them. Before her arrival in Fingerbone, Sylvie was living as a transient, riding the rails and sleeping in bus stops and on park benches. By the end of the novel, the community decides Sylvie is unfit to be entrusted with the care of children. She then returns to the life of a drifter and takes Ruth with her, after setting fire to the grandmother's house. Meese calls this final defiance of the confinement of 'women's work' to a private sphere a 'gesture to the permanence of family relationships, one that stands in strict contrast to Kerouac's male fantasy of life on the road'.[40] The novel ends with the two women never knowing for certain whether the house was actually destroyed or whether Ruth's sister Lucille might be living there, since Lucille had rejected Sylvie's alternative economy of the home by running away to live with her Home Economics teacher. Through the choices the two sisters make, Ruth accepting Sylvie's way of life and Lucille accepting a conventional gender role, the narrative asks the reader to choose one or the other of these two perspectives and thus to undertake the political act of either endorsing or rejecting Ruth and Sylvie's rebellion.[41] But the novel contextualizes the alternative Sylvie represents in other ways, as well.

Early in the novel, the grandmother's relation to society is defined in terms of her exclusion from access to the public domain. She looks forward to her death, Ruth tells us, because it will result in the execution of her will: 'Since my grandmother had a little income and owned her house outright, she always took some satisfaction in thinking ahead to the time when her simple private destiny would intersect with the great public processes of law and finance – that is, to the time of her death' (*H*, 27). Significantly, the only men to appear in the narrative are public figures, a school principal and a sheriff who arrives to legislate Ruth and Sylvie's family arrangements. The specification of death as the point when this woman would gain the power to exert her will within the public realm is important for an understanding of the novel's ending, where this standard narrative of women's powerlessness is revised even as it presents Ruth and Sylvie's decision to become drifters as a kind of death. The ending foregrounds and dramatizes the contradictions women live when they refuse to abide within their 'proper place', but it also implies the possibility of putting these contradictions into practice as a form of historical agency with potentially radical results. The grandmother's death prefigures the way of life Ruth and Sylvie choose by leaving the house. At the time of her death 'all the habits and patterns and properties that had settled around her, the monthly checks from the bank, the house she had lived in since she came to it as a bride, the weedy orchard that surrounded the yard on three sides where smaller and wormier apples and apricots and plums had fallen every year of her widowhood, all these things would suddenly become liquid, capable of assuming new forms' (*H*, 27). The significance of linking the separation of public and private spheres to ownership will become apparent in Sylvie's attitude toward private property, especially when she 'steals' a boat. Sylvie's economy of the home will be marked by a fluidity in the structures effecting that separation, a fluidity the grandmother could imagine occurring only after her death. Sylvie will reject the logic of exclusion that circumscribes the grandmother's life and will bring Ruth to reject it also.

Still, Ruth demonstrates her sensitivity to the values of a traditional female consciousness by trying to think back through her grandmother and imagine how this woman felt while hanging up clothes to dry and while working in her garden, which Ruth presents as a 'resurrection of the ordinary' (*H*, 18). But the grandmother's moment of self-consciousness about the value of her way of life is accompanied by a recognition of the limitations imposed on her by the domestic enclosure that forms the material basis of that way of life. This recognition appears as a feeling of loneliness, in response to which 'old women she had known, first her grandmother and then her mother, rocked on their porches in the evenings and sang sad songs, and did not wish to be spoken to' (*H*, 18). Ruth expresses the same dissatisfied awareness of limits in describing how the grandmother combined her private life and personal habits with her social function of caring for the girls: 'Say that my grandmother sang in her throat while she sat on her bed and we laced up her big black shoes. Such details are merely accidental. Who could know but us?' (*H*, 116). Ruth's question indicates an awareness that the openness and productive complexity the grandmother's attitude displays is confined to the domestic sphere and excluded from the standard life stories in which 'such details' would be 'merely accidental' to the real plot. As long as the home continues to define a rigid boundary between public and private spaces, the potential alternative to that public/private dichotomy will remain a private experience rather than a social movement or practice.

In contrast to the grandmother, the girls' mother, Helen, had internalized a masculine concept of individuality as detachment rather than the engagement prominent in the grandmother's behavior. Ruth refers to her mother's 'gentle indifference' toward her children and the abstraction which often made them think there was someone else in the room with her that they could not see. Ruth's comment about being left on the grandmother's porch before Helen drove her car into the lake at Fingerbone is, 'At last we had slid from her lap like one of those magazines full of responsible opinion about discipline and balanced meals' (*H*, 109–10). Besides having had to jettison the traditional role of mother to the extent that it interfered with her need to make a living, Helen's status as a working mother and the actual division of her time between the marketplace and the home had become part of her way of life even within the home. Unlike the grandmother, Helen excluded the children from her private thoughts and feelings and made them feel excluded, just as she denied them access to information about their absent father in maintaining that it was her business and hers alone (*H*, 52). She treated domestic work as the kind of regimen that might be contained in one of those 'magazines full of responsible opinion' and subordinated her private life to her public activities, as if nothing private could make 'any significant demands on her attention' (*H*, 109). This division is presented as the major factor in her decision to commit suicide.

The girls' mother corresponds to the first generation in Kristeva's model, an entry into history made on masculine terms, an appropriation of the detached position of the male subject. The return to the grandmother, then, performs a narrative function equivalent to the rejection of official history that characterizes the second moment in Kristeva's model. Sylvie's appearance marks the beginning of the third generation, the combination of these two attitudes. Soon after Sylvie's arrival, the lake by Fingerbone rises, and the grandmother's house is flooded. When they come down to check on the ground floor, Ruth describes how 'Sylvie took me by the hands and pulled me after her through six grand waltz steps. The house flowed around us' (*H*, 64). The remark prefigures both the change Sylvie will introduce into the traditional domestic economy and the relationship she establishes with Ruth.

Meese refers to Sylvie's housekeeping as a 'tending to and nurturing of the exterior world, an opening up of the outside to the inside'.[42] Her housekeeping is the other side of her vagrancy, which treats the exterior world and public spaces like parks as if they were a domestic space where one would be perfectly justified in satisfying a need, say, to sleep.

Ruth remembers Sylvie walking around the house with a scarf around her hair and a broom in her hand, but at the same time the house began to accumulate leaves in the corners, along with scraps of paper bearing phrases like 'Powers Meet' and 'I think of you' (*H*, 84–5). The change occurs as a function of Sylvie's belief that air is the best cleaning agent, since she would open doors and windows and not think to close them. Ruth tells us 'it was for the sake of air that on one early splendid day she wrestled my grandmother's plum-colored davenport into the front yard, where it remained until it weathered pink' (*H*, 85–6). In Sylvie's hands, the house becomes 'attuned to the orchard and the particularities of weather, even in the first days of Sylvie's housekeeping', with the leaves in the corners 'lifted up by something that came before the wind' (*H*, 85).

Another of Sylvie's habits underscores her rejection of the home as a mechanism of exclusion. She prefers to leave the lights off when evening arrives and to eat dinner in the dark. Ruth says that Sylvie 'seemed to dislike the disequilibrium of counterpoising a roomful of light against a worldful of darkness. Sylvie in a house was more or less like a mermaid in a ship's cabin. She preferred it sunk in the very element it was meant to exclude. We had crickets in the pantry, squirrels in the eaves, sparrows in the attic. Lucille and I stepped through the door from sheer night to sheer night' (*H*, 99). Sylvie works against the binary logic of 'counterpoising' an inside and an outside. One night, while eating dinner in the moonlight, Lucille suddenly turns on the lights in the kitchen. The passage suggests that Sylvie's housekeeping and the attitude toward women's social situation to which it corresponds can only be criticized from within the dualistic structures of thought and social existence to which Sylvie's way of life stands as an alternative. Turning on the light restores the separation of interior and exterior that Lucille wishes to uphold: 'The window went black and the cluttered kitchen leaped, so it seemed, into being, as remote from what had gone before as this world was from the primal darkness. We saw that we ate from plates that came in detergent boxes, and we drank from jelly glasses. . . . Lucille had startled us all, flooding the room so suddenly with light, exposing heaps of pots and dishes, the two cupboard doors which had come unhinged and were propped against the boxes of china' (*H*, 100–1). The episode ends with a comic detail that looks ahead to what Ruth and Sylvie will eventually feel forced to do to the house, since another thing they can see is a curtain 'which had been half consumed by fire once when a birthday cake had been set too close to it. Sylvie had beaten out the flames with a back issue of *Good Housekeeping*, but she had never replaced the curtain' (*H*, 101).

Being inside a lighted room establishes a barrier between those inside and the exterior, making it difficult to see outside; but the lights make it easier for those outside to see in. In this way, Robinson's novel encodes women's confinement and the masculine privilege of moving freely between the public sphere and the family space. At the same time, that privilege sets substantive male existence outside the home, so that the traditional position of men within the domestic space resembles the picture Ruth conjures up of her grandfather 'just outside [the women's] conversation, like a difficult memory, or a ghost' (*H*, 96). That description also conveys a sense of the woman-identified quality of Ruth's imagination and narrative. This ghost is the only figure in the text offered to male readers to situate themselves in opposition to the sheriff, the law, with respect to the events and characters of the narrative. To take the position of that ghost, a reader like me must acknowledge that feminist discourses both speak critically to me and demand a reply that heeds the various boundaries by which women define themselves. As male critic, *I* must make this ghost speak. This essay is, I hope, marked by a sense of the political urgency and the risks such an undertaking carries.

. . .

Prefiguration and practice

Like Kristeva's historical model of the development of feminist responses to marginalization, *Housekeeping* offers some support for the conclusion that women have in practice already begun 'to operate from displacement as such'.[43] Kristeva and Marilynne Robinson's writings together imply that there is a social subtext to the female thematics of the home, as an enclosure frequently conflated with the female body itself. Sandra Gilbert and Susan Gubar argue that the 'paradigmatic female story' centers on 'the psychic split between the lady who submits to male dicta and the lunatic who rebels', a paradigm derived from *Jane Eyre*.[44] Kristeva and Robinson, however, construct narratives grounded in social practices and the possibility of social transformation.

Housekeeping and 'Women's Time' also offer some insight into a psychodynamic of women's writing that would connect textual production to women's prefigurative social practices. The problem women writers have to negotiate may not always be a sense of 'belatedness' or even a gender-based 'anxiety of authorship', as in Gilbert and Gubar's appropriation of Harold Bloom's ideas.[45] As Annette Kolodny points out, Bloom's theory of the anxiety of authorship applies only to authors who think of themselves as securely working within a tradition where their texts can be situated.[46] As Emily Dickinson's line, 'I lingered with Before –' suggests, women trying to produce literary texts may suffer from a sense of earliness, of writing in advance of a tradition that would accord their work the same significance male texts receive.[47] Kolodny implies that women's writing often anticipates its own misreading by men.[48] I would argue that women can use strategies of anticipation by writing *as if* there were already a tradition and a community of readers prepared to receive their work. Such strategies would empower individual women but could also have a collective effect, giving meaning to existing practices by helping to create the conditions for a significant body of women's texts to come into being. This proleptic troping of a possible future condition would be prefigurative – in Rowbotham's sense of the word.

Kristeva's theoretical writing calls for a prefigurative practice like the one Rowbotham describes in *Beyond the Fragments*: 'We need to make the creation of prefigurative forms an explicit part of our movement against capitalism. I do not mean that we try to hold an imaginary future in the present, straining against the boundaries of the possible until we collapse in exhaustion and despair. This would be utopian. Instead such forms would seek both to consolidate existing practice and release the imagination of what could be.'[49] In 'Women's Time' Kristeva uses the term 'future perfect', in quotes, with reference to the cyclic temporality that she later associates with the traditional ideas of women's subjectivity recuperated by the separatist moment in her model (*WT*, 32).[50] For Derrida, the logic of the future perfect only objectifies the future as what will have been and so 'reduces the future to the form of manifest presence'.[51] But for Kristeva, this logic of anticipation can also operate as a form of critical negativity, opening the possibility of transforming present conditions by bringing to light elements or potentialities that have been repressed and excluded. Alice Jardine summarizes Kristeva's future perfect as 'a modality that implies neither that we are helpless before some inevitable destiny nor that we can somehow, given enough time and thought, engineer an ultimately perfect future'.[52] The idea is not to hold an imaginary, perfect future in the present, as Rowbotham says, but to hold and practice a possible future, whose possibility is precisely what the dominant culture ensconced in that present tries to deny. Kristeva's third generation is nonsynchronous in relation to linear history, but this heterogeneity is no longer the remnant of an overtaken past. It is rather a future like that of the young in Ernst Bloch's analysis: '[Women] turn away from the day that [they have]. It is a day that [women] do not have today', but are in the process of creating.[53]

In her historical and political analysis of male avant-garde writers like Leautréamont, Kristeva argues that their work is 'social' because it 'speaks to subjects in immediate desire for play, knowledge and constructive activity'; it is addressed to a new collective subjectivity before the fact, since that subjectivity's 'realization is impossible in the interior of the present social body'.[54] In 'Women's Time' and women's writing like Robinson's we find that it *is* possible to proceed from the marginality of an aesthetic avant-garde 'to linking the placing in process/on trial of the subject in a text to social subversion, to the struggle for a society where production will not be the imperative rule and where expenditure will be the principle of a constant renovation of ephemeral structures'.[55]

Notes

I would like to thank Jane Marcus for her readings of this paper, her support, and her encouragement, as well as the other participants in her seminars at the University of Texas on women's writing and feminist criticism.

1. See ELIZABETH A. MEESE, *Crossing the Double-Cross: The Practice of Feminist Criticism* (Chapel Hill: University of North Carolina Press, 1986), esp. chaps. 5 and 8; CELESTE M. SCHENCK, 'Feminism and Deconstruction: Re-constructing the Elegy', *Tulsa Studies in Women's Literature* 5, no. 1 (Spring 1986): 13–27; and GAYATRI CHAKRAVORTY SPIVAK, 'Displacement and the Discourse of Woman', in *Displacement: Derrida and After*, ed. Mark Krupnick (Bloomington: Indiana University Press, 1983), 169–95.

2. JULIA KRISTEVA, 'Women's Time', trans. Alice Jardine and Harry Blake, in *Feminist Theory: A Critique of Ideology*, ed. Nannerl O. Keohane, Michelle Z. Rosaldo, and Barbara C. Gelpi (Chicago: University of Chicago Press, 1982). Subsequent citations of this article will appear in parentheses in the text as *WT*. The main exception is TORIL MOI, *Sexual/Textual Politics: Feminist Literary Theory* (London: Methuen, 1985), 12–13, who offers a schematic outline of Kristeva's model and uses it to argue for the need to deconstruct male/female gender roles.

3. Socialist feminist work discussed below will include JOAN KELLY, *Women, History, and Theory: The Essays of Joan Kelly* (Chicago: University of Chicago Press, 1984); ELIZABETH FOX-GENOVESE, 'Placing Women's History in History', *New Left Review* 133 (May–June 1982): 5–29; MICHÉLE BARRETT, *Women's Oppression Today: Problems in Marxist Feminist Analysis* (London: Verso, 1980); and (more briefly) SHEILA ROWBOTHAM, LYNNE SEGAL, and HILARY WAINWRIGHT, *Beyond the Fragments: Feminism and the Making of Socialism* (Boston: Alyson Publications, 1981). MICHAEL RYAN, *Marxism and Deconstruction: A Critical Articulation* (Baltimore: Johns Hopkins University Press, 1982), chap. 9, treats socialist feminism in relation to dialectics and deconstruction. Gayatri Spivak's work is concerned with the same issues, and Meese sets out 'to provoke critical theory, especially American manifestations of deconstruction, to be more radically political' (x).

4. JULIA KRISTEVA, 'Semiotics: A Critical Science and/or a Critique of Science', trans. Sean Hand, in *The Kristeva Reader*, ed. Toril Moi (New York: Columbia University Press, 1986), 85. Kristeva takes this term from PHILIPPE SOLLERS's distinction between linear and monumental histories in his 'Programme', *Tel Quel* 31 (Autumn 1967): 3–7. See JACQUES DERRIDA, *Positions*, trans. Alan Bass (Chicago: University of Chicago Press, 1981), for an indication of what this concept came to mean in French theoretical discourse. In an interview from this collection, Guy Scarpetta asks Derrida if it is not possible to retain a notion of 'history conceived no longer as a linear scheme, but as a stratified, differential, contradictory' group of social practices (56).

5. ERNST BLOCH's essay, 'Nonsynchronism and the Obligation to Its Dialectics', *New German Critique* 11 (Spring 1977), offers a way of reading Kristeva's notion of women's time. Bloch begins: 'Not all people exist in the same Now. They do so only externally, by virtue of the fact that they may all be seen today. But that does not mean that they are living at the same time with others. . . . One has one's times according to where one stands corporeally' (22). Writing originally in response to the rise of fascism in the 1930s, Bloch points to the prefiguratively nonsynchronic position of young people, a position Kristeva also claims for women: 'For the most part, *Youth* turns away from the day that it has. It is a day that the young do not have today. But their dreams are nourished just as materially by an empty condition of being-young, which is not of the present' (23).

6. JULIA KRISTEVA, 'Oscillation between Power and Denial', in *New French Feminisms*, ed. Elaine Marks and Isabelle de Courtivron (New York: Schocken, 1981), 165–7.

7. Ibid., 166; Kristeva, 'Women's Time', 44–8.

8. JULIA KRISTEVA, *Revolution in Poetic Language*, trans. Margaret Waller (New York: Columbia University Press, 1984), 75.

9. LUCE IRIGARAY, *This Sex Which Is Not One*, trans. Catherine Porter (Ithaca, N.Y.: Cornell University Press, 1985), 166.

10. Kristeva, 'Women's Time', 48–9; JULIA KRISTEVA, 'Stabat Mater', trans. Arthur Goldhammer, in *The Female Body in Western Culture: Contemporary Perspectives*, ed. Susan Rubin Suleiman (Cambridge: Harvard University Press, 1986), 99–118.

11. TEMMA KAPLAN, 'Female Consciousness and Collective Action: The Case of Barcelona, 1910–1918', in Keohane, Rosaldo, and Gelpi, eds. (n. 2 above), 55–76, esp. 55–7, 75–6. See SONDRA HALE, 'The Wing of the Patriarch: Sudanese Women and Revolutionary Parties', *Merip: Middle East Report* 16 (January–February 1986), 28–30, for an application of Kaplan's ideas to one group of non-Western women. Rather than revalorizing domestic space, Hale proposes that Sudanese women could draw upon other, culturally specific women-only spaces in order to avoid a cooptation that ignores women's issues. Hale also relates these spaces to what Sheila Rowbotham in *Beyond the Fragments* (n. 3 above) calls 'prefigurative forms', which I will discuss in the last section of the present essay. Susan Willis makes an argument about domestic space similar to mine in her book on Afro-American women's writing. See WILLIS, *Specifying: Black Women Writing the American Experience* (Madison: University of Wisconsin Press, 1987), 159–60.

12. MARY JACOBUS, 'The Difference of View', in *Women Writers and Writing about Women*, ed. Mary Jacobus (Totowa, N.J.: Barnes & Noble, 1979), 10–21, esp. 14.

13. MARGARET HOMANS, ' "Her Very Own Howl": The Ambiguities of Representation in Recent Women's Fiction', *Signs: Journal of Women in Culture and Society* 9, no. 2 (Winter 1983): 186–205, esp. 186–7; ELAINE MARKS, 'Women and Literature in France', *Signs* 3, no. 4 (Summer 1978): 832–42, esp. 835–6. Homans's essay defines one such conjunction when she argues that contemporary women's fiction displaces the French feminist concern with women's exclusion from the symbolic order of language onto the thematic level, thus continuing to use and to revise given discursive forms (205).

14. ADRIENNE RICH, 'Compulsory Heterosexuality and Lesbian Existence', in *Blood, Bread, and Poetry: Selected Prose 1979–1985* (New York: Norton, 1986), 63.

15. Irigaray, *This Sex* (n. 9 above), 135.

16. Ibid., 159.

17. LUCE IRIGARAY, *Speculum of the Other Woman*, trans. Gillian C. Gill (Ithaca, N.Y.: Cornell University Press, 1985), 139.

18. Kristeva, *Revolution* (n. 8 above), 68.

19. Kelly (n. 3 above), 59–60.

20. Fox-Genovese (n. 3 above), 7.

21. Ibid., 14.

22. Ibid.

23. Ibid., 29.

24. Georg Lukacs, *History and Class Consciousness: Studies in Marxist Dialectics*, trans. Rodney Livingstone (Cambridge, MA: MIT Press, 1971), 199.

25. Ibid., 224.

26. Barrett (n. 3 above), 226.

27. Ibid., 134–8.

28. Kelly (n. 3 above), 61.

29. Kristeva, 'Oscillation' (n. 6 above), 166.

30. Derrida, *Positions* (n. 4 above), 41. These negative political effects are what Moi seems to chance or to attribute to Kristeva when she describes Kristeva's model simply as a deconstruction of gender roles; see n. 2 above.

31. Derrida, *Positions*, 42.

32. Ibid., 66.

33. Kristeva, *Revolution* (n. 8 above), 142.

34. STANLEY ARONOWITZ, *The Crisis in Historical Materialism: Class, Politics, and Culture in Marxist Theory* (New York: Praeger, 1982), 31.

35. Ibid., 24–34, 116–17, 121; Bloch (n. 5 above), 38; see Ryan (n. 3 above), 73–81, on Adorno.

36. JACQUES DERRIDA, *Spurs/Eperons*, trans. Barbara Harlow (Chicago: University of Chicago Press, 1979), 65.

37. ALICE JARDINE, *Gynesis: Configurations of Woman and Modernity* (Ithaca, N.Y.: Cornell University Press, 1985), 194–5, points out how Derrida seems to endorse Nietszche's perspective on feminism in this passage, treating it merely as a moment of inversion which fails to challenge the hierarchies of man/woman or truth/untruth. Kristeva's model asks whether the moment of inversion is necessary to give purpose to 'skepticism' and 'dissimilation' (Jardine, 194) as social practice and to link it to a material subject position, thus giving substance to her critique of grammatology for remaining silent about the subject.

38. Jean Bethke Elshtain, *Public Man, Private Woman: Women in Social and Political Thought* (Princeton, N.J.: Princeton University Press, 1981), 12, describes a logic of the supplement in the separation of the Greek *polis* from the household: 'First the relations and activities occurring within and serving as the *raison d'être* of the *polis* were defined as existing outside the realms of nature and necessity. Second, the free space of the *polis*, though apart from necessity, existed in a *necessary* relation to those activities lodged within the private realm, held by the Greeks to be the sphere of unfreedom.'

39. Marilynne Robinson, *Housekeeping* (New York: Farrar, Straus, & Giroux, 1980), subsequent citations of this novel will appear in parentheses in the text as *H*; Meese (n. 1 above), 57.

40. Meese, 64.

41. Ibid., 61.

42. Ibid., 59.

43. Spivak, 'Displacement' (n. 1 above), 186.

44. Sandra M. Gilbert and Susan Gubar, *The Madwoman in the Attic: The Woman Writer and the Nineteenth-Century Literary Imagination* (New Haven, Conn.: Yale University Press, 1979), 82.

45. Ibid., 48–9.

46. Annette Kolodny, 'A Map for Rereading: Gender and the Interpretation of Literary Texts', in *The New Feminist Criticism: Essays on Women, Literature, and Theory*, ed. Elaine Showalter (New York: Pantheon, 1985), 47–8.

47. *The Complete Poems of Emily Dickinson*, ed. Thomas Johnson (Boston: Little, Brown, 1955), 300.

48. Kolodny, 51–2, 57–8.

49. Rowbotham, Segal, and Wainwright (n. 3 above), 147.

50. Kristeva's earliest use of this term takes it from Jacques Lacan; Julia Kristeva, *Séméiotiké: Recherches pur une sémanalyse* (Paris: Editions du Seuil, 1969), 242, n. 32. For Lacan as for Derrida, this kind of anticipation is a reification, underlying the formation of the autonomous ego in the mirror stage; Lacan, *Ecrits: A Selection*, trans. Alan Sheridan (New York: Norton, 1977), 306–7. Louis Althusser makes a similar argument about the negative effects of tropes of anticipation in his discussion of how 'expecting' a child already assimilates her or him to a position in a preexisting ideological formation; Althusser, *Lenin and Philosophy and Other Essays*, trans. Ben Brewster (New York: Monthly Review Press, 1971), 176.

51. Jacques Derrida, *Dissemination*, trans. Barbara Johnson (Chicago: University of Chicago Press, 1981), 7. However, in an earlier text, Derrida uses the term 'future perfect' in a more positive way; Jacques Derrida, *Of Grammatology*, trans. Gayatn Chakravorty Spivak (Baltimore: Johns Hopkins University Press, 1976), 5 (Derrida here uses the French phrase for the verb tense of the future perfect, *futur antérieur* and it is translated literally as 'future anterior').

52. Alice Jardine, 'Introduction to Julia Kristeva's "Women's Time"', *Signs* 7, no. 1 (Autumn 1981): 5–12, esp. 5.

53. Bloch (n. 5 above), 23.

54. Julia Kristeva, *La révolution du langage poétique* (Paris: Editions du Seuil, 1974), 419, my translation. The English version contains only the first section of this longer work.

55. Ibid., 366.

Other feminist and deconstructive approaches to Robinson's work are by Paula E. Geyh, 'Burning Down the House? Domestic Space and Feminine Subjectivity in Marilynne Robinson's *Housekeeping*', *Contemporary Literature* 34, 1 (1993): 103–22; Siân Mile, 'Femme Foetal: The Construction/Deconstruction of Female Subjectivity in *Housekeeping*, or NOTHING GAINED', *Genders* 8 (Summer 1990): 129–36; and Karen Kaivola, 'The Pleasures and Perils of Merging: Female Subjectivity in Marilynne Robinson's *Housekeeping*', *Contemporary Literature* 33, 4 (1993): 670–90.

5 Making *Familia* from Scratch: Split Subjectivities in the Work of Helena María Viramontes and Cherríe Moraga*

Norma Alarcón

French feminism once again proves useful in analysing contemporary American fiction by women. Norma Alarcón engages Julia Kristeva and Luce Irigaray to consider the nature of the 'sociosymbolic structures' of 'home', 'family', and 'woman' in a Mexican American cultural context. Following the trajectory of fictional characters in works by Helena María Viramontes and Cherríe Moraga, Alarcón traces their exploration of 'the subjectivity of the speaking subject'. Her assumption, like Yarbro-Bejarano's in the first essay of this collection, is the following: if gender stereotypes ('semantic charters') can be exposed as oppressive cultural constructs, then self-knowledge and self-determination will follow. This is, of course, one more version of the American dream – the promise of endless and unencumbered self-making – but with the difference that the self-making occurs in a culturally contested and gendered space. Alarcón argues for the deconstruction of repressive power relations in service of personal empowerment, concluding her essay with a kind of idealizing call to action in the form of a 'self-conscious grasp of the engendering process'.

Chicana writers are increasingly employing female-speaking subjects who hark back to explore the subjectivity of women. Often in their writings this subjectivity takes as its point of departure 'woman's' over-determined signification as future wives/mothers in relation to the 'symbolic contract' within which women may have a voice on the condition that they speak as mothers.[1] The female-speaking subject that would want to speak from a different position than that of a mother, or a future wife/mother, is thrown into a crisis of meaning that begins

---

* Reprinted from *Chicana Creativity and Criticism: Charting New Frontiers in American Literature.* Ed. María Herrera-Sobek and Helena María Viramontes (Houston, TX: Arte Público Press, 1988), pp. 147–59.

with her own gendered personal identity and its relational position with others. Paradoxically, as we shall see, a crisis of meaning can ensue even in the case of a female who may have never aspired to speak from a different position than that of a wife/mother.

First, to start the exploration of the question of 'woman', I want to discuss Helena M. Viramontes' story 'Growing'. What young girl can fight a father (and an assenting mother) when he roars 'Tú eres mujer'?[2] As Naomi, the protagonist notes, the phrase is uttered as a verdict. It is a judgment meant to ensure the paternal law and view of woman's cultural significance. Within this symbolic structure, Naomi is not supposed to counterspeak her sense of herself as different from what her father says it is. In his view her subjectivity has been decided *a priori* by what is perceived as the body of a woman. The fact that she is compelled to report the phrase in Spanish only points to a particular Chicano/ Mexicano rigidity with respect to the signifying system that holds the dyad woman-man in place, and which provides her father with his authority. By switching codes to 'mujer', he knows more precisely what his judgment of Naomi ought to signify. If he said 'woman', he would be on precarious ground. He is not quite sure what it may mean in Anglo culture, a culture within which he may well feel that he has no authority. Thus, though we may conjecture that Naomi's family transacts some of its communication in English, Spanish is employed in this sentence to guarantee parental authority. Naomi, on the other hand, has learned that 'woman' is different from 'mujer'. As a result, she attempts to assert her difference from what is expected of Mexican/Chicana girls by appealing to the Anglo code. Thus Naomi notes that for the girls 'in the United States' experience is different (31).

Though Naomi is correct in her perception of the difference in social experience between girls due to the relatively different cultural/racial codes (perhaps class-rooted codes as well), she is also too young to apprehend that in the 'symbolic contract' virtually all women will sooner or later reach a limit with regard to the speaking position that they may take up as 'woman'. How rapidly that limit is reached and how she may speak thereafter will vary in accordance with the specific 'semantic charters' that her cultural linguistic ground offers her.[3] Often that limit is set by how her father (and assenting mother) perceive her body which is always that of a 'woman' and underpinned by what her father perceives as her sexual/maternal function. As a result, Naomi feels increasingly imprisoned by the concept 'mujer', which her father wields as a weapon against her. Yet, she is hard put to fight him because his evidence for her meaning as 'woman' is her own changing body, that is, menarche and breasts. In a sense, then, her very physical experience is used to press her to live out concepts such as 'woman' and make Naomi become *'the practical realization of the meta-physical . . .* operating in such a way,

moreover, that subjects themselves, being implicated through and
through, being produced in it as concepts would lack the means to
analyze it. Except in an after-the-fact way whose delays are yet to be
fully measured . . .'.[4] Within such a 'semantic charter' Naomi is too
young to understand what is happening to her. She views her sexuality
as a very confused mass. Though it may take her the rest of her life to
apprehend what may have taken place as a result of the verdict 'Tú eres
mujer', the narrator of Naomi's circumstance is not too young to conclude
as follows: 'Now that she was older, her obligations became heavier both
at home and at school. There were too many expectations. . . . She could
no longer be herself and her father no longer trusted her, because she was
a woman' (38). All manner of things that she is obliged and expected to
do are derived from the 'fact' that she is a 'woman'. Her body is enlisted
in a stream of sociosymbolic activities which she also experiences as a
splitting her from herself. As Irigaray comments,

> Participation in society requires that [her] body submit itself to a
> specularization, a speculation, that transforms it into a value-bearing
> object, a standardized sign, an exchangeable signifier, a 'likeness' with
> reference to an authoritative model. *A commodity – a woman – is divided
> into two irreconcilable 'bodies'*: her 'natural' body and her socally valued,
> exchangeable body, which is a particular mimetic expression of
> masculine values. (180)

Within Mexican/Chicano culture the authoritative model, however
unconscious, to which fathers (masculine values) have recourse is the
Catholic Holy Family and its assumed social authority. Viramontes,
the constructor of this narrative world, is quite aware of that since many
of her stories allude to religious expectations and dogma. Given that
Naomi feels split from herself when she is pressed to become a 'woman'
for social and symbolic purposes, who is that self? If *it* could speak what
would it say? It is at this point that many a woman of letters of Hispanic
origin, in her quest for her subjectivity has turned to mysticism. Santa
Teresa is our paradigm in that instance. Others, and here Sor Juana Inés
de la Cruz is our paradigm, have opted for the convent (a retreat) so that
no one could verify she was a 'woman': 'Yo no entiendo de esas cosas; /
sólo sé que aquí me vine / porque, si es que soy mujer, / ninguno lo
verifique.'[5] In order to avoid these resolutions which are no solution at
all for the contemporary Chicana critic and writer as speaking subjects,
I want to pursue an alternate course with reference to two very different
female-speaking subjects: Viramontes' own Olga Ruiz in 'Snapshots' and
Cherríe Moraga's Marisa in *Giving Up The Ghost*.[6] I choose these because,
unlike Naomi of 'Growing', they speak their subjectivity directly, without
the intervention of a narrator who has greater 'knowledge'. Moreover,

in assessing their crisis of meaning with regard to their own gendered personal identity, they have to look back as older women. Naomi is too young to have much to look back to except those moments of play when she experienced herself as forgetting that she was a 'woman', though, as we shall see, that in itself can be significant. Both Marisa, who is in her late 20s, and Olga Ruiz, who is past 50, have had an opportunity that Naomi has yet to go through, that is, the increasing pressure to become that 'woman' in the sociosymbolic contract. In looking back (and so many Chicana writers have their speaking subjects look back – Sandra Cisneros in *The House on Mango Street*, Ana Castillo in *The Mixquiahuala Letters* and Denise Chávez in *The Last of the Menu Girls* to name a few), Marisa and Olga Ruiz enact, as Irigaray asserts, an analysis 'after-the-fact' of the treacherous route on the way to becoming a 'woman' or not becoming a 'woman'.

Virtually all the readers I have talked with are put off by the story 'Snapshots'. Since there is nothing wrong with the story *qua* story, I ask why? Neither older women nor young women students like Olga Ruiz. Since Olga is the sole speaking subject in the story, as readers we are called upon to enter her world, and her view of it. Only one reader has admitted to me that she feels like Olga Ruiz and she said it with a sigh. Hardly anyone can, or wants to, recognize their subjectivity in Olga Ruiz. Olga Ruiz holds up a deadly mirror for women. If, as Pierre Maranda states, 'the text is the light on my face that enables me to see myself in the one-way mirror that I hold in front of it; the text allows me, Narcissus, to marvel at my mind, to believe in myself and, consequently, to have the impression that I live more competently' (191), then Olga Ruiz holds up to us the potential psychosis that awaits us if we live a life like hers. As readers we refuse to take up her 'I' as our own, to fuse our 'I' with hers. Female readers could come away feeling that they live 'more competently', but they are not sure. Olga Ruiz may well remind us of our mothers, or we may even recognize ourselves in Olga's own daughter Marge, whose only advice to her mother is to keep busy. Marge has brought Olga enough skeins of wool to stock a retail shelf. Even the daughter, that is, younger readers, are caught speechless as to what they may say to help Olga Ruiz out of her crisis of meaning. In short, Olga Ruiz has lived the life of a 'woman'. How can we help a woman who according to cultural models has lived her life 'correctly' and who is now cynical and embittered?

Olga Ruiz has been *framed* by cultural expectations and is now so removed from her sensibility, her contact with her own body and its reality that she states, 'I don't know if I should be hungry or not' (98). Was her grandmother right? Did her grandfather's camera, which split the sexes into men who mill 'around him expressing their limited knowledge of the invention' (98), and women whose pictures are taken,

cut her from her soul? Given her desperate situation, Olga Ruiz appeals
to folk beliefs in order to give closure to her crisis of meaning as wife/
mother. If she can accept that she was 'killed' since infancy, then maybe
she can stop her obsessive-compulsive desire to find clues for meaning in
the family album. Yet she will be left to wonder if her grandmother's
antidote worked to save her, 'My grandmother was very upset and cut
a piece of my hair, probably to save me from a bad omen' (99). The
grandmother's effort to counter the camera's evil work may have
worked, in which case Olga Ruiz may be forced to conclude that
she did not save herself, that she colluded with society and thus is
responsible for her situation. Obviously, she stops short of completely
blaming herself, and leaves a seed of doubt, a very small one, since
not to doubt that indeed that is the meaning could throw her over the
edge into total psychosis.

According to her own account, Olga stands on the threshold of
psychosis after thirty years of marriage. However, as Olga remembers it,
she had an earlier crisis of meaning as a 'woman' after the birth of her
daughter, Marge. The discomforts of pregnancy send her into her first
quest for self-meaning in the family album as if it were a bible: 'I began
flipping through my family's photo albums . . . to pass the time and the
pain away' (94). She labels her compulsive behavior an 'addiction' to
'nostalgia'. Giving birth becomes for Olga the first occasion in which she
feels split from herself. Julia Kristeva has suggested that for many women,

Pregnancy seems to be experienced as the radical ordeal of the
splitting of the subject: redoubling up of the body, separating and
coexistence of the self and of an other, of nature and of consciousness,
of physiology and speech. This fundamental challenge to identity is
then accompanied by a fantasy of totality – narcissistic completeness
– a sort of instituted, socialized, natural psychosis.[7]

According to sociosymbolic 'semantic charters', Olga Ruiz should
have found her gendered meaning and should surrender herself to a
'narcissistic completeness' in the child, which she subsequently does.
However, at that moment Olga found herself divided between the past
as the moment of separateness from the child and the future which will
demand an uneasy and continued coexistence. Though nothing comes of
this critical moment, the sense that she should be separate is signalled
by the nostalgic neurosis. By contemplating the family photo album,
Olga hopes 'some old dream will come into my blank mind' (94). She is
depressed 'because every detail, as minute as it might seem, made me
feel that so much had passed unnoticed' (94). What dream or desire
should make itself evident in the photographs? Whatever 'had passed
unnoticed' is not accompanied by any speech that would help Olga grasp

the difference between what she wanted and what she got. Her mind is blank with regard to that self who may have dreamed of another life. She already knows that she has been very capable of devoting herself to the details of homemaking. She is so much the automaton that she cannot stop, though it is no longer necessary that she continue homemaking for others. The only words she can come up with, that can describe what might have been different from the muteness that enveloped her life, are nostalgia, indulgence, anticipation. She cannot come to terms with the separate self that could articulate an alternate past, present or future than what she has had.

Her solution to this particular blankness is brilliant given its truth currency: 'Both woman and child are clones: same bathing suit, same pony tails, same ribbons' (97). However, truth does not necessarily grant one a new purchase on life. The snapshot of Olga, Marge and Dave is uncannily like the one of Olga with her parents. In a sense it is like that of the Holy Family triad – father, mother and child – except that the child is a girl, and indeed that is what problematizes the 'snapshot'. The girl-child does not have a sublime transcendent story. Her story according to that 'semantic charter' is to duplicate the wife/maternal tale. How can any meaningful memory stand out in the redoubling of this snapshot? Certainly Olga could not get close to her passionless mother, just as Marge cannot get close to Olga, nor does she appear to want to. They are as distanced from feeling as they are from their core responsive sensibility/sexuality, not only from men but from each other. Mother and daughter are so much alike one would think they could comfort each other, but they cannot. To do so Olga or Marge would have to take up a different speaking position with respect to each other. Before they can see themselves as more than a relational unit of mother–daughter, Olga or Marge would have to take up a different speaking position in their bodies. This position would entail entering into their emotional lives in ways that would strengthen and renew the bond differently, which may shut men out (temporarily?). (Let us remember that the Holy Family is the family of the son not the daughter.) Thus, to contemporanize the situation Marge would have to be capable of speaking to Olga, who is on the verge of madness, in the words of Luce Irigaray, as follows:

> And here you are, this very evening, facing a mourning with no remembrance. Invested with an emptiness that evokes no memories. That screams at its own rebounding echo. A materiality occupying a void that escapes its grasp. A block sealing the wall of your prison. A buttress to a possible future which, taken away, lets everything crumble indefinitely:
> Where are you? Where am I? Where to find the traces of our passage? From the one to the other? From the one into the other? (. . .)

No one to mark the time of your existence, to evoke in you the rise of a passage out of yourself, to tell you: Come here, stay here. No one to tell you: Don't remain caught up between the mirror and this endless loss of yourself. A self separated from another self. A self missing some other self. Two dead selves distanced from each other, with no ties binding them. The self that you see in the mirror severed from the self that nurtures. And, as I've gone, I've lost the place where proof of your subsistence once appeared to you.[8]

Olga's middle-of-the-night phone call to Marge is her cry to have Marge reunite her with herself, 'I don't know if I should be hungry'. To start from the beginning as if she were a baby, so they can 'make *familia* from scratch'. Since Marge may not possess the wherewithal to respond, the call is rendered irrelevant. Before a crisis of meaning can be effected in the relationship between Olga and Marge as mother–daughter–mother, the husbands interfere. It is clearly not in their interest to have these two women renegotiate the sociosymbolic contract by effecting a different dialogue between themselves. If we go on the report that Olga gives us of Marge, Marge herself cannot even begin to grasp that she, too, is abducted from herself, 'Immobilized in the reflection he expects of [her]. Reduced to the face he fashions for [her] in which to look at himself. Traveling at the whim of his dreams and mirages. Trapped in a single function – mothering.'[9] In short Marge is already also *framed* in her great grandfather's camera-eye which he passed on to the sons. It will be some years before Marge arrives at the speaking position her mother presently holds, by which time it may be too late. For indeed, grasping one's gendered meaning 'after-the-fact' entails the removal of the buttress (that is, Mother) which 'lets everything crumble indefinitely'. In the crumbling may be the speaking position from which to transform the sociosymbolic contract.

In *Giving Up The Ghost*, Cherríe Moraga offers us a heroine who has refused to become a 'woman', who has refused to be framed by the camera's eye, 'immobilized in the reflection he expects of [her]'. On the contrary Marisa desires to take up his 'camera's eye', his gaze. In short, Marisa wanted to be a 'man' when she was a child. Uncannily, as if the lines of communication between Olga Ruiz and Marisa had been inverted, Marisa implicitly uses the metaphor of the camera except, like a 'man', she uses it to frame or trap women. Through Corky, her younger 'male' self, Marisa 'after-the-fact' reports:

> when I was a little kid I useta love the movies
> every saturday you could find me there
> my eyeballs glued to the screen
> then during the week my friend Tudy and me

we'd make up our own movies
one of our favorites was this cowboy one
where we'd be out in the desert
'n' we'd capture these chicks 'n' hold 'em up
for ransom we'd string 'em up 'n'
make 'em take their clothes off
jus' pretending a'course but it useta make me feel
real tough
strip we'd say to the wall
all cool-like. . . .
I was a big 'n' tough 'n' a dude (5)

Corky's imaginary play, however, the fact that in her mind she was a 'dude', is put into action one day. Corky and her friend Tudy (a boy), strip Chrissy down completely, and Corky reports that 'after that I was like a maniac all summer' (12). In stripping Chrissy down, Corky looks into the vaginal mirror which makes her a little crazy as she also remembers that 'deep down inside / no matter / how / I tried to pull the other / off' (6), she always knew she was a girl. As in Naomi's case, Corky is reminded that she is a girl, and consequently a 'woman-to-be' through the body, except that Corky refuses to enter the 'semantic charter'. We are not sure what will come to Naomi, though she did report that she experienced sexual neutrality during childhood play. There is no neutrality for Corky ever, and even as she puts into play the dyad man-woman, it is in some sense unacceptable. However, she first internalizes the dyad in such a way that, though her body always reminds her that she is a girl/woman, her imaginary desire, the site of her subjectivity, is experienced as that of a 'man'.

Marisa, the adult Corky, is catapulted into a dance of 'symbolic identifications' with the concepts of 'man' and 'woman' that is always too close for any female's comfort, because they constantly run the risk of being socialized into poses. Because Marisa is a lesbian, one of these is the famous lesbian dyad of the 'butch-femme' split. In some sense, Marisa is split asunder between her male-like subjectivity and behavior, and her literal female body. For Marisa neither alternative 'butch' (man) nor 'femme' (woman) is acceptable. At this point, one can say that Marisa, out of necessity, either conjures Amalia into her life or that Amalia appears out of nowhere to save her. Both Marisa and Amalia speak their subjectivity 'after-the-fact' of the relationship and hold a conversation that hardly ever is enacted face-to-face. It is as if Moraga knows that in 'real' life these two women may not be able to speak to each other directly in any effective way, thus we must enter their sociosymbolic lives, in a dialogue that is always a near miss. Thus Moraga effects a process of potential transformations between two

women as unlike each other as we could ask for – the lesbian with the
subjectivity of a 'man' and the traditional heterosexual 'woman', who
may also be our mother.

There are ways in which one can see the ghostly face of Olga Ruiz in
Amalia, except that given the sexual interchange between Marisa and
Amalia, Amalia is less repressed than Olga. Yet Amalia is in some ways
a stereotypic heterosexual Mexican 'woman'. Amalia is framed by the
eye of her male lovers, the ones for whom she wanted to be an object
of desire. Amalia cannot bring herself to desire Marisa until her ideal
male lover dies, and his ghost reenters her body so that she may feel
enough a 'man' to desire Marisa (28). In this fashion we are cued from
a different angle, that active sexual desire has been marked masculine.
By the end of this 'after-the-fact' indirect dialogue both Amalia and
Marisa have learned as much about themselves as we have about the
variety of gendered crises of meaning.

The subjective agency of desire, the ineffable energy that may help us
transform our world has heretofore been the province of whoever 'man'
is. As a lesbian-identified woman, Marisa does not want just a 'woman'
(a 'femme'), that is a muted object of desire, but as she says: 'It's not that
you don't want a man, / you don't want a man in a man. / You want a
man in a woman. / The woman-part goes without saying. / That's what
you always learn to want first' (29). The implication that a girl learns to
want a woman first through her relationship to her mother, and places
the girl-child in competition with the boy-child for the body of the
mother is very suggestive. It brings us face to face with the fantastic
cultural silence, religious or Freudian, with regard to what the girl's
position is in the Holy Family or Oedipal triad. This lays bare the fact
that in that sociosymbolic contract a girl-child may not speak except as
would-be mother or mother. In taking refuge in a male identity, Corky/
Marisa acquire a speech that is at odds with the body, thus in a different
way they are forced into two irreconcilable selves. Amalia, however, thinks
that Marisa wanted her so that Marisa could feel (be) the woman in her:
'Sometimes I think, with me / that she only wanted to feel herself / so
much a woman / that she would no longer be hungry for one' (53). If
this is so, then Marisa goes to Amalia, the maternal/heterosexual, for
the reconciliation with her female body. As bereft daughter, Marisa
reverses the 'narcissistic completeness' that Kristeva suggests mothers are
expected to attain through the child: 'But then was the beautiful woman
/ in the mirror of the water / you or me?' (27). Moraga here suggests
the daughter's quest to unite with the mother in ways that only sons get
to do within a too rigid patriarchy. It is clear at the end of the dramatic
monologues, that Marisa's severed pieces have come together to enable
her creativity, 'so I cling to her in my heart, / my daydream with pencil
in my mouth, / when I put my fingers / to my own forgotten places' (58).

In my view, in *Giving Up The Ghost*, Moraga puts into play the concepts 'man' and 'woman' (and the parodic 'butch/femme'), with the intuitive knowledge that they operate in our subjectivities, so that it is difficult to analyze them, except in the way she has done. Women speaking with each other in a spiralling way, not quite face-to-face, but with the recollection that at least once they were so close to each other that they could effect a transfusion so as to avoid the extremes – that is a muted 'woman's' speaking position, and a male-identified subjectivity. It is to Moraga's credit that she puts the dyad man-woman into play in such a way that she brings into view three relational trajectories – the lesbian butch who is killing herself by the implied rejection of her literal body, the mother–daughter relation where the daughter may be forced to take the son (or father's) position so as to get close to her mother, and the hope that the heterosexual woman will not be put off by the lesbian due to homophobia.

For young Chicana writers (and critics) the crisis of meaning as women has increasingly led to a measuring 'after-the-fact' of the speaking subject's meanings. The most exciting explorations are those that 'measure' the intricacies of relationship between and among women. Yet if actual social experiences have the potential of effecting a complex and heterogeneous subjectivity, the symbolic contract within which 'woman' is the repository of meaning and not the agent, constantly presses her to align herself with the symbolic; in this way she is forced to live the life of a 'woman/mother'. To refuse to live the life of a 'woman', which is both literal (body) and symbolic (iconic/linguistic configurations), throws her into a crisis of meaning. As young Corky makes clear, if you don't want to be a girl, society as well as she then take it that you want to be a boy. Corky's 'error' is that she does not refuse both. How could she? Perhaps, as the older and wiser Marisa suggests, we must make *'familia* from scratch' (58). Marisa, who wanted to save her own mother (14) and later Amalia, by having them remember their own 'forgotten places' beyond womanly duty, would, unlike Marge, be capable of saying to Olga Ruiz: 'Where are you? Where am I? Where to find the traces of your passage? From the one to the other? From the one into the other?'

In my view, Julia Kristeva goes a long way towards charting a course for the dissident (female) speaking subject. The speaking subject today has to position herself at the margins of the 'symbolic contract' and refuse to accept definitions of 'woman' and 'man' in order to transform the contract. However, as Kristeva's critics have pointed out, a female-speaking subject today has to walk with one foot inside and another outside the interstice that would stake the boundary of what a 'woman' may speak. Toril Moi's critique reads as follows: 'political reality (the fact that patriarchy defines women and oppresses them accordingly) still makes it necessary to campaign in the name of women, it is important to recognize that in this struggle a woman cannot *be*: she can only exist negatively, as it were, through the refusal of that which is given'.[10] Moi adds that as a result Kristeva can state 'I therefore understand by "woman", that which cannot be represented, that which is not spoken, that which remains outside naming and ideologies (163). Thus, it is that both Naomi and Marisa leave their futures open-ended, and Naomi in her way too can challenge her father, for to believe that one 'is a woman' is as absurd and obscurantist as to believe that one 'is a man' (163).

As Chicana writers explore the subjectivity of their speaking subjects, they are bound, as most of us are, to explore sexual identities as they have been bequeathed. However, as I hope I have made clear, each speaking subject takes positions that vary according to her self-conscious grasp of the engendering process, which constantly throws girls/women into a crisis of meaning as women. That self-conscious grasp will be very much dependent on age, cultural ground, and on how she understands herself in relation to others, after the fact. The task before us is to continue to measure the delay and its painful implications.

Notes

1. 'Symbolic contract' is the term Julia Kristeva sometimes employs to refer to the Patriarchal Law and/or linguistic domain. In her work the subject, who is almost always male, is conjectured as one who finds 'his identity in the symbolic, [and] *separates* from his fusion with the mother'; in 'Revolution in Poetic Language', *The Julia Kristeva Reader*, Ed. Toril Moi (New York: Columbia University Press, 1986), 101. In Kristeva's theoretical perspective the Mother is posited, for the male subject, as an almost inarticulable site (i.e. a site of the Freudian/Lacanian unconscious). I do not take up that line of inquiry in this essay because in asking what our place as female subjects may be within the symbolic contract, the Mother is more than a theoretical site. We are asked to fill the site symbolically and socially. In 'Women's Time', from which my epigraph is taken (23–4), Kristeva suggests that women speaking subjects may want to adopt an attitude where 'the very dichotomy man/woman as an opposition between two rival entities may be understood as belonging to *metaphysics*' (33). That attitude is the one I have attempted to take *vis-à-vis* the writers discussed in my essay. See *Signs: Journal of Women in Culture and Society*, 7:1 (Autumn 1981), 13–35.

    The second epigraph was written by BRUCE BUURSMA in the *Chicago Tribune* and subsequently reprinted in the *Des Moines Register*, Sunday, October 17, 1987, n.p.

2. *The Moths and Other Stories* (Houston: Arte Público Press, 1985), 32. All subsequent citations for both 'Growing' and 'Snapshots', will be noted in the text.

3. Pierre Maranda suggests that 'Semantic charters condition our thoughts and emotions. They are culture specific networks that we internalize as we

undergo the process of socialization' (185). Moreover these charters or signifying systems 'have an inertia and a momentum of their own. There are semantic domains whose inertia is high: kinship terminologies, the dogmas of authoritarian churches, the conception of sex roles' (184–5). See his essay 'The Dialectic of Metaphor: An Anthropological Essay on Hermeneutics', in *The Reader in the Text: Essays on Audience and Interpretation*, Eds. Susan R. Suleiman and Inge Crosman (Princeton: Princeton University Press, 1980), 183–204.

4. LUCE IRIGARAY, *This Sex Which Is Not One*, Trans. Catherine Porter (Ithaca, NY: Cornell University Press, 1985), 189. The ellipsis occurs in the original as if calling for the measurement itself which is what our research is about. In the chapter 'Women on the Market' (170–91), from which I cite Irigaray, she also argues that this process turns women *qua* woman/mother into commodities so as to sustain economic systems and infrastructures that exploit women. Further citations to this work will be noted in the text.

5. For a discussion of Sor Juana's passage from 'woman' to 'non-woman', see OCTAVIO PAZ, *Sor Juana Inés de la Cruz o Las Trampas de la Fe* (Mexico: Fondo de Cultura Económica, 1982), 291.

6. *Giving Up The Ghost* (Los Angeles: West End Press, 1986). References to this work will be cited in the text.

7. 'Women's Time', *Signs*, 31.

8. LUCE IRIGARAY, 'And the One Doesn't Stir Without the Other', Trans. Helene Vivienne Wenzel, *Signs: Journal of Women in Culture and Society*, 7:1 (Autumn 1981), 64–5.

9. Irigaray, 'And the One Doesn't Stir Without the Other', 66.

10. *Sexual/Textual Politics: Feminist Literary Theory* (New York: Methuen, 1986), 163.

See also MARÍA ELENA DE VALDÉS, 'In Search of Identity in Cisneros's *The House on Mango Street*', *Canadian Review of American Studies* 23, 1 (Fall 1992): 55–72.

6 Native American Aesthetics: An Attitude of Relationship*

Sidner Larson

Several essays in this volume refer to indigenous American cultures, but Sidner Larson's essay does so differently. His primary references are to cultural anthropologists (Clifford, Campisi, Sturtevant) rather than literary theorists. Indeed, his only reference to literary theory serves his anthropological intentions. Larson applies Bakhtin's theory of 'dialogism' to literary works that dramatize orally transmitted narratives in order to contrast cultural assumptions about history and its modes of expression.

Larson's central concern in this essay is with the 'standards of identity' applied to Native Americans. Weighing 'acculturation' against 'assimilation', he takes as his primary text a trial involving the Mashpee tribe in the state of Massachusetts. That trial involved a lawsuit contesting land ownership that hinged upon the Mashpees' tribal identity, which in turn hinged upon the competing claims of historians and anthropologists about race, territory, community, leadership, historical and legal documentation. Based upon the information drawn from this trial, Larson posits cultural characteristics common to contemporary Native American writing: the related thematics of identity and curing; the prevalence of ethnographic and orally transmitted content; the revision of Western generic forms and narrative techniques – what he calls the 'flagrant violation of the "statutes" of Eurocentric esthetics'.

Native American people are in the process of identifying or re-identifying features that distinguish them as individuals and in relationship to others. In doing so they are tied to elements of history, property, and identity. At the present time, Native Americans are a minority defined by the majority culture and as a result they are dependent on notions of identity developed by others. This is in direct opposition to their former historical, place-oriented notion of themselves.

---

* Reprinted from *MELUS* 17, 3 (Fall 1991–92): 53–67.

A sense of place is very traditional in Native American culture and ironically is closely related to European concepts of property that figure critically in their present circumstances. An example of this is land-claim lawsuits filed by east coast Indians in the late 1960s and 1970s. In one case this resulted in an unprecedented trial 'whose purpose was not to settle the question of land ownership but rather to determine whether the group calling itself the Mashpee Tribe was in fact an Indian tribe' (Clifford 277).

Perhaps the most publicized east coast Indian litigation was a suit by the Passamaquoddy and Penobscot tribes resulting in an award of $81.5 million and an entitlement to 300,000 acres in the state of Maine. Although the Mashpee claim was similar to the Maine Indians', it had a different result due to a court ruling that they were not sufficiently 'Indian'.

Some of the history of the Penobscot and Passamaquoddy cases helps to explain the result in the Mashpee trial. Although they served as favorable legal precedent, and helped to clarify some standards for judging identity, they also cut the other way. Part of the publicity of the cases was a strategy by defense counsel to paint a picture of suburban whites being thrown out of their homes by newly enfranchised Indians. In fact, only large tracts of undeveloped land were in question, but that was not the popular perception in Maine. There were repercussions, politicians lost office, and the Mashpee trial received negative publicity as a result.

The vastly superior force in the litigation was the Supreme Court of the United States. The court had made it clear in an earlier case that the only reason the Indians were in court in the first place was pure generosity. The court stated that, 'Indians are dealing with the magnanimity of a rich and powerful nation, one that is not about to divest itself or its non-Indian citizens of large acreage in the name of its own laws' (Clifford 284). This was a clear indication of the court's intention to place arbitrary limitations on such litigation.

The plaintiffs in the land claim suits, however, had found a way to gain some power. Based on the Non-Intercourse Act of 1790, legislation that declared that alienation of Indian lands could be legally accomplished only with permission of Congress, and with direct intervention from then President Jimmy Carter, the Maine tribes had reclaimed some of their land. The resulting picture was one of Indians who were no longer safely vanishing. Instead, they were portrayed as winning court cases and becoming carried away with their new found power by attempting to do such things as run high-stakes bingo games. One of the results of this was that the all-white jury in the Mashpee case was confronted with a series of threatening images as part of their task of coming up with a way to define tribal status and individual Indian identity.

The Mashpee owned only fifty-five acres of land, did not speak a native language, did not practice a native religion, had no tribal political system, and had intermarried extensively with non-Mashpee people. On the other hand, they had lived in the town of Mashpee, Massachusetts, for centuries, and it was known as an Indian town. Because of this, as James Clifford has said, 'Looked at one way, they were Indian; seen another way, they were not. Powerful ways of *looking* thus became inescapably problematic. The trial was less a search for the facts of Mashpee Indian culture and history than it was an experiment in translation, part of a long historical conflict and negotiation of "Indian" and "American" identities' (289).

The experiment was conducted in a court of law and the translators were a few members of the Mashpee community attempting to explain why they felt they were Indians, and professional anthropologists and historians who provide 'expert' testimony. The defense used a historical approach, presenting a documented record of Mashpee history that attempted to show that the Mashpee had been assimilated into American society, that their Indian identity had been lost long ago. The Mashpee argued that they had kept their Indian identity alive; that they had only acculturated to the white culture, rather than having been assimilated by it.

Jack Campisi, anthropologist and expert witness for the Mashpee, testified that in his opinion the Mashpee were a tribe. As part of his testimony he provide a definition of 'tribe', something the court had refused to do up to that point. Campisi listed five criteria: '(1) a group of Indians, members by ascription – that is, by birth, (2) a kinship network, (3) a clear consciousness of kind – "we" versus "they", (4) a territory or homeland, and (5) a political leadership' (Clifford 319). Vine Deloria, apparently the only Indian expert witness, also testified for the Mashpee, defining tribe in the following manner: 'As I use it and as I understand other Indian people using it, it means a group of people living pretty much in the same place who know who their relatives are. I think that's the basic way we look at things' (Clifford 323). Although the differences in definition here may seem essentially negligible, they point up an essential difference in the White and Indian view. Campisi's definition reflects a picture of human beings that envisions their freedom and security in terms of elements that foster bounded spheres. Deloria's definition is less overly analytical and more of an imaginative synthesis allowing for acceptance rather than restriction. The boundary metaphor becomes very important in discussion of the Mashpee trial and in later discussion of other forms of Native American discourse in that it illustrates a wrong focus for exploring the best possibilities of human autonomy.

As a further illustration of the invocation of boundaries as rigid walls rather than being fluid, shifting, and permeable, the defense in the Mashpee trial relied in part on the testimony of Jean Guillemin, a sociologist with some experience among the Canadian Micmac Indians. The Mashpee generally would not speak with her because they felt she was too unfamiliar with their situation, as well as being obviously unsympathetic. As a result, the defense had fifty Mashpee subpoenaed and deposed, and she formulated an opinion on the basis of this unwilling testimony, stating that 'Mashpee Indians never had a distinct culture and never were a tribe' (Clifford 324).

William Sturtevant, of the Smithsonian Institution, provided additional general concepts from the witness stand. He distinguished acculturation from assimilation, pointing out that acculturation is a borrowing process while assimilation is the incorporation of one society into another so that the assimilated society no longer exists – a complete loss of identity. He also pointed out that acculturation is common among all Indian tribes, and that 'there are other universally recognized tribes as acculturated as the Mashpee' (Clifford 325). Sturtevant went on to say that it is also characteristic of many Indian tribes that their people often move to different areas for a period of time often as long as their working lives, then return to the tribe to live out their retirement years.

As this sort of testimony accumulated, standards of identity that can be applied to Native Americans, rightly or wrongly, began to emerge. For example, during cross-examination Sturtevant was confronted with an article he had written about Indian communities in 1968. In the article Sturtevant claimed that a restrictive definition of Indian identity has caused much suffering. When asked if he could illustrate how this suffering was caused, he replied, 'yes: insisting that you can't be an Indian unless you are a member of a federally recognized tribe. Or saying you can't be an Indian if you have black ancestry. Or defining Indianness by "some fairly high degree of blood quantum"' (Clifford 326).

When both sides had rested their cases the judge specified the legal definition of tribe that would apply. Departing significantly from the information provided during the trial, he chose the definition provided in a 1901 case, *Montoya* v. *United States*: 'A body of Indians of the same or similar race united in a community under one leadership or government and inhabiting a particular, though sometimes ill defined, territory' (Clifford 334). For the Mashpee to win, the key factors of race, territory, community, and leadership had to be continuously present since July 22, 1790.

After twenty-one hours of deliberation the jury emerged with a verdict, finding that the Mashpee were not a tribe on July 22, 1790, although they were a tribe on March 31, 1834 and March 3, 1842; they were again not a tribe, however, on June 23, 1869, nor were they a tribe on May 28, 1870; finally, the jury found that the Mashpee did not continuously exist as a tribe from July 22, 1790 to August 26, 1976.

July 22, 1790, was the date of the first Federal Non-Intercourse Act, paternalist legislation decreeing that Indians could not transfer land to

whites without the consent of Congress. March 31, 1834 was the date
Mashpee received district status, a move the Mashpee were forced to
make in order to have legal title to their land. March 3, 1842 is the date
Mashpee land was partitioned to individuals. June 23, 1869 marked the
end of alienation restraints. May 28, 1870 was the date of incorporation
of the Town of Mashpee. August 26, 1976 was the date of the
commencement of the lawsuit.

In selecting these dates the judge tied the decision-making process to
certain historical events marking the development of white culture
surrounding Mashpee. At the same time, Mashpee was expected to
remain aboriginal in order to be recognized as a tribe. The injustice is
that compromises the Mashpee were forced to make to keep from being
engulfed were seen as abandonment of culture by an unsympathetic jury.
James Clifford analyzes the dynamics further by pointing out that the
likely tribal way of settling such things was by prolonged discussion
intended to arrive at a consensus. He further notes, 'this process is
preserved in an enclave of orality within the vast writing machine of the
law: the jury room' (328). The jury in this case, however, was not a jury
of 'peers', nor is the system designed to produce a judgment that will
satisfy everyone; it instead determines who wins and who loses. Clifford
states, 'In this sense the law reflects a logic of literacy, of the historical
archive rather than of changing collective memory. To be successful the
trial's result must endure the way a written text endures' (329). Indian
life in Mashpee, largely a remembered and talked about thing, could
only be 'proven' where it existed in written form. In recognizing this
unfortunate fact, it also becomes clear how important other forms of
discourse, for example, oral literature, are to Native American identity.

From the Mashpee trial have come certain features of tribal identity:
race, territory, community, leadership, and documentation. It is
significant that a people has attempted to 'fix' so amorphous a thing as
identity. It is significant that their struggle for identity became a struggle
between history and anthropology. In so many ways they have become,
literally, men and women made of words. In light of the Mashpee trial to
establish tribal identity, it seems likely that someday an individual will
bring a lawsuit to establish individual Indian identity. Some of the
features of individual identity are discernible in history, anthropology,
and law, but they are also discernible in Native American songs,
storytelling, and in various later forms of written literature.

Some understanding of key issues of identity is helpful in looking
forward to Native American literature. It is well-recognized that the
original Native American notion of identity was communal, or tribal.
With colonization, however, came extreme pressure to abandon the tribal
notion of identity in favor of individuality, a divide and conquer
strategy. In order to accomplish this, Whites imposed a policy of

assimilation on Indian cultures. For many, this was the most devastating historical blow to tribalism and the Indian way of life. The linchpin for this policy was the Dawes Severalty Act, which is also known as the General Allotment Act of 1887. President Theodore Roosevelt most forcefully described the purpose of the Act as 'a mighty pulverizing engine to break up the tribal mass' (Pommersheim 255).

In order to individualize Indians, the Bureau of Indian Affairs was empowered to allot 160 acres of tribal land to each head of household and forty acres to each minor. Allotments were to remain in trust for twenty-five years so the Indians would not be swindled out of them. This twenty-five year trust period was soon undermined by the Burke Act of 1906, however, which allowed the transfer of title to land to 'competent' Indians prior to the expiration of the trust period. Competency commissions were established to determine which Indians could have clear title, which would enable them to sell their land. These commissions often made perfunctory findings, including whether the individual was one-half degree Indian blood or less. Thus began the fragmentation of individual Indian identity that remains one of the most important issues to be addressed among Indian people and the systems with which they interact.

The importance of individual identity comes about in many ways. For example, the Fort Belknap Reservation, where I was raised, is the home of the Gros Ventre and Assiniboine tribes. The two tribes, traditional enemies, were forces to live together as a consequence of colonization. At Fort Belknap 'here first' stories exist among the two tribes as an expression of political conflict, mainly over who is more entitled to scarce resources as a consequence of having been on Fort Belknap lands first. In order to be entitled to such things as treaty money payments or education grants, an individual must be an enrolled member of one of the tribes.

In order to be enrolled an individual must be able to 'prove' at least one-quarter Indian blood. The establishment of an enrollment commission at Fort Belknap in 1921, to determine who would receive the allotments discussed above, demonstrates political maneuvering associated with individual identity. In her book *Shared Symbols, Contested Meanings*, Loretta Fowler has pointed out the fact that the commission offered an opportunity for Gros Ventres 'to control the criteria for allotment and thereby attain greater self-determination and demonstrate primacy in relation to the Assiniboines. Apparently the Gros Ventre member of the commission dominated the proceedings, for seventy-six individuals who were living among the Assiniboines were rejected for the allotment roll' (217). The struggle for enrollment identity was demonstrated recently at Fort Belknap when the tribes were awarded a large sum of money on the Sweet Grass Hills treaty claim. When the award was publicized, many people sought to have themselves or their children enrolled so they could share in the bounty. Most applications were rejected on the basis of a blood quantum that had been established almost whimsically years before.

Adding to the unreliability of using degree of Indian blood as the determining factor of identity is the fact that there is no chemical analysis for 'Indian blood'. This points to the necessity of using a 'cultural' definition of identity more rationally related to certain connections rather than being specifically tied to absurd quasi-scientific criteria. The concept of culture was dealt with at some length in the Mashpee trial. In testimony for the Mashpee, Lawrence Shubow defined culture as 'a group's total body of behavior' (Clifford 337). This might be narrowed somewhat by what Brian Swann has said, 'that Native Americans are Native Americans if they say they are, if other Native Americans say they are and accept them, and (possibly) if the values that are held close and acted upon are values upheld by the various native people who live in the Americas' (Clifford 208). Some of the elements of cultural identification, then, might include self identification, community identification, and identification with Native American values. This three-part process differs considerably from the criteria originating with allotment identity abuses in that it is not autonomous or arbitrary and provides for reasonable validation.

The third element of the proposed model for cultural identification is identification with Native American values. Although these values have been written about extensively by anthropologists, ethnographers, and historians, an additional source is the literature spoken and written by Native Americans themselves. Contained within this body of literature are features of the Native American aesthetic, a direct reflection of the values that are held close and acted upon by the various native people who live in the Americas.

The broad features of American Indian literature are comprised of both spoken and written elements. The spoken elements are related to native oral tradition, the practice of telling and re-telling stories that have been passed down from generation to generation. The oral telling of stories is very functional in its social and educational aspects. It provides an opportunity for gathering, communicating, and passing on information, whether it be exploits, history, or warning children to stay away from the river. It is also a way of ordering things. In one sense it is a way of dealing with a chaotic world in a more organized manner by providing explanations and making associations. In another sense it is an interweaving process that bends time and sequence to its own purposes and is ever-changing with each re-telling of stories.

Written representations of Native American literature are even more multi-dimensional. Most broadly, they are comprised of a combination of the elements of oral tradition and the elements of Euramerican tradition, which is almost strictly based on the written word. Some of the features of Native American literature include: enhanced levels of participation stemming from the oral tradition of storytelling; a 'curing' phenomenon related to cultural bridging and regard for all forms of life as well as the environment; seeming fragmentation of thought and use of circular rather than linear time, resulting in unique structures; a more individualized concern with identity; and an increased incidence of ethnographic and historical content. These features are things that have been much talked about in the scholarly literature of the 1970s and 1980s. It is important to note, however, that in addition, the stories that are accepted and being told within native communities today, and the way they are being told, is very much a part of the literature. The telling of stories in 'Red English', lacking in subject-verb agreement, full of substandard expressions, ungrammatical conjunctions and elliptical sentences, yet vital and vivid, is an example. A more dramatic example is Anthony Mattina's observation of the Colville Peter Seymour telling the story of *The Golden Woman*, wherein Seymour tells a European story into a western technology tape recorder in such a way that Colville tradition is illustrated and preserved.

One of the things that makes the American Indian novel American Indian and not part of the mainstream is active participation on the part of writer and readers. This stems from the oral tradition, a literature based on live performance in front of a live audience, with all the attendant dimensions of both individual and group dynamics. This element of performance, whether sung, chanted, spoken, or delivered through drums, allows the performer to exploit and develop a number of opportunities. Among these, qualities such as emotional atmosphere, dramatic suspense, characterization, and the effective build-up through repetition can be conveyed not just in the words but in their performance. The Native American author, closer to live performance in her imagining, provides more of these qualities in her attempt to engage the audience. Part of the way this happens is that performance of traditional stories and the criticism of those stories is a simultaneous process. For example, Larry Evers has said 'Each time a storyteller tells a story he tells his own version of it. He gives his interpretation of it; he recreates it. If it works for others, they repeat it. Through his critical act it survives' (73). Native American written literature is traditional in this sense. It is comprised of stories, the authors' telling of stories they have heard, and it is criticism, a story about those stories.

There is a 'curing' phenomenon that is also a distinctive feature of Native American literature. The first element of curing is related to cultural bridging, an attempt to take Indian culture forward and Euramerican culture back, for their mutual benefit. Native American people have been doing this for some time. In one case, as Paula Gunn Allen has said, 'the people who formed the Laguna settlement were from several different Pueblos and they included some Navajo. They were mediational people. They were people who chose to live together and then to work out their differences' ('Psychological Landscape' 19). In addition, new blood, new ways, new ceremonies are at the very heart of Leslie Marmon Silko's novel *Ceremony*, especially where she writes that change is necessary for life, because 'things which don't shift and grow are dead things' (126). Colonization, of course, accelerated this process for Native Americans, forcing them to live and act between cultures in whatever ways would enable them to survive.

The second element of curing, concern for the environment as well as for forms of life other than higher mammals, is proving to be a valuable lesson for Euramerican culture. This kind of thinking has, until recent times, been taken as simple-minded romanticization. Talking about respect for insects is sentimental and unproductive, many people have said, a romanticizing of the past which keeps us from coming up with real solutions to our problems. In a lecture at South Dakota State University in 1979, Charles Woodard said:

> Scientists are increasingly telling us that the small things of the earth must be preserved. That as our problems are increasing, the natural world variety which may contain solutions to those problems is *de*-creasing, and at alarming rates. It will not be enough, they tell us, to save those elements of creation which we have sentimentalized to positions just beneath us in some Great Chain of Being. It will not be enough to preserve the lion and the rose. We need to work to preserve all of the gene pool, scientists tell us, if we are to pull back from the edge of environmental disasters which are now everywhere apparent. And those people we call poets are increasingly telling us what traditional Native Americans have believed for centuries: the *any* reduction of the natural world stands to reduce us in spirit. The Blackfeet poet and novelist James Welch calls spiders 'snow country weavers.' He says: 'I saw your spiders weaving threads/to bandage up the day.' Implicit in this statement is an environmental ethic and an attitude of earth relationship which is in my opinion invaluable.

The themes of curing run through virtually all of Native American literature, represented by the tendency to bridge cultures rather than destroy them, and consideration of all forms of life. This is a new way of looking at life in general, or a return to an older, saner way of looking. Paula Gunn Allen, in her article 'The Sacred Hoop: A Contemporary Perspective', has pointed out that separating nature from humanity is antithetical to tribal thought; that all things of creation are necessary parts of a balanced whole. In addition, she notes that Native Americans do not separate what is material and what is spiritual, instead seeing the two as different expressions of the same reality, and concluding that, 'The closest analogy in Western thought is the Einsteinian understanding of matter as a special state or condition of energy. Yet even this concept falls short of the American Indian understanding, for Einsteinian energy is believed to be unintelligent, while energy, according to the Indian view, is intelligence manifested in yet another way' (8). Land is so intrinsic to Native Americans as to be considered their Mother. It is not just a romantic notion, but a cultural centerpiece providing spiritual sustenance as well as subsistence. This is in contrast to Euramerican culture, which tends

> to *take* possession without becoming possessed: to take secure hold on the lands beyond and yet hold them at a rigidly maintained spiritual distance. It was never to merge, to mingle, to marry. To do so was to become an apostate from Christian history and so be lost in an eternal wilderness. (Turner 238)

For Native Americans, this connection often determines the values of the human landscape.[1] They needed the land too much to permit destructive use and ecological impairment.[2] This attitude of relationship is so prevalent that it is an obviously recurring theme in contemporary Native American literature.

Seeming fragmentation of thought is also specifically Native American. Underlying this is the Native American experience of living in both white an Indian cultures, an experience that often provides disparate elements when reflected in writing. An example of this is N. Scott Momaday's novel *House Made of Dawn*, a story told simultaneously on levels of modern white society, Catholic and Pueblo religion, and Pueblo culture. In this novel fragmentation of thought is represented by fragmentation of time, making a coherent pattern difficult to find. This lack of coherence is related to concepts of circular and linear time. *House Made of Dawn* is constructed of circular images that force the reader to reorient her sense of structure from linear to circular. In the words of Martha Kimble, the novel's protagonist, Abel, 'moves in a different kind of zone from those narratives we are accustomed to reading which have initial conflicts, climaxes, and the like' (65). More specifically, the book doesn't start at the beginning, progress in a straightforward manner through a middle, then finish with an ending in linear fashion. There is instead a kind of interweaving, a moving back and forth through time and place, from Jemez Pueblo to the Army, to San Francisco, and back to Jemez. Larry Evers has said, 'it seems to me that in a good many examples from oral tradition, you see a narrator working back and forth in time and not following a strict time frame in the storytelling' (66). This combination of oral tradition and western form is particularly Indian in its seeming effect of fragmentation.

Considering how hard Native Americans have had to struggle with issues of assimilation, acculturation, acceptance, and rejection, it is no wonder that concern with identity surfaces so frequently in Native American literature. It is an ongoing process of identity with self, place, and with others, often as they perceive and are perceived through storytelling. James Ruppert, then a teacher at Navajo Community College, has observed, 'the people I know are so totally involved in where they're from, who they are, and what they think of the land or how another person thinks of it, and how they are incorporated into others' stories that they have a sense of identity totally different from ours' (69). This fixation with identity occurs for good reasons. In Leslie Silko's *Ceremony*, the protagonist, Tayo, suffers serious discrimination from his own family as a result of his identity, his status as the product of his mother 'and that white man' (30). On the other hand, Lulu, from Louise Erdrich's *Love Medicine*, celebrates her identity, and is empowered by it, threatening to expose the council to scandal for turning the Lamartines off the land:

> By then there were a hundred people in the room. 'All those Lamartine sons by different fathers.' That voice was loud enough to be heard. And then it said: 'Ain't the youngest Nector's?' So I had no choice in what I did. I turned around. I looked straight out at the people sitting in their unfolded chairs. There was many a man who found something to study on the floor.
> 'I'll name all of them,' I offered in a very soft voice. 'The fathers ... I'll point them out for you right here.' (224)

In this scenario is revealed the evolved power of identity. Identity opens doors, closes off possibilities, marks the boundaries of dark blood imagined in unspeaking regions of the brain, boundaries that apply to corporations as well as reservations.

A prevalence of ethnographic and historical content is another characteristic of Native American literature. A large amount of anthropological work was conducted among North American Indian tribes early in the century in order to 'salvage' what remained of their cultures. As a result, to some extent a book such as *House Made of Dawn* has come to be judged authentically American Indian to the degree that its content agrees with the information disseminated by ethnographers. Similarly, such novels are often judged historically accurate according to whether or not they agree with an author such as Dee Brown. Although such information is valuable to a certain extent, Larry Evers has pointed out that, 'too often our search for what is "American Indian" in texts is reduced only to these ethnographic and historical facts. . . . We place stories, along with the pot sherds and squash blossoms, in what one critic unblushingly calls "The Museum of Manitou"' (74). In another sense, the elements of oral tradition in Silko's *Ceremony* are ethnographic in nature, as is the obviously historical content of James Welch's *Fools Crow*, and these elements are prevalent in other Native American writing as well.

Additional features of Native American literature can be identified by making certain comparisons with Euramerican narrative forms. Euramerican culture structures narrative in the four modes traditionally designated as romance, tragedy, comedy, and irony. This differs considerably from Native American narrative structure. In his book *For Those Who Come After*, Arnold Krupat has said that the traditional modes of romance, tragedy, comedy, and irony 'are by no means operative in non-Western cultures' (112).

For Those Who Come After illustrates how the four modes of western narrative were structurally imposed on Native American autobiographies, which were essentially recordings of the stories of Native Americans by white biographers. Krupat presents Walter Dyk's *Left-Handed: Son of Old Man Hat* as an example of the ironic mode in that 'its subject seems merely to live through one episode of his life after another . . . presented as simply the facts of the case, the things that just happened to happen' (112–13). Gilbert Wilson's *Goodbird the Indian* is said to use a comic pattern of integration and reconciliation. 'For Goodbird, the loss of the old can be accepted without pain or "anger"; his view is optimistic and progressive, a sober but cheerful, reconciliation to what the future . . . holds' (114). Krupat says John Neihardt's *Black Elk Speaks* is structured romantically, as a story that 'celebrates the transcendence of what is and must be. . . . The mode of transcendence . . . is not tragedy but romance' (131). Lucullus McWhorter's story of the Nez Perce warrior, *Yellow Wolf*, illustrates the final mode of tragedy, representing 'the stories of those Indians who would not enthusiastically embrace the new, yet could not, for all their intense longing, live the old' (115).

It is interesting to note that the modes derived from the Euramerican literary tradition have practically been elevated to the position of literary statutes in opposition to other, non-Western, forms. The effect is to repress other forms of narrative, which then become designated as alien, or truly 'other'.

McWhorter's work with Yellow Wolf is more informative about 'other' forms of narrative that it is a simple example of the Euramerican mode of tragedy. McWhorter's technique was to indicate as many of the circumstances of the narration as possible, or to tell the story of how the story was told. This included internal breaks in the narration in which McWhorter described such things as pauses, hesitations, tones of voice, and gestures. This was a distinct departure from the Euramerican approach of author as God and was derived from the communal nature of oral tradition as observed by McWhorter. Krupat notes that McWhorter's procedure insisted upon the performed quality of Yellow Wolf's story, 'Unlike those editors of Indian autobiography who strove to produce a *text* that would *read* as a smooth and seamless verbal object, McWhorter does not let us forget that this text is a recitation, with all the gaps and fissures of what we have come to call everyday discourse' (119).

In permitting others besides Yellow Wolf and himself to speak, McWhorter provide perhaps as much objectivity as is possible in the recreation of oral events. Krupat terms this a 'movement away from monologic presentation and univocal authority in the direction of – in the sense of Bakhtin, a Russian contemporary – the dialogic' (120). This 'dialogic' style of presentation can also include notes, appendices, and extensive quotation from any source in an effort to provide as much context as possible. McWhorter learned this from his interviews with the Nez Perce, whose custom it was to include witnesses to the telling of coup stories. These witnesses were encouraged to interject, to authenticate, or to correct if they felt it was necessary.

It is important to note that coup stories are not self-centered. For example, Krupat discovered that McWhorter had some difficulty getting Yellow Wolf to tell things the way McWhorter wanted him to. Krupat says, 'Yellow Wolf attempted to adhere to the Plains sense of the coup story, the story of actions performed in war, as the central meaning of the request to "tell his story." But McWhorter is true to the Western conception of autobiography as the story of a whole life, and it is that conception that prevails' (123). This is opposed to Eurocentric private ownership of stories and identifies a more truthful hero than Euramericans have evolved so far.

McWhorter's technique makes for a book in flagrant violation of the 'statutes' of Eurocentric esthetics, one similar to Native American narrative in its repetition and lack of unification, as modernist critics would have it. In opposition, the Eurocentric tradition valorizes the text as object, not performance, 'removing it from history, and celebrating foremost those individual talents whose original works relate to no history but literary history, or tradition' (126).

For Those Who Come After illustrates how Native American autobiographies were transposed into the Euramerican literary modes of irony, comedy, romance, and tragedy. The significance of this is two-fold. First, it reveals the Euramerican tendency to sacrifice truth in favor of literary closure. Part of the problem seems to be that 'Western narrative has no convention for the representation of the ongoing and un-ended; . . . Western authors have always sought to provide at least "the sense of a ending" . . .' (130). It seems as though if reality must bend to fit one of the literary modes, so be it. Second, the book points out the Native American characteristics of dialogic storytelling to ensure veracity, and the lack of a proprietary interest in stories. Both these Native American characteristics are directly opposite Eurocentric tradition.

In his later book, *The Voice In The Margin*, Arnold Krupat identifies additional features of Native American literature in the context of Local, National, and Cosmopolitan literature. Referring to Jack Forbes's consideration of the question 'What is Indian Literature?', Krupat notes that 'it is the oral and periodical literature that is for him the only discourse being produced today that may appropriately be called *Indian* literature because these alone are primarily for an Indian audience by authors whose primary self-identification is Indian, working in forms historically evolved by or at least currently most readily accessible to that primary audience' (207).

This is problematic because it excludes from the category of Indian literature writing of the sort done by Momaday, Silko, and others whose writing is influenced substantially by the forms and genres of Eurocentric literature. Krupat goes on to say that Fredric Jameson's definition of 'third world literature' might do except for the fact that 'it tends to obscure the importance of local, internal, or Indian modes of literary expression *within* texts that externally appear to fit the Western typology of "novels", "poems", and "short stories"' (214). Krupat then indicates that his term for this is indigenous literature:

> *Indigenous literature* I propose as the term for that form of literature which results from the *interaction* of local, internal, traditional, tribal, or 'Indian' literary modes with the dominant literary modes of the various nation-states in which it may appear. Indigenous literature is that type of writing produced when an author of subaltern cultural identification manages successfully to merge forms internal to his cultural formation with forms external to it, but pressing upon, even seeking to delegitimate it. (214)

This last feature is related to the curing phenomenon in Native American literature observed by earlier commentators, and is perhaps the most important feature of the Native American aesthetic. If cultures can be bridged by merging literary forms, a significant accomplishment will have been achieved – a possible deliverance from racial polarization and an education of the populace to alternatives which could improve all of society. Although the features of Native American literature I have enumerated in this discussion are important, it is also important that they are only part of an ongoing, living thing. In the words of Leslie Silko, from *Ceremony*, 'Things which don't shift and grow are dead things' (126). Hopefully the search for features of Indianness in personal lives and in literature will continue to be an ongoing thing that will help heal both Native American and Eurocentric culture.

Notes

1. LESLIE SILKO, 'Landscape, History, and the Pueblo Imagination'. In *On Nature*, D. Halpern, ed. (1987) 83–94; BARRY LOPEZ, *Crossing Open Ground* 61–71 (1988).

2. See, e.g., JOHN NEIHARDT, *Black Elk Speaks* (1932) and LUTHER STANDING BEAR, *The Land of the Spotted Eagle* (1933) for the most forceful descriptions of these observations.

Works cited

ALLEN, PAULA GUNN. 'The Psychological Landscape of *Ceremony*'. *The American Indian Quarterly* 5 (February 1979).

——. 'The Sacred Hoop: A Contemporary Perspective'. In *Studies in American Indian Literature*. New York: The Modern Language Association of America, 1983.

CLIFFORD, JAMES. *The Predicament of Culture*. Cambridge: Harvard U P, 1988.

EVERS, LARRY. 'A Response: Going Along with the Story'. *The American Indian Quarterly* 5 (February 1979).

FOWLER, LORETTA. *Shared Symbols, Contested Meanings*. Ithaca: Cornell U P, 1987.

KIMBLE, MARTHA. 'A Discussion of *Ceremony*'. *The American Indian Quarterly* 5 (February 1979).

KRUPAT, ARNOLD. *For Those Who Come After*. Berkeley: U of California P, 1985.

——. *The Voice in the Margin*. Berkeley: U of California P, 1989.

POMMERSHEIM, FRANK. 'The Reservation as Place: A South Dakota Essay'. *South Dakota Law Review* 34.2 (Spring 1989).

RUPPERT, JAMES. 'A Discussion of *Ceremony*'. *The American Indian Quarterly* 5 (February 1979).

SILKO, LESLIE MARMON. *Ceremony*. New York: Viking Press, 1977.

TURNER, FREDERICK. *Beyond Geography: The Western Spirit Aainst the Wilderness*. New Brunswick: Rutgers U P, 1983.

WOODWARD, CHARLES. Lecture delivered at South Dakota State University, Brookings, South Dakota. 1989.

7 Claiming and Making: Ethnicity, Gender, and the Common Sense in Leslie Marmon Silko's *Ceremony* and Zora Neale Hurston's *Their Eyes Were Watching God**

Toni Flores

Toni Flores is trained as an anthropologist and folklorist, but her approach to Leslie Marmon Silko's *Ceremony* and Zora Neale Hurston's *Their Eyes Were Watching God* is phenomenological and existential. She coins the metaphor of 'common sense' to mean not that which is practical or sensible but rather that which is known to an individual in a given cultural community through his or her own experiences of/in that community. To recognize an individual's 'common sense' and 'claim' it in a literary work, the writer (and reader) must give credence to the 'authority of experience'. Flores explicitly contests poststructuralist paradigms by arguing as follows: Silko and Hurston realize that the 'opposition is always deferred by what it opposes', so they do not oppose dominant power structures but rather redefine them in ways that avoid 'the old dualisms'. In so doing, they are empowered to 'claim' their own 'common sense' of race and gender in their respective cultures.

The writer in the modern world necessarily lives and works within a context of domination, whether in the arena of race-ethnicity, nationality, language, class, sexual orientation, gender, or any of a number of others. To be in a context of domination is to suffer. A writer who is a member of a dominating group will suffer the constrictions and limiting visions of those who rely on privilege and command. A writer who is a member of a dominated group may suffer from a lack of confidence, and certainly will suffer from a lack of influence and opportunity. On the other hand, as hard as it is to be a member of a nondominating group, it is also possible for the writer to turn this very position to artistic, moral, and imaginative advantage. Clearly, there is no virtue, in itself, in being a victim. Still, the writer who has not participated fully in the culture of the victimizer, who writes from the margins or, better, from another center, will have a different world view from that of the dominating

* Reprinted from *Frontiers* 10, 3 (1989): 52–8.

culture, a different perspective. One way to express this perspective is to take domination and resistance as a subject, as Toni Morrison has in the shining *Beloved*. Another way, the one that interests me most, is to use one's experience of non-elite, nondominating ways of being in constructing new and nonexploitative definitions of power.

To do this, however, the writer must first deeply know the other way of life, in considerable fullness, and not just as a wistful, wispy longing for some fancied utopia. She or he must really understand, whether through birthright or through long study, the 'common sense' of a different way of life. By 'common' sense I mean what is joint or shared, and also what is ordinary, daily, unexceptional, on the ground, unelevated, even material. The common sense of a culture is its bedrock, that which underlies its various traits and which, being rooted in the daily material world and the habits of daily survival, most persistently and consistently forms and orders the disparate impulses of geography and history and political power.

Second, in order to use a common sense to construct new visions of the world, the writer must have claimed its validity and intrinsic worth, with no apology and relying on no authority other than, in Arlyn Diamond and Lee Edwards's felicitous phrase, the authority of experience.[1]

When that has happened, when the writer has both known and claimed a way of life whose center is not one of the dominant centers of power, then she or he may use that common sense, not just incidentally (as local color or embroidery) and not simply in opposition (as opposition is always defined by what it opposes) but as a real grounding for a new edifice.

It is my belief and the argument of this paper that precisely this process may be seen in the work of two extraordinary twentieth-century American writers, the Native American novelist Leslie Marmon Silko, author of *Ceremony*, and the black novelist-anthropologist-folklorist Zora Neale Hurston, author of *Their Eyes Were Watching God*. Both of these people come from 'off the center'. The one is of Indian and Mexican descent, the other is black, and both are women. Both have been deeply immersed in the lives of their own people, yet both have navigated their way in the dangerous waters of the patriarchal, bourgeois, and white elite world of literature and academia. Both have used the common sense of their own cultures to redefine power in ways that avoid the old dualisms. Both, it is my contention, have turned their origins, which might have been seen to be and might indeed have been liabilities, into advantages and strengths.

Leslie Marmon Silko's *Ceremony*

The story of *Ceremony*, published in 1977, revolves round the illness and cure of a young Laguna pueblo man. At the outset, Tayo has returned from World War II, from battle in the Philippines. He is 'crazy', withdrawn, hallucinating, despairing. He mourns the death of his brother Rocky, who died from wounds and gangrene and the jungle. He mourns his own inability to save Rocky or to substitute for him. He mourns for the Japanese killed in the war; although he himself has not killed any, he perceives an identity between the Japanese and his own people (a correct racial identity, of course), and he recoils in horror at his own complicity, willed or not, with both sides in this slaughter. He mourns the death while he was away of his uncle Josiah, his mother's brother, and the only one of his kin to be unequivocally kind to him. He mourns the drought in the Southwest, and the death it causes, and he feels himself guilty of bringing it on, since in the steaming jungle, with Rocky dying of the damp, he had committed the sacrilege of cursing the rain. He rages over white racism. He mourns the loss to Native Americans of the land, of freedom, of the old things and the old ways, of self-respect. He rages against, all the while being complicitous in, Indian drunkenness, thievery, prostitution, poverty, violence, and despair. He doubts the efficacy of the old ways, but he fears change. He mourns his mother's shame in going with white men and bearing him illegitimately; he mourns her desertion of him; he is wounded by his family's grudging acceptance of him and in particular by his mother's sister's insistence on the stigma he both bears and inflicts. He feels unwanted, unloved, and misplaced. In Tayo there is a coming together of the sicknesses of the land, nature, the social order, power relations, the family, and the soul.

Eventually, Tayo returns to or reestablishes health through his willing participation in the creative act of story-telling and in the ritual acting out of story in ceremony. First, he leaves the VA mental hospital and comes home, where people have known him all his life and where he can't be invisible. He allows himself to be taken care of by old Grandma and Auntie, even though the care is partial and edgy; he accepts love, however flawed it may be. He undergoes a ritual with a Laguna medicine man, a ceremony meant to put back in their proper places the ghosts of those slain in war. This helps a little, and he begins to eat and to retain food, but he is far from well. Still he dwells on death and dwells in anger, especially when he is with his friends, young men who, like himself, are returned from war but deeply dislocated by it. Then he is brought to old man Betonie, a Navajo curer, who has under his care not just the Navajo, not just the Southwest, not just America, but the entire universe. Betonie starts for him a long curing ceremony, gives him the pattern (a mountain, a particular constellation of stars, certain cattle, and a woman) that will guide him through the ceremony, teaches him the history of the ceremony and the curers, and tells him that he must complete the ceremony himself. Tayo has no idea how he is to do that, but when he goes searching for the cattle his uncle Josiah bred, cattle that are themselves half-breeds, full of meat like domestic Anglo cattle but wild and rangy like Indian stock, he turns toward a life-sustaining activity, toward change and synthesis, and he begins to take a more active and creative role both in his relationship to nature and his people and in his own cure. In the search for the cattle, he meets a woman, a mysterious and powerful medicine woman who can make the rain and the snow come, who cares for his cattle for him, and who gives him food and makes love to him. He spends the summer with her, centering himself in the present and in love, living with the land and with animals and with the body, allowing himself to be loved and to feel worthy of love, at once making and accepting the harmonious pattern of the universe. Strengthened and filled, he is able at last to face a final encounter with evil and to conquer it, not with more hate but with a resolute turning away from violence and toward life and all that is life-sustaining. At the end, Tayo faces east and greets the sunrise.

This novel, as its popularity attests, can speak to a wide audience; at the same time it is so deeply placed in the American Southwest, so deeply rooted in the Native American culture and situation of that place, that it is difficult for mainstream readers to appreciate its richness, and perhaps even its point, without knowing something about that context.

For one thing, Tayo works out his cure, not solely within himself, but largely by going *home*, among people who know him deeply and who are known by him because he has been part of their stories. He has been in the Pacific, he has been to California, but he can't get well away from the desert land with which his people have interacted so long and so intensely that the two are interwoven: land and people are one entity.

Most of the major events and themes of the novel are traditional to that land and that people: a preoccupation with drought and rain; a focus on the fertility of soil, animals, and humans; a concentration on herds and flocks and on the material well-being they bring and represent; an involvement with the work life of farmers and herders. In this world there is a proper order to the universe, an order that includes humans, sentient and nonsentient material beings, and spirits; all evil, illness, misery, and natural disasters result from a disruption of this proper order. Material well-being, health, morality, happiness, long life, and proper function can be attained only by restoring proper order and, especially, properly harmonious relations between humans and the rest of nature. The novel expresses, as well, a traditional concern over evil-dealing, over witches and witchery, socially engendered violence, gossip and social control, the search for ritual cures to deal with evil, and the absolute necessity of turning resolutely away from witchery, death, and death-dealing and toward life. Linked with these ancient themes and preoccupations are the more modern ones centering on this culture's contact with whites – loss of the land, loss of cultural autonomy, loss of dignity and self-respect, poverty, prostitution, prejudice, drunkenness, theft, and, most of all, the dissolution of the old ways, old certainties, old beauties. Southwestern and Native American too are the affirmation of kin ties and community nets, the deep identification with land and place, a peculiarly pervasive and material spirituality, and a deep respect and longing for the embrace of the Mother (in all her social, biological, and spiritual manifestations). Finally, both the novel and the culture in which it is rooted are deeply committed to the conviction that story-telling is creation, in the most literal sense. For Tayo, for the Navajo and Pueblo peoples, and for Silko also, to tell a story is to make a reality; to act out a story is to make a world.

Ceremony is, then, for all its modern concern with the individual, with the Western problem of guilt, with interior angst, with nuclear war and social prejudice, with art as itself the prime subject matter of art, at the same time a most specifically Indian production. In this sense, the novel must be seen as a claiming of Native American and especially Laguna ways of being in the world. It is, clearly, based in the Laguna common sense, a sense built slowly, over probably millennia, as this Pueblo people have lived out their daily, ordinary, material lives, interacting with each other and with the land, creating their own definitions and solutions to the problems and possibilities for life on that land and with that people. At exactly the same time *Ceremony* is also a making: out of the confrontation between the ancient and autonomous Native American common sense and the dilemmas and imperatives of the modern white world of power, it makes a new vision of how one might define and deal with power, a new understanding of what illness and evil are, and a new sense of where and how one might place one's hope and confidence.

In *Ceremony*, the claiming of ethnicity, then, surely serves as one base for making new possibilities for human existence. I would suggest that gender serves as another, in that it too offers a region where common sense may be claimed and a new vision cultivated, for Silko and for the people about whom she writes. For Tayo and the other southwestern Indians Silko portrays, gender relations have gone all awry. The Mother principle, so strong in all these cultures, matrilineal or not, has been swamped, pressed down by the weight of the white patriarchal culture. On the personal level, Tayo has been damaged. He has been abandoned by his actual mother, who was over come by her shame; he is hurt by his aunt, his surrogate mother, who is ashamed of his illegitimacy, as though having an Indian mother were not enough to make him acceptable; he feels unnurtured, unloved. In southwestern society, gender relations have been warped; the fine Indian balance between male and female, the mutual respect and sense of equality, have been replaced by the obscene preying of white men on Indian women (always the ultimate objects of conquest), the desperate grab of Indian men for the acquisition of white women (not people but symbols of power, the jewels in the white scepter), and the resultant disruption and tenuousness between Indian men and women. The southwestern land, the ultimate source of nurture, has been raped, stolen, and sold into bondage. And politically and globally, the male principle has gotten all out of hand. Without the balance of the female power, the male hunters and killers, so necessary for food and protection, have gone on an insane rampage, killing for conquest, for ego-satisfaction, and, worst of all, for pleasure. Tayo's desperate task is to cure the gender-sick world, that is, to reestablish the proper harmony of the engendered universe by reestablishing respect for the female principle and the bedrock necessary willingness to be loved by and to love the Mother.

He does this by remembering, recreating, ties with the Mother in the guise of a series of women. First, he goes home to his aunt and his grandmother, living in their house (which, in this culture of matrilineal succession, is also his mother's house), sleeping on his childhood bed, eating the food that they give him, and, ultimately, taking responsibility for herding their sheep and cattle. Next he allows himself the memory of the Night Swan, the half-breed Mexican-Indian, green-eyed woman who had been his uncle Josiah's lover, who was the source of Josiah's half-breed cattle, and who had once made love to Tayo himself. Then he listens to the tales old man Betonie, the Navajo curer, tells of his own grandmother, an ochre-eyed Mexican girl who was a curer full of power. In learning about her, Tayo learns about the timelessness, the cyclical nature, of the Mother, learns that she is Changing Woman, who is the maiden, the matron, the crone, all at once and successively, cycling through the years, ever-changing, ever-persistent. He learns that he must himself become one with Thought-Woman, Spider-Woman. Changing-Woman, that is, the teller of the story, the creative principle, Finally Tayo meets Her, the woman who helps him find and tend uncle Josiah's cattle, who controls the rain and snow, who is a curer and mistress of the curing plants, who tends and feeds him, who makes love to him and takes him into herself. She is, of course, the goddess herself, the nurturer, the land, and, most important, the mother principle in all humans, male and female. She makes him realize that he is loved, has always been loved, and therefore can love himself and can himself love.

Through these epiphanies of the Mother, Tayo is strengthened and guided in his task of telling the correct story, setting the world right. He establishes that race is an unreal category and that intercourse between races is a vital aspect of change. He establishes that his mother, his aunt, his grandmother have always loved him, that they have always done their best under difficult and complex conditions. He establishes that the land has not been stolen, that land cannot be stolen because it cannot be property, and that, on the contrary, the people belong, as they have always belonged, to the land. He learns that violence cannot be defeated by violence but only by a resolute turning east, a balancing of killing with life-begetting, of death-dealing with curing, of anger with nurture. In short, Tayo reestablishes the female principle in himself and thus in the moral universe, the political arena, and the social world.

Silko, in her character Tayo, has rejected the patriarchal, authoritarian, bourgeois, and Western set of ideas about what it is to be male, what it is to be female, and what relations one must expect between male and female, and she has, instead, claimed the authority of a different vision of gender, a vision based on that of the mother-centered Native American peoples of the Southwest *and* on the collective experience of women in many cultures of the world. In a sense, she may be seen as working from a double folk, that of the Pueblo-Navajo peoples and that of women, relying on these two collective common senses.

Ultimately, and tellingly, Silko is staking a claim, not just to the authority of established ways of being but also to a newly made territory, a new telling of the story. She claims Laguna-Navajo patterns of belief, cosmology, and morality, but she casts them into new forms. In a deliberate use of one culture's forms for another's content, Silko opts not for telling a myth or performing a chantway but for writing a novel. It is not so much that she imitates or even preempts the modern bourgeois literary form as that she unites it with Native American meanings and transforms both into an entirely new existence, a form suitable to twentieth-century American life and accessible to its people. The hero is not the boy adventurer of old myths but a modern person. In this new version of renewal, Tayo, who is of mixed blood and living under the conditions of mixed culture, learns that he does not have to choose between white and red but must learn to accept what he is so that he can become what he can become. A man, of a white father and thus carrying the blood of the dominant and dominating culture, Tayo learns to accept alliance with the female, to accept the Mother in himself. He comes to terms with that part of his past which is implicated in the actions of the victimizer – American, violent, male – and with that part which is implicated in the role of the victim – Indian, suffering, female. Resolved to accept neither of these roles, rejecting the necessity of dichotomizing them, he tells the story in a new way, making good rather than evil and active creation rather than passive suffering the salient principles.

In effect, Silko the novelist has made herself into an epiphany of Betonie the curer, for whom nothing is lost, who keeps everything, who keeps the ceremonies alive, precisely by changing them. Silko is with her people, responding to their shared needs, evolving lives, and continually changing common sense; at the same time, she has expanded the Laguna world to include, in her vision of possible changes, the world of the dominant and dominating culture as well. Ultimately, of course, Indian and Anglo, female and male, are part of one system that can be healed only as a whole.

Zora Neale Hurston's *Their Eyes Were Watching God*

The story of *Their Eyes Were Watching God*, first published in 1937 and republished in 1978 as part of the revival of interest in the work of black novelist-folklorist-anthropologist (and perhaps feminist) Zora Neale Hurston, revolves around the life and development of Janie Crawford, a black woman from Florida.

The story opens with Janie's return to town after a two-year absence with Vergible 'Tea Cake' Woods, a man a good bit younger than she and much below her in status. Naturally, the town smacks its lips over the good story her return without Tea Cake implies, and eventually Janie relates that story, her story, to her friend Phoeby.

It's a story that begins, really, with Janie's grandmother, Nanny, born into slavery and, like so many other slave women, the mother of a child by the white master. To escape the wrath of the mistress, Nanny flees with her infant daughter Leafy into the swamps and survives there until the war's end. 'Emancipated', she goes to work for a white family, her sole aim to 'make the sun shine on both sides of the street for Leafy',[2] to raise her daughter to a higher and more comfortable place than she has had. It doesn't work that way, because Leafy is raped, gives birth to Janie, and, ruined and shamed, runs off, leaving Nanny with another girl child to raise, yet another set of hopes and fears. As she wanted Leafy to be, she wants Janie to be well off, to be comfortable, to be safe. Janie has other ideas. In a most beautifully written passage, Janie has a vision of the erotic, of an intense connection with life and with life's possibilities for connection and love and pleasure and human reality. Under the influence of this vision, of the springtime eroticism of bees and pear trees, and of her own blossoming sexuality, Janie takes a step into the world – and Nanny reacts in terror, lest the world harm her Janie. Her response is to marry Janie off to Logan Killicks, an older man with a house and sixty acres, a good name, no imagination, and dirty feet. Janie tries hard to love him, but there is little enough in Logan Killicks for a young girl to love, and nothing in his property and respectability. Hurt by her inability to appreciate him, Logan reacts by trying to put her down, to turn her into an obedient drudge, what Nanny says a black woman is, 'the mule of the world'. Unable to accept this, Janie runs off, in search of life and the horizon, with Jody Starks, an ambitious, big-talking, heavy-handed man. Jody aims to and does make himself a prosperous man, a big man, the mayor of the all-black town of

Eatonville, and in the process he tries to turn Janie into Mrs. Mayor Starks, a respectable lady, sitting up on a high chair above the common world, her hands folded. But Janie longs for the life of the common world around her, the passionate, messy, creative life of the ordinary people, and increasingly she resents Jody's attempts to make her into his image of a proper wife, his restraints on her, his lack of knowledge of or respect for her. The relationship between them shuts down, and Janie withdraws into an interior life. When Jody dies after twenty years, Janie begins to live. Quietly, she begins to enter the life around her, to do as she likes, and to become herself. Finally she meets Tea Cake Woods, a man twelve years her junior, a gambler by trade, without property or name, but with a vast love of life, a ready acceptance of people, and a quick and ready humor. Tea Cake and Janie enter into one of the great love relationships of literature, a connection in which each accepts the other for exactly what he or she is. Janie blossoms. Fulfilling her girlhood vision of the bee and the pear blossoms, she embarks with Tea Cake on a life full of work, laughter, fighting, tears, passion, acceptance, love and respect, dancing and song, and plenty of other people. In the end, Tea Cake is bitten by a rabid dog while trying to save Janie, gets rabies himself, goes mad, and dies when Janie, in self-defense, shoots him as he attacks her in his madness. Janie buries Tea Cake, returns to Eatonville with her memories, and tells the story to Phoeby.

The very basis of this novel, then, are the twin concerns of power-wielding and autonomy. If Janie moves to an everincreasing sense of self and of autonomy, she moves, as the novel moves, pushing against a background of powerlessness. Nanny, formed by her experience of being the helpless object of her master's desire and the nearly powerless victim of her mistress's rage, by her realization of the precariousness of her reliance on kind white folks, and by the tragedy of Leafy's rape and victimization, can only hope to provide for Janie some bulwark against outrage. She concentrates herself on wanting Janie safe; she neglects to want her free. Logan Killicks, with his house and sixty acres, offers Janie security, but at the extortionate price of her love. When he fails to get that, he, a black man, begins to use the little power he might have in the white man's world, the power over his woman. He seeks to tame her, punish her, harness her, almost literally make her into his mule. Jody Starks, realizing that his world is arranged in hierarchies and that he doesn't want to be at the bottom, decides that he had better become the master, or at least as much a master as any black man can be. He accepts dominance as a way of life. He has to control everybody who might possibly be brought under his control: not only Janie but all the people of Eatonville. The difference is that Janie, as Mrs. Mayor, is to be not only under his control but also the very symbol of his control and his position. The struggle for autonomy, both personal and cultural, is then set at the very heart of the novel.

The struggle leads in two parallel directions, a claiming of autonomy along racial and cultural lines, and a claiming of autonomy along gender lines.

For the first part, Janie refuses to be kept apart from the life of the people and most particularly refuses to participate in the exercise of power over that life. She seeks not to control the life of the people around her but to participate in it. She embraces the common life of the people, the life that is both shared and ordinary. Relieved of being Mrs. Mayor, she experiences the work life of the bean fields and the muck. She participates in the shifting social life, the song, the dance of jook joints, spontaneous jumps, and eating houses. She has always been a good cook, but now learns to serve and share great pans of baked beans, barbecue, sweet potato pie. She learns to hunt. She watches the gambling, the drinking, the teasing-testing games of the men, and the flirting games between women and men, and she swims in all of it. Above all, she revels in the talk, with all its richness and salt, and she learns to participate in it herself.

Much of this life, which Hurston describes so vividly, is what we might usually include under the term folklore. These elements are not incidental touches of local color; they appear on virtually every page as part of the very substance of the work and the life it describes. The people speak in proverbs, traditional sayings, and common metaphors, in the most natural and complete way in the world. To give a proper example one would almost have to quote the whole book, but perhaps a sample will give the flavor of the thing. Commenting on Janie, one gossiping woman says, 'She sits high, but she looks low.' Phoeby says of the gossipers, 'An envious heart makes a treacherous ear.' Nanny tells Janie, 'Dat's how come de ole folks say dat bein' uh fool don't kill nobody. It jus' makes you sweat.' Sitting on the front porch of the store, the men discuss Jody Starks:

'But now, Sam, you know that all he do is big-belly round and tell other folks what tuh do. He loves obedience out of everybody under de sound of his voice.'

'You kin feel a switch in his hand when he's talking to yuh,' Oscar Scott complained. 'Dat chastisin' feelin' he totes sorter gives yuh de protolapsis uh de cutinary linin'.'

'He's uh whirlwind among breezes,' Jeff Bruce threw in.

'Speakin' of winds, he's de wind and we'se de grass. We bend which ever way he blows,' Sam Watson agreed, 'but at dat us needs him. De town wouldn't be nothin' if it wasn't for him. He can't help bein' sorta bossy. Some folks needs thrones, and ruling-chairs and crowns tuh make they influence felt. He don't. He's got uh throne in de seat of his pants.'[3]

Story-telling, and especially the telling of tall tales, is an important and common element of the communicative life of Janie's people. For example, in an extended and hilarious series of stories about Matt Bonner's yellow mule, the men amuse themselves, compete in cleverness, and at the same time gently but pointedly let Matt know what the community thinks about his stinginess. Boasts play their part; at one point in a gambling game, Sop, a black 'ring-tailed roarer' if ever there was one, declares, 'Ah can look through muddy water and see dry land.'[4] They frequently play the sometimes dangerous game of the dozens. Folk heroes like High John de Conquer are back of everyone's eyes. Blues and spirituals and folk preaching are on everyone's tongue; when Jody puts a lamppost on the town street, for example, the dedicatory lighting is marked by a sermon and spiritual, and when Matt Bonner's yellow mule finally dies, his passing is marked by an exuberant mock funeral, with all the wonderful details of preaching and getting the spirit a funeral requires.

What is more, the folklore is not only a major part of the substance of the novel, it is also part of its structure. Tea Cake's life is the life of High John de Conquer, who survives on his high spirits, his cleverness, and his bravery. Janie's story is the very stuff of the blues. And in the episode that marks the real turning point for Janie, the point at which she begins to be an active shaper of her own life, she plays the deadly game of the dozens with Jody and beats him.

The main point, of course, about these forms of folklore is not just that they are there or even that they form the substance and structure of the novel, but that they are *claimed*, by the character Janie and by the author Hurston. At the same time that Janie lays claim to her self and her life, she lays claim to the common ways of the common people. And at the same time that Hurston lays claim to the world of black people as a valid subject for narrative, she lays claim to the voice and speech of that world as her own. It is interesting to note that at the beginning of *Their Eyes Were Watching God*, there is a difference between the voice of the narrator, a cool, distanced voice speaking standard English, and the voices of the folk, who speak in dialect. Midway through the novel, when it begins to take on power and meaning, the narrator loses her distance and takes on the voice of her subjects; from the time Janie takes up with Tea Cake and takes on her own life, the story is related almost entirely in dialect. The rural black southern world has become not just object but subject; it is telling its own story, in its own words.

Something similar can be said about gender, for here, I would suggest, is a novel not only about a woman but by a woman and, more importantly, from a woman's point of view. Hurston has her character Janie reject power relations between men and women. She leaves Logan Killicks, not simply because she doesn't love him (although it is true that she finds the trade-off of love for security unacceptable), but because and when he tries to make her a mule, a docile work animal. She resents and ultimately rejects Jody Starks's use of her as a symbol of his power over others, as she resents his efforts to define and limit her very being. Janie does not meet power with power and she does not want to rule; she simply does not want to be ruled. In the one real love in her life, she and Tea Cake are equals. She accepts him for what he is – a gambler, a common man, a pleasure-giver and pleasure-taker – and she accepts herself, completely unmoved by incidentals like her age and her social status. Except for the incident in which he beats her to demonstrate to Mrs. Turner's brother that she is *his* woman (and I must admit that this is a very big exception and, to my mind, a disturbing anomaly), Tea Cake never attempts to exercise power over her, always asks her voluntary compliance in being and doing with him, meets her as an equal in all matters including jealousy and passion, and never denigrates her or undervalues her. He is proud and pleased at her accomplishments even when, as with her shooting ability, they eclipse his own.

At the same time that Janie comes to claim her rights to autonomy and self-respect, she comes also to reject victimization, to refuse the role of victim. In the terrible moment when the rabid Tea Cake attacks her and in self-defense she has to kill him, or kill the rabies in him, she heroically refuses to confuse love with self-sacrifice or victimization. Through Tea Cake's love and through her relationship with him, she has come to love and respect herself enough to kill the person who would kill her, even if it happens to be Tea Cake himself. In a tender and appropriate irony, in teaching her to shoot so well Tea Cake has given her the means to defend herself, even from him.

Finally, in the very first lines of the book, Hurston herself suggests that Janie's story, which she is telling Phoeby and which Hurston is telling us, results from claiming the authority of woman's experience:

> Ships at a distance have every man's wish on board. For some they come in with the tide. For others they sail forever on the horizon, never out of sight, never landing until the Watcher turns his eyes away in resignation, his dreams mocked to death by Time. That is the life of men.
>
> Now, women forget all those things they don't want to remember, and remember everything they don't want to forget. The dream is the truth. Then they act and do things accordingly.[5]

This, then, Hurston is saying, is a woman's story as a woman would remember and want to tell it. It is a story, not about her horizons or world-making, but about human relationships, emotional connections, and real eroticism, in Audre Lorde's definition of the erotic as that which is life-supporting, life-enhancing, connecting, and enlarging.

There is an interesting double claiming going on here. On the one hand, the character Janie Crawford Woods is claiming her own people, the common life and her right to the common speech. As a woman, she is claiming connectedness, mutuality, desire, and the right to be what body you happen to be. And she is claiming herself, the right to be herself and, both figuratively and literally, to live her own life.

Simultaneously, the author Zora Neale Hurston is laying a series of parallel claims. Educated in New York, at Barnard and Columbia, into the white, scholarly world, she was trained as an anthropologist, folklorist, and linguist. In one sense, *Their Eyes Were Watching God* might be seen as an ethnography of the black rural South, or could have been turned into one. It isn't that really, however, and my sense is that this is deliberate and even emphatic. Trained as an anthropologist, Hurston eschews any attempt at or pretense of scholarly distance, instead overtly identifying scholar with community, the knowing subject with the known object. At the same time, she claims the right to transform her material (the speech, beliefs, folkways of the black community) into whatever form she sees fit and necessary – in this case not the ethnography but the novel. Finally, as a novelist, she rejects the usual models offered by the literary world of her time and takes the enormous risk of writing a novel not only about black life but also largely in black dialect. Simultaneously, she claims the validity and worth of black speech and asserts her own right to that speech. In valuing the voice of her people, she finds or makes her own voice, and in doing so she greatly expands the possibilities for new voices, new stories, and new realities in American literature and American life. *Their Eyes Were Watching God* stands squarely within the context of domination and yet sees autonomy, the rejection of domination, and the right to be one's own proper self not only as vital to a fully lived existence but also as possible. Janie claims her own people and her own self, and she makes her own story. Zora claims her own vision, and she makes a story that not only illustrates but powerfully persuades us of the believability of that vision.

In both of these novels the authors as well as their protagonists have claimed commonality and identity with the culture and the gender that nurtured them. At the same time, they have claimed personal vision, individual value, and the right to change. Both have insisted on alternatives to white, Western, patriarchal power, rejecting the choice between victimizer and victim, between dominance and submission. Instead, both Silko and Hurston have claimed autonomy, the ability to self-direct. They have insisted on the authority of their own experience, both cultural-racial and gender-personal. They have taken on the right and the responsibility to seek change and new possibilities, and they have insisted on their rights and abilities to create new meanings, tell new stories. It is not accidental that the stories of *Ceremony* and *Their Eyes Were Watching God* are about people (Tayo and Janie) telling their stories. Nor is it accidental that the stories are about people attempting to escape or, rather, to change altogether the context of domination. In claiming as valuable their respective ethnicities and their gender, Silko and Hurston have simultaneously claimed a version of ethnicity, gender, and power that is different from the version of the white male world, and they have newly envisioned what the world might be if we were to understand power not as dominance but as autonomy.

Notes

1. ARLYN DIAMOND and LEE R. EDWARDS, *The Authority of Experience: Essays in Feminist Criticism* (Amherst: University of Massachusetts Press, 1977).

2. ZORA NEALE HURSTON, *Their Eyes Were Watching God*, 2nd ed. (Urbana and Chicago: University of Illinois Press, 1978), 36.

3. Hurston, 12, 16, 41, and 78–9.

4. Hurston, 20.

5. Hurston, 9.

Other relevant essays on Silko are by EDITH E. SWAN, 'Laguna Symbolic Geography and Silko's *Ceremony*', *American Indian Quarterly* 12, 3 (1988): 229–49; EDITH E. SWAN, 'Healing via the Sunwise Cycle in Silko's *Ceremony*', *American Indian Quarterly* 12, 4 (1988): 313–28; BERNARD A. HIRSCH, ' "The Telling Which Continues": Oral Tradition and the Written Word in Leslie Marmon Silko's *Storyteller*', *American Indian Quarterly* 12, 1 (1988): 1–26; ANN FOLWELL STANFORD, ' "Human Debris": Border Politics, Body Parts, and the Reclamation of the Americas in Leslie Marmon Silko's *Almanac of the Dead*', *Literature and Medicine* 16, 1 (1997): 23–42.

By LESLIE MARMON SILKO, see 'Language and Literature from a Pueblo Indian Perspective', in *English Literature: Opening Up the Canon*, eds Leslie A. Fiedler and Houston A. Baker, Jr. (Baltimore, MD: Johns Hopkins University Press, 1981), pp. 54–72; and interviews with PER SEYERSTED, 'Two Interviews with Leslie Marmon Silko', *American Studies in Scandinavia* 13 (1981): 17–33, and with KIM BARNES, 'A Leslie Marmon Silko Interview', *The Journal of Ethnic Studies* 13, 4 (1986): 83–105.

See also MAGGIE HUMM, 'Simultaneous Translators: Zora Neale Huston and La Malincha', in *Border Traffic: Strategies of Contemporary Women Writers* (Manchester: Manchester University Press, 1991), Chapter 3, pp. 94–122.

8 Initiation in Jamaica Kincaid's *Annie John**
DONNA PERRY

Jamaica Kincaid was born in Antigua, West Indies, in 1949, and emig-
rated to the United States at the age of seventeen; her novel *Annie John*
is set in Antigua and traces the individuation of an autobiographical
protagonist. To discuss Kincaid's work, Donna Perry offers a revision
of psychoanalytic criticism by engaging three central aspects of West
Indian cultural identity. In so doing, she implicitly substitutes a Jungian
model that privileges collective cultural archetypes and mythic patterns
over a Freudian model that privileges individual intergenerational struggles. Though we might think that this revision is simply a substitution
of one colonizing version of selfhood for another, Perry's reference to specific cultural practices and gender scripts in the West Indies belies this
thought. Her analysis of Kincaid's novel ultimately combines Western
psychological insights with postcolonialist cultural critique to 're-examine
old models of what autonomy means for women'. Perry affirms her revision by linking Kincaid to other women writers of colour (Paule Marshall,
Maya Angelou, Toni Morrison, Maxine Hong Kingston) who have also
dramatized 'successful struggles' between mothers and daughters in
ways that complicate Western models of the singular self.

Two recent studies attempt to trace the mythic patterns contained in
women's fictions, particularly those written by white, middle-class,
Western women: Annis Pratt's *Archetypal Patterns in Women's Fiction*
(1981) and Rachel Blau DuPlessis's *Writing beyond the Ending* (1985).[1]
These studies are significant not because they can help us better understand
Annie John (or the work of other black women writers) but because they
so clearly outline the parameters of the so-called Western tradition in
literature. A short summary of the texts will demonstrate what I mean.

---

* Reprinted from *Caribbean Women Writers: Essays from the First International Conference.*
Ed. SELWYN R. CUDJOE (Wellesley, MA: Callaloux Publications, 1990), pp. 245–353.

Annis Pratt singles out two dominant patterns in novels of development written by women. The first, the 'growing down' story, is the conservative extreme, a model of how to prepare for marriage, behave, and learn humility, stoicism, and self-abnegation. The message is that submission to suffering and sadism prepares one for life; an example is Fanny Fern's popular *Rose Clark* (1856). The more common pattern in women's fiction, according to Pratt, is the move from the green (matriarchal) world, which is restorative, positive, and nourishing, to the enclosed patriarchal world. The message here is that the world of nature belongs to women, but no other world does. Nature keeps women in touch with their selfhood, but this state of innocence is usually destroyed with the onslaught of the patriarchal world. Often there is a 'green world' lover (who is more desirable than the socially acceptable one), and a rape trauma is necessary to overturn the matrilinear society. Examples would be Emily Brontë's *Wuthering Heights* (1847) and Margaret Atwood's *Surfacing* (1972). These nature myth narratives are rooted in Greek mythology in which the woman, raped by the gods, turns herself into another life form (Daphne becoming a laurel tree after her rape by Apollo, for example). Sometimes the women find solace, companionship, and independence in nature.

DuPlessis explores the way Western women writers subvert the marriage plot of the novel through themes of reparenting, female bonding, mother–child dyads, and brother–sister pairs. She studies a number of modern texts in which women 'find themselves' in ways other than through romance (Dorothy Richardson's *Pilgrimage*, the fiction of Virginia Woolf, the poetry of H.D. and Adrienne Rich). But, as she demonstrates, often the cost for these women is great – the female protagonist may remain isolated, commit suicide, or go insane.

The problem with these two studies is that they look, for the most part, at the writing of white middle- and upper-middle-class women who saw themselves as part of a literary tradition that glorified marriage and romantic love. DuPlessis spends only fourteen pages out of two hundred on Zora Neale Hurston, Gwendolyn Brooks, Toni Morrison, and Alice Walker, and Pratt cites Paule Marshall, Margaret Walker, Hurston, and Morrison only in passing.

I am suggesting that fiction by women of color and Third World women offers new myths of female development and new definitions of success. As Paule Marshall and Alice Walker have demonstrated, black women have been forced outside the 'happily ever after' world of white middle-class privilege to find the story of their lives closer to home. Both describe turning to their mothers for those stories. Marshall recalls learning from 'the poets in the kitchen', her mother and the other women from Barbados, who urged one another to talk ('Soully-gal, talk yuh talk!') and gained power through their language ('In this man world you got to take yuh mouth and make a gun!').[2] Walker found her mother's life to be poetry, and the 'ambitious' gardens she grew were her daughter's legacy. As Walker generalizes: 'And so our mothers and grandmothers have, more often than not anonymously, handed on the creative spark, the seed of the flower they themselves never hoped to see: or like a sealed letter they could not plainly read'.[3]

Novels by women of color, particularly women from outside the United States, draw on different traditions and reflect a different set of cultural assumptions from those that writers like Pratt and DuPlessis define as universal. In many cultures (West Indian, with its roots in Africa, for example) images of strong, autonomous women abound; women are often seen as powerful, even awe-inspiring. African tradition featured women as tribal leaders and *obeah* women, trained in witchcraft and knowledgeable about herbal medicine and cures. Older women were revered as storytellers and keepers of the family history. In short, a woman functioned in other ways than solely in her relationship to men.

I am suggesting that in fiction by women of color, particularly that written by women who have lived or live outside of the industrialized West, there are other development patterns for women. The 'green world' harmony that Pratt describes can survive, if transformed, but DuPlessis's romance plot will wither away. A close study of Jamaica Kincaid's novel *Annie John* (1985) suggests a possible paradigm for female development that represents an alternative to the victim models we find in most recent fiction (and in life).

Annie John, Kincaid's only novel, began as a series of short stories and sketches in the *New Yorker*. It is an initiation tale about a young girl's movement from childhood to maturity – from life in lush, fertile Antigua to her eventual move to London at seventeen, when the novel ends. In one sense, Annie's life is just beginning as she leaves her island home for 'civilized' Europe, but her apprenticeship in Antigua has prepared her adequately for the world she will face beyond it.

Three aspects of West Indian culture contribute to Annie's development and empower her to leave home and create an independent life: the storytelling tradition; the tradition of the obeah woman who reads nature's signs (storm, cuts that won't heal) and who curses and cures using the materials of nature (herbs, dead animals); and matrilinear bonding – the strong blood tie of women through the generations.

The storytelling tradition among people connects the present with the past (thus suggesting timelessness and immortality), establishes a sense of community, and testifies to the power of language not only to record but to transform reality.

At an earlier time, an enslaved people had to depend on this oral tradition to transmit and maintain their cultural heritage. The tradition of storytelling is an integral part of African culture and was continued in the West Indies among Africans brought there by British, French, and Dutch colonizers. Its continuation in the United States among West Indian immigrants is clear from Paule Marshall's *Brown Girl, Brownstones* (1959), in which young Selina Boyce learns her ethnic identity from her mother and the other Barbadian immigrant women as they talk in her Brooklyn kitchen. In 'The Making of a Writer: From the Poets in the Kitchen' (1983), Marshall says that she first learned the power of language through hearing stories.

Storytelling plays a central part in *Annie John*. In an interview, Jamaica Kincaid said, 'Clearly, the way I became a writer was that my mother wrote my life for me and told it to me.'[4] Significantly, Kincaid claimed that she never read twentieth-century writers until she left Antigua at age seventeen. Her models were stories she heard – ritual retellings of her own and her people's pasts.

There is very little in *Annie John* about the influence of 'traditional' writers Annie studied in school, probably because they had little meaning for her. She is forced to copy out Books I and II of *Paradise Lost* as punishment for her rebelliousness – an example of the Western tradition being used punitively – and the novel she cites as her favorite, *Jane Eyre*, is about a woman who is a rebel. The tradition – predominantly white, male, middle-upper class – could not speak to her as her mother's stories could.

What are the effects of this African storytelling tradition? First, Annie becomes the hero of her own life, in sharp contrast to the fate of Western heroines, who are usually forced into prescribed roles and scripts as Pratt and DuPlessis suggest. Significantly, it is Annie's mother who is the weaver of the tale. In the often-repeated ritual of going through Annie's baby trunk, Annie Senior goes through the contents, piece by piece, holding up each item and recreating her daughter's past through vivid accounts of its significance. The christening outfit, baby bottles (one shaped like a boat), report cards, first notebook, and certificates of merit from school become both relics and omens – symbols of the girl she was and the woman she would become – through her mother's transformative language. The narrator remembers: 'No small part of my life was so unimportant that she hadn't made a note of it, and now she would tell it to me over and over again.'[5]

But there is method in the telling. The stories woven were designed to stress Annie's assertiveness, her accomplishments, and her independence: the slipped stitch in the christening dress happened when Annie, still in her mother's womb, kicked. Annie's mother creates the myth of Annie for her so that her past becomes as real to her as her present. Like Greek heroes who chanted the litanies of past glories to prepare themselves for battle and to awe their opponents, Annie's mother sings her daughter's praises and empowers the child.

Another function of storytelling in the novel is to provide an impetus for Annie's emergence as a writer. At twelve, she is asked by her British schoolteacher to write an 'autobiographical essay'. She tells the story of the time she went swimming with her mother and her mother disappeared from view. She recreates the panic she felt when her mother disappeared and the joy when she reappeared. But Annie changes the ending both to suit her audience and to please herself. In life Annie's mother shrugged off the event's significance; in Annie's imaginative reconstruction, mother embraces daughter lovingly. Annie wins the adoration of her classmates and her teacher – teary-eyed, Miss Nelson adds the story to the class's library of books. And Annie manages, through telling and transforming her story, to begin the imaginative reconstruction process that is autobiographical fiction.

The most significant implication of storytelling, the power of language in the book, is that it gives Annie a potential source of resistance. From childhood, Annie uses her imaginative versatility to make up elaborate lies to tell her mother when she disobeys. But, more important, stories become a way to rewrite the history of an oppressed people. In *Resistance and Caribbean Literature* (1980), Selwyn Cudjoe says, 'The purpose of colonial education was to prepare obedient boys and girls to participate in a new capitalist enterprise.'[6] He quotes Sylvia Wynter, who adds, 'To write at all was and is for the West Indian a revolutionary act.'[7]

The revolutionary potential of language is dramatically illustrated in an episode entitled 'Columbus in Chains', depicting the navigator's ignominious return to Spain after he offended the representative of King Ferdinand and Queen Isabella. The narrator remembers: 'How I loved this picture – to see the usually triumphant Columbus brought so low, seated at the bottom of a great boat just watching things go by' (pp. 77–8).

Having seen this picture in her textbook, Annie connects Columbus with patriarchal tyranny in general when she overhears her mother talking about Annie's grandfather. The old man who once dominated her life has now become infirm, according to Annie Senior's sister, who still lives in Dominica. Reading her sister's letter telling her of her father's ill health, Annie's mother laughs and says, 'So the great man can no longer just get up and go.'

Echoing her mother's scorn of patriarchal privilege, Annie writes under the Columbus picture: 'The Great Man Can No Longer Just Get Up and Go.' For this rebellious act she is stripped of power (she is removed as class prefect) and made to ingest a heavy dose of Western culture – Books I and II of *Paradise Lost*, which she is forced to copy.

Although neither Annie the child nor Annie the narrator focuses on the full implications of colonization, the racism that was a part of West Indian life, the confusion and anger it caused are evident. The narrator remembers:

Sometimes, what with our teachers and our books, it was hard for us to tell on which side we really now belonged – with the masters or the slaves – for it was all history, it was all in the past and everybody behaved differently now; all of us celebrated Queen Victoria's birthday, even though she had been dead a long time. But we, the descendents of the slaves, knew quite well what had really happened, and I was sure that if the tables had been turned we would have acted differently; I was sure that if our ancestors had gone from Africa to Europe and come upon people living there, they would have taken a proper interest in the Europeans on first seeing them, and said, 'How nice,' and then gone home to tell their friends about it. (p. 76)

The narrator's political consciousness is still in an embryonic state, however, since this childish perception is neither challenged nor commented on. Although there are hints of outrage at colonial oppression, the book, for the most part, emphasizes Annie's personal growth, not the political situation in the West Indies. Jamaica Kincaid is not a 'political' writer in the sense that the Jamaican writer Michelle Cliff is, although these references to oppression suggest that in later works she might more fully explore the political implications of colonialism.

A second source of strength for Annie lies in the obeah tradition. Two facts about obeah deserve note: the obeah was believed to be in communication with the devil and other spirits, and she was thought to have full power to exempt one from any evils that might otherwise happen.

Annie's mother consults the obeah woman (as well as her own mother and a friend) when ominous signs appear – a small scratch on Annie's instep does not heal, a friendly dog turns and bites her, a prized bowl suddenly slips and breaks. The obeah woman reads and interprets: one of the many women from her husband's past is putting a curse on them. The cure would be a ritualistic bath in water in which the barks and flowers of special trees had been boiled in oils.

As a child, Annie fantasizes about such supernatural power when she is in love with her secret friend, the unwashed, barefoot, tree-climbing 'Red Girl'. When this friend moves away, Annie dreams of rescuing her after a shipwreck and escaping with her to an island where they can get their revenge on the adult world: 'At night, we would sit on the sand and watch ships filled with people on a cruise steam by. We sent confusing signals to the ships, causing them to crash on some nearby rocks. How we laughed as their cries of joy turned to sorrow' (p. 71).

Like her mother's stories, the obeah woman's charms have the power to transform reality: they can undo curses, heal wounds, even destroy enemies. From this obeah tradition Annie learns the power of working with nature, of trusting in signs and symbols, of trusting one's instincts.

The matrilinear bond between Annie, her mother, and her grandmother proves to be the most empowering force of all. The two women present striking generational contrasts: Ma Chess, the grandmother, who lives in Dominica, more skilled in obeah than anyone Annie knows, appears in person only once in the novel, though her influence is felt throughout. When Annie becomes seriously ill at age fifteen, her grandmother mysteriously appears 'on a day when the steamer wasn't due' and nurses Annie back to health. As Annie's mother had done before, the grandmother feeds and bathes Annie, literally taking her granddaughter back into the womb: 'Ma Chess would come into my bed with me and stay until I was myself – whatever that had come to be by then – again. I would lie on my side, curled up like a little comma, and Ma Chess would lie next to me, curled up like a bigger comma, into which I fit' (pp. 125–6).

This image of Annie as a fetus protected by its mother is an apt description of the 'paradise' of the early part of the novel, when Annie and her mother lived in harmony. With the onset of adolescence came inevitable mother–daughter tensions, and Annie struggled to free herself from life in her mother's shadow. It is as though the maternal sheltering is surfacing again – symbolically – through the nurturance of the grandmother. This nurturance does not smother the adolescent girl but serves as a source of strength, for she has already become a separate being. Her mysterious illness at the end of the novel corresponds to the death of her child self – a dependent self that must grow into freedom. But her grandmother's nurturing clearly suggests that she is not to break away from her past, as most male artist-heroes do (we think of James Joyce's Stephen Daedalus or D.H. Lawrence's Paul Morel). Instead, she must grow into her new, freer self, with maternal blessing. Remember, it was Annie's mother, earlier in the novel, who encouraged her daughter to become independent.

Annie's mother remains her strongest role model. The older woman left Dominica at sixteen to escape a domineering father and gave birth to Annie, her only child, at thirty, after marriage to a man thirty-five years her senior who already had grown children older than she was. This is no romance plot, at least not in the conventional sense, but one based on mutual respect and admiration.

Like all mothers in all cultures, she tries to train her daughter in proper sexual conduct, respectful behavior, and appropriate customs and rituals, but Annie's mother knows the importance of independence and is strong enough to force her child out of the nest: when Annie is twelve her mother stops their communal baths, dressing alike, and being inseparable. She wants her daughter to become a woman.

In 'The World and Our Mothers', in the *New York Times Book Review*, Vivian Gornick claims that mother–daughter struggles are more complex than those between fathers and sons because they are fraught with more ambivalence. Speaking of the child's struggle, she says: 'Our necessity, it seems, is not so much to kill our fathers as it is to separate from our mothers, and it is the daughters who must do the separating.'[8]

Gornick's thesis is borne out in the recent pioneering work by Nancy Chodorow and others, but she is mistaken when she claims that 'nowhere in literature is there a female equivalent of the protagonist locked in successful struggle, either with the father or with the mother, for the sake of the world beyond childhood' (10). This may be true of the fiction of white women, but several women of color have immortalized 'successful struggle(s)' between mothers and daughters in fiction and autobiography: I think of Paule Marshall's *Brown Girl, Brownstones* (1959), Maya Angelou's *I Know Why a Caged Bird Sings* (1970), Maxine Hong Kingston's *The Woman Warrior* (1975), and Toni Morrison's *Beloved* (1987), as well as *Annie John*.

But the paradigm here is different: in a racist society in which the world beyond the family denies her autonomy, the female hero of color looks to her mother – and the world of women – to find models of strength and survival. As Mary Helen Washington explains the situation of the black woman writer in America:

> The literature of black women . . . is about black women; it takes the trouble to record the thoughts, words, feelings, and deeds of black women . . . and few, if any, women in the literature of black women succeed in heroic quests without the support of other women or men in their communities. Women talk to other women in this tradition, and their friendships with other women – mothers, sisters, grandmothers, friends, lovers – are vital to their growth and well-being.[9]

Whereas Gornick and others, following the lead of modern psychoanalysis, claim that our greatest source of tension and conflict resides in the family, black women writers (and many writers of color) recognize that these familial tensions cannot be seen apart from the broader reality of racism. Thus, for the woman of color, her mother and the women in her family and/or community provide strength, self-confidence, an individual and communal history, and heavy doses of reality. For whatever the tensions these characters encounter at home are minor annoyances compared to their oppression in a racist culture.

Annie John is not an overtly political novel, but it challenges us to reexamine old models of what autonomy means for women. At the end of the novel, seventeen-year-old Annie leaves for London and a career as a nurse. Some readers might say that her initiation has not yet begun – that Antigua has been a womb, a paradise from which she must escape – but I disagree. Annie John is as developed as her mother was at sixteen when she packed her belongings into a single trunk and left home alone. And like her grandmother, she has magical powers – her language can transform her life into art.

Notes

1. ANNIS PRATT, *Archetypal Patterns in Women's Fiction* (Bloomington: Indiana University Press, 1981); RACHEL BLAU DUPLESSIS, *Writing beyond the Ending: Narrative Strategies of Twentieth-Ccentury Women Writers* (Bloomington: Indiana University Press, 1985).

2. 'The Making of a Writer: From the Poets in the Kitchen', *New York Times Book Review*, January 9, 1983; rpt. in *Reena and Other Stories* (Old Westbury, N.Y.: Feminist Press, 1983), p. 7.

3. 'In Search of Our Mothers' Gardens', *Ms.*, May 1974; rpt. in *In Search of Our Mothers' Gardens* (New York: Harcourt Brace Jovanovich, 1983), p. 240.

4. Quoted in PATRICIA T. O'CONNER, 'My Mother Wrote My Life' (interview with Jamaica Kincaid), *New York Times Book Review*, April 7, 1985, p. 6.

5. JAMAICA KINCAID, *Annie John* (New York: Farrar, Straus & Giroux, 1985), p. 22. All references are to this edition and are given in the text.

6. SELWYN CUDJOE, *Resistance and Caribbean Literature* (Athens, Ohio: Ohio University Press, 1980), p. 21.

7. SYLVIA WYNTER, 'We Must Learn to Sit Down Together and Talk a Little Culture: Reflections on the West Indian Writing and Criticism, Part 1', *Jamaica Journal, Quarterly of the Institute of Jamaica* 3 (December 1968): 31; cited in Cudjoe, *Resistance*, p. 3.

8. VIVIAN GORNICK, 'The World and Our Mothers', *New York Times Book Review*, November 19, 1987, p. 52.

9. MARY HELEN WASHINGTON, Introduction, *Invented Lives: Narratives of Black Women, 1860–1960* (Garden City, N.Y.: Doubleday Anchor Press, 1987), p. xxi.

Other relevant critical essays that combine psychoanalytic and postcolonialist perspectives in the context of familial relations are GLORIA WADE-GALES, 'The Truths of Our Mothers' Lives: Mother–Daughter Relationships in Black Women's Fiction', *SAGE: A Scholarly Journal of Black Women* 1, 2 (1984): 8–12; EBELE EKO, 'Beyond the Myth of Confrontation: A Comparative Study of African and African-American Female Protagonists', *Ariel* 17, 4 (1986): 139–52; CONNIE R. SCHOMBURG, 'To Survive Whole, To Save the Self: The Role of Sisterhood in the Novels of Toni Morrison', in *The Significance of Sibling Relationships*, eds JoAnna Stephens Mink and Janet Doubler Ward (Bowling Green, OH: Bowling Green State University Popular Press, 1993), pp. 149–57; HELEN TIFFIN, 'Cold Hearts and (Foreign) Tongues: Recitation and the Reclamation of the Female Body in the Works of Erna Brodber and Jamaica Kincaid', *Callaloo* 16, 3 (1993): 909–21. See also KAY BONETTI, 'An Interview with Jamaica Kincaid', *The Missouri Review* 15, 2 (1992): 125–42.

Similar issues in the Asian American cultural context are treated by WALTER SHEAR, 'Generational Differences and the Diaspora in *The Joy Luck Club*', *Critique* 34, 3 (1993): 193–9; and MARINA HEUNG, 'Daughter-Text/Mother-Text: Matrilineage in Amy Tan's *Joy Luck Club*', *Feminist Studies* 19, 3 (1993): 597–616.

9 The Geography of Female Subjectivity: Ethnicity, Gender, and Diaspora*

SUSAN KOSHY

Susan Koshy critiques Bharati Mukherjee's novel, *Jasmine* (1989), focusing on her depiction of an immigrant woman who is engaged in the parallel processes of establishing cultural and gender identities. She contrasts this novel to an earlier one by Mukherjee that is also about assimilation, *Wife* (1975), finding that *Jasmine* has been co-opted by the American ideology of a 'mainstream' in which cultural differences must be homogenized rather than respected and maintained. Koshy's argument is Foucauldian in its premise that women must demystify the obfuscations of patriarchy, and Marxian in its awareness of the gender prescriptions of capitalism. She charges Mukherjee with creating a 'geography of female subjectivity' that fails to map the cultural heterogeneity necessary for her protagonist to construct a 'postcolonial and postmodern' self.

And I very deliberately set the story in V.S. Naipaul's birthplace because it was my 'in' joke, challenging, if you like, Naipaul's thesis of tragedy being geographical. Naipaul's fiction seems to suggest that if you are born far from the center of the universe, you are doomed to an incomplete and worthless little life. You are bound to be, if you're born like a Jasmine, an Indian in the Caribbean, a comic character, you come to nothing. So I wanted to say, 'Hey, look at Jasmine. She's smart, and desirous, and ambitious enough to make something of her life.'

Bharati Mukherjee

Female subjectivity forms the primary site of dislocation in Bharati Mukherjee's stories of the making and imagining of immigrant identities in America.[1] The experience of diaspora displaces the cultural narratives that write identity and womanhood in the home country; her stories

* Reprinted from *Diaspora: A Journal of Transnational Studies* 3, 1 (1994): 69–83.

reveal the vexed and ambivalent renarrations of 'woman' produced by the dissemination of identities. This essay will examine the negotiations involved in the insertion of female subjectivity into the cultural space of 'America' by focusing on the way Mukherjee's fictions appropriate and interrogate the narratives of assimilation and feminism that provide paradigmatic texts of gender, as well as of ethnic and racial identity, in the United States and Canada.

First, I will argue that Mukherjee's celebration of assimilation is an insufficient confrontation of the historical circumstances of ethnicity and race in the United States and of the complexities of diasporic subject-formation.[2] Second, while it is important to indicate the feminist concerns in Mukherjee's writing, I will try to show that such an analysis is incomplete if it does not also address the narrativization of these concerns in her work. Since gender does not exist as a unitary text but is variously intersected by race, class, religion, and nationality, an interpretation that focuses only on the liberatory feminist motifs misses theorizing their production within other traversing relations. My interest in Mukherjee's writing is in the ways in which 'woman' disrupts the homogeneities of national and ethnic identity *and* in the ways in which 'woman' is used as a signifier to cover class discriminations. A comparison between *Wife* (1975), an early novel, and *Jasmine* (1989) will form the basis of my analysis, which will highlight the shifts in Mukherjee's articulation of emergent female subjectivity and the assimilationist narrative.

Mukherjee's representations of female subjectivity have consistently engaged western liberal feminism's paradigmatic texts of emergent selfhood. Mukherjee has staked out a position that she claims is distanced from mainstream American and European feminism, and she has frequently indicated her disapproval of 'the imperialism of the feminists' whose 'tools and rhetoric' cannot be applied 'wholesale and intact' to the situations of 'some non-white, Asian women' (Connell 22). Despite this declaration, Mukherjee's is both a more mediated position than her statements would allow *and* it is one that has changed significantly in the course of her career. She has moved since her novel *Wife* toward a celebration of what Norma Alarcón has described as 'the most popular subject of Anglo-American feminism . . . an autonomous, self-making, self-determining subject' (357). Thus, her work, despite its stated opposition to mainstream feminism, is also deeply complicit with some of its underlying assumptions.

The difficulty can be located in Mukherjee's tendency to frame issues in terms that always claim maximum marginalization for her main characters. Insofar as they are victims, they are shown as being marked by racial, religious, or class conflicts; but Mukherjee obscures similar social relations in situations where they are part of the structures of dominance. Since her main characters are usually middle-class

Indian women, *class* becomes the ground of greatest obfuscation and ambivalence in her fiction. Quite often, Mukherjee stages confrontations so that the gender conflicts overwrite and obscure class conflicts. One of the key moments in 'The Management of Grief' presents a confrontation between Shaila Bhave and a petty Indian customs official; he refuses to clear the coffins and Shaila abuses him in public.[3] For Shaila, her outburst becomes a measure of her liberation. It signals growth within a feminist emancipatory narrative: 'Once upon a time we were well brought up women; we were dutiful wives who kept our heads veiled, our voices shy and sweet' (184). The narrative shifts from 'I' to 'we', from the particular to the representative, but it is unclear who the 'we' is – all Indian women, all Indian women returning from America? – and how this shift is made. Generalizing the episode enables Shaila to extend the scope of the claims she can make about its significance. Her past is cast as mythical and unchanging; hence, her achievement in breaking out of mythical femininity into historical subjectivity. Her prior submissiveness is represented through the highly overdetermined metaphors of veiling and silence. When Shaila challenges the official, we are asked to view her challenge in the perspective of her personal history, but what is the context in which we are to understand him? He is physically revolting (boils that swell and glow with sweat) and bureaucratic. There is no mention of the fact that the class differences between them mitigate the threat signified by his gender or that as a nonresident Indian 'foreign-returned', Shaila has acquired a status that confers substantial power in India. The heroism of a woman yelling at a customs official can only be posited by constructing the image of earlier Indian womanhood in entirely abject terms and obscuring the status difference between them.

Thus, it is important to note the ways in which Mukherjee's feminist themes are themselves susceptible to reinscription by liberal and capitalist discourses, all of which conjoin in positing the seductive appeal of the American dream in her fiction. In a strange alliance of liberal feminism, capitalism, and neocolonialism, Mukherjee's critique of the patriarchal practices of indigenous and diasporic Indian culture gets narrativized, in *Jasmine*, as the emancipatory journey from Third to First World, a journey into the possibilities of a 'developed' subjectivity characterized by individualism, autonomy, and upward mobility. According to Hazel Carby, this emancipatory trajectory also characterizes popular and feminist representations of Asian women in Britain:

> The media's 'horror stories' about Asian girls and arranged marriages bear very little relation to their experience. The 'feminist' version of this ideology presents Asian women as being in need of liberation, not in terms of their own history and needs, but *into* the 'progressive' social mores and customs of the metropolitan West. (216)

Carby's comments describe a feminist discourse of salvation produced in metropolitan centers about Asian immigrant women that invites comparison to Mukherjee's production of narratives that are assimilationist because they reconstruct their emancipation within hegemonic feminist narratives.

Mukherjee's engagement with feminist discourse is evident in her attempts to appropriate, subvert, and rewrite the female bildungsroman. Within immigrant writing, one might argue that the genre itself undergoes a metamorphosis so that the novel of formation becomes the novel of *trans*formation. In *Wife*, Dimple's transformation is depicted through the devolution of the female bildungsroman. The novel of formation charts a unified subject's progress from youth to maturity; the immigrant female subject's emergence, however, resists assimilation into linear fictions of growth. Instead, it is articulated in moments of incoherence, disruption, and splitting. In Dimple's story, the practice of arranged marriage and the repressive conformity of the immigrant community ironize the possibility of romance and individualism that is the mainstay of the bildungsroman. The text uncovers that genre's parochialism by presenting a heroine for whom individualism and self-determination are sources not of potentiality but of bafflement and perversion. By contrast, *Jasmine*'s confident appropriation of the Jane Eyre story simultaneously reaffirms and revises what Gayatri Spivak calls a 'cult text of feminism' ('Three Women's Texts' 244). *Jasmine* undercuts the domestic ideology that articulates the fulfillment of romance in marriage. Nonetheless, romantic love underpins the novel's celebration of individualism, ambition, and upward mobility through the rhetoric of desire. Although repetition and rupture threaten the heroine's mobility, *Jasmine* is finally assimilable to a fiction of becoming articulated not so much in terms of individual achievement as of an imagined cultural geography – Jasmine's story is a fable about coming to America. As Jonathan Raban has astutely observed, Mukherjee's stories are 'a romance with America itself, its infinitely possible geography' (2).[4]

Wife depicts the unraveling of the unified and socially integrated subject of the bildungsroman, an unraveling effected by displacement. Cultural pressures relentlessly close off the possibility of growth for Dimple Dasgupta before and after her marriage. Immigration to America signifies escape from the joint family and, therefore, the possibility of independence. But the constraints of the joint family are unexpectedly recreated in the suffocating proximity of the Indian immigrant community in New York. To the oppressiveness of her derivative identity as wife is added the burden of preserving ethnic identity within the home, in order to shore up her insecure husband in an alien culture. When Ina Mullick, the most sophisticated of the Indian women, offers her a drink, Dimple is caught between Ina's thinly veiled challenge and her husband's hasty reply that she does not like to drink: 'She felt that Amit was waiting for just the right answer, that it was up to her to uphold Bengali womanhood, marriage and male pride' (78). The perceived threat to ethnic identity intensifies the investment in preserving 'tradition', an embattled communal response that recasts 'tradition' as the woman's proper role and responsibility. As Kumkum Sangari and Sudesh Vaid explain: 'The ideologies of women as carriers of tradition often disguise, mitigate, compensate, contest, actual changes taking place. Womanhood is often part of an asserted or desired, not an actual cultural continuity' (17). Amit curtails Dimple's opportunities to move outside the apartment; he refuses to allow her to work, discourages her friendship with Ina, and accompanies her everywhere, even to the grocery store. The only form in which America is allowed to enter the apartment is through the television screen and through the avid consumerism that becomes the index of success among the immigrants. Shut in by her husband's rules, surrounded by blenders, toasters, and microwave ovens, eyes riveted to the keyhole, fearful of rapists and killers, Dimple implodes.

By depicting the experience of diaspora from the perspective of a wife, Mukherjee highlights the production of ethnic identity as a patriarchal construct within the immigrant community.[5] As wife, Dimple is relentlessly written into a role that denies her a voice. She is never able to speak to her husband; her anxieties are brushed aside as 'craziness' and her questions as ignorance. Isolated, Dimple discovers self-expression in her surreal fantasy life – dreams, delirious visions, and hallucinations. But her fantasy life shuts her off more completely from the external world; it represents paradoxically a form of speech that is also the 'unspeakable'. She hides her feverish inner life from her husband, meticulously obliterating all signs of her excesses from the apartment before his return: 'She didn't tell him about these imaginary beginnings. She didn't tell him about her immoderate daytime sleeping either. They were unspeakable failings' (113).

Dimple is increasingly afflicted by silence after her arrival in New York. To her long-time Calcutta friend Pixie she manages only awkwardly patronizing letters: 'Conveying New York, Ina Mullick, her nightmares, the "phase" (as Amit called it) she was going through – all impossible to talk about, let alone describe in English or Bengali. There were no words she'd ever learned to describe her daily feelings' (120). She finds herself less and less able to speak about herself to Amit and her Bengali friends: with them 'she talked in silences' (191).

One possibility for resistance that the novel engages is the emancipatory discourse of mainstream feminism. It offers the heroine an alternative trajectory for emergence. Ina tries to force Dimple into self-expression by getting her to vent her anger and fear. She badgers, provokes, harangues Dimple to speak. But for Dimple the language of feminist liberation that Ina speaks is intimidatingly alien: Ina's sessions with her consciousness-raising group, where Ina strips to reveal her hernia scar, are, for Dimple, grotesque metaphors of the violent and farcical self-exposure required by Ina's injunctions to speech. Dimple answers Ina's urgings by barricading herself behind politeness. In one of the harshest scenes in the novel, Leni and Ina, both card-carrying feminists, revel in Leni's decision to appear in public without her dentures, oblivious to Dimple's wretchedness as she serves them tea. Thus, Mukherjee shows how despite their rhetoric of sisterhood, the concerns and practices advocated by mainstream feminists serve only to further silence the voices of those nonwhite women, who, unlike Ina, are unwilling to assimilate.

The discourses contained in the novel that purport to offer solutions to her situation fail altogether in addressing it. Dimple scours women's magazines in search of solutions to problems that she has not articulated to herself. She writes an agonized letter to a columnist, 'Miss Problem-Walla c/o Eve's Beauty Basket', searching for a cure for flat-chestedness. The letter is never answered. The letters to the editor in Indian women's magazines contain debates on the position of women in modern India, but the debates are carried on in English, shutting her off from participation. Her response is to weave stories around the women she hears of in these columns, giving them happy endings to resolve their painful dilemmas. Similarly, the liberal rhetoric of Ina's feminist friends confuses and intimidates her. Leni is infuriated by Dimple's refusal to involve herself in the discussion, but the conditions for participation require obscenely public disclosures that terrify Dimple. When discussion fails, Ina tries leaving Dimple novels about adulterous women – her tacit prescription for emancipation – but 'the books, which were often about middle-aged women committing adultery on their own premises, had nothing to offer Dimple and were returned with only the first chapters and the last pages read' (137). The novel explores Dimple's silencing in terms of her failure to constructively engage existing narratives, either 'Indian' or 'American'. In an ironic twist, the violence that the immigrants insistently identify with the alienness of America provides the means for Dimple's self-assertion and becomes a symptom of her collapse.

Wife is often dismissed by critics because its heroine 'fails' to make the transition from one world to another; she is, therefore, judged to be 'weak' (Chua 54). But what is often assumed in such arguments is that agency, selfhood, and resistance assume similar, if not identical, forms across cultures. This is precisely the assumption that Mukherjee problematizes in *Wife* and dramatizes through Dimple's antagonism toward her feminist friends. *Jasmine*, on the other hand, has been widely acclaimed because the heroine has a 'positive' attitude toward assimilation, is active and venturesome. Such a reading overstates her assertiveness by equating agency with success and mobility, when very often the novel highlights the operation of fate and emphasizes Jasmine's passivity in certain circumstances. It is also important to remember that much of the narrative momentum is generated by the power of Jasmine's beauty. Indeed, the optimism of *Jasmine* has been as consistently misread as has the pessimism of *Wife*.

It frequently appears as if Mukherjee's celebration of assimilation in the United States is written from her bitter disillusionment with the implied racism of the official Canadian multicultural policy of the mosaic. There is a discernible shift between those of Mukherjee's stories written in Canada and those written after her move to the United States – a transition she discusses in the introduction to *Darkness*. The overt color bar in Canada defines South Asians as racially other; the policy of the mosaic works to support ethnic differentiation. According to Mukherjee, this liberal policy has had the inadvertent effect of fostering racism. Mukherjee has also denounced the discriminatory policies codified in the Canadian Green Paper of 1975, and her earlier stories lay bare the racist attitudes toward 'visible minorities' in Canada. Although *Wife* is nominally set in New York, Mukherjee says, 'in the mind of the heroine, it is always Toronto' ('An Invisible Woman' 39). Toronto is the proper name for the perpetual estrangement of the immigrant from national identity in her fiction. No longer Indian, not yet Canadian.

By comparison, the situation of South Asian immigrants in the United States is more ambiguous and is worth discussing in detail in order to gain a perspective on Mukherjee's fictions of the United States. The racially ambiguous position of South Asians here has created much uncertainty even within the community. South Asians in the United States had, until 1980, been classified as Caucasians based on their supposed Aryan origins;[6] in 1975, however, they lobbied for and eventually won minority status as Asian Americans.[7] There were deep splits among the political groups representing the community about the legitimacy of highly educated South Asians claiming minority status, since it would enable employers to fill affirmative action quotas while continuing to discriminate against seriously disadvantaged groups. However, some political groups, arguing from a comparison with the profiles of Japanese and Korean immigrants and from discrimination based on skin color, pressed the claim for minority standing. The legacy of these divisions remains and is further compounded because, as Sucheta Mazumdar has lucidly pointed out, for South Asians 'questions pertaining to racial identity and skin color have had a particularly convoluted history' (25).[8] Mazumdar points out that the myth of the Aryan origins of upper-caste Hindus is still perpetuated among many South Asians and has been used in post-Independence India to justify class hegemony. Many immigrants bring over this cultural baggage

when they arrive in the United States and draw on it to negotiate
their ambiguous location here, officially codified as nonwhite
Caucasian-Asian-Americans (this obviously does not include other
linguistic and religious identifications that may be operative).[9] The
relative affluence of this diasporic community and its English language
skills also foster the willingness to assimilate, a willingness that is
reinforced by the concept of the melting pot. But assimilation offers a
scenario in which class and caste prejudices can be recast in the act of
claiming a new national identity as Americans. So the question is not
really whether Mukherjee's writing celebrates assimilation or whether
this celebration reveals a positive attitude toward immigration. The
question is, how is assimilation constructed in her texts?

Mukherjee's fiction enacts its cultural identifications within an unstable
and highly ambivalent field.[10] Without a recognition of the location of her
stories at the intersection of different cultural narratives, one runs the
risk of neglecting the historical specificity of ethnicity and producing
readings that point to 'optimistic' or 'pessimistic' phases in her work.
In representing assimilation entirely as a matter of desire – which
Mukherjee does in *Jasmine* – and as something that happens if one wants
it to, in a process that requires only being 'smart, desirous and ambitious
enough', Mukherjee's novel avoids confronting the predicament of
ethnicity in the United States. A discussion of *Jasmine* will help elucidate
this argument.

A mythography of shared racial origins allows Mukherjee to represent
ethnicity, in Jasmine's case, as an attribute that can be shed. Except
through the traces of the exotic (signs of mysterious beauty, skill with
esoteric languages and foreign cuisine), Jasmine's ethnicity is not
manifested and does not interfere with her prospects. In fact, the
narrative movement of *Jasmine* (and several other stories by Mukherjee)
contravenes the claim made by Werner Sollors about the status of
ethnicity in American literature since the 1960s: 'In contemporary usage
ethnicity has largely been transformed from a heathenish liability into
a sacred asset, from a trait to be overcome in a conversion and rebirth
experience to a very desirable identity feature to be achieved through yet
another regeneration' (33). Sollors's analysis overlooks the ambivalence
that many immigrant writers, in particular, bring to ethnic identities
available to them in America, identities that undercut and reconfigure
class, religious, or racial affiliations by which they may have defined
themselves before they came to America. Jasmine's story enacts just such
an ambivalence. Jasmine describes the reaction of the Iowa farmers to
her foreignness as follows: 'They want to make me familiar. In a pinch,
they'll admit that I might look a little different, that I'm a "dark-haired
girl" in a naturally blond county. I have a "darkish complexion" (in India
I'm wheatish), as though I might be Greek from one grandparent. I'm

from a generic place, "over there," which might be Ireland, France, or Italy' (33). By resisting the inscription of ethnic difference as racial difference, Mukherjee is able to circumvent the intransigence of race in the elaboration of a fiction of American possibility.[11]

Mukherjee's *Jasmine* explores the emergence of the individualistic subject, that emergence which *Wife* briefly engages but abandons as a viable option for its heroine. However, by writing emergent female subjectivity within a narrative of assimilation, Mukherjee is caught in the position of equating feminism and westernization. Her narrative becomes deeply compromised and merely reproduces Eurocentric assumptions about the subjection of Third-World women. Chandra Mohanty points out that frequently western feminist representations of Third-World women imply their own self-presentation as more modern and sexually emancipated. She concludes, 'These distinctions are made on the basis of the privileging of a particular group as the norm or referent' (337). According to Trinh Minh-ha, feminism that develops out of such biases betrays an ethnographic ideology: 'Feminism in such a context may well mean "westernization"' (106).[12] Her comments are useful in uncovering the weaknesses underlying Mukherjee's confident espousal of individualism in her celebration of Jasmine's growth and transformation. Trinh adds: 'One can say that fear and insecurity lie behind each attempt at opposing modernism with tradition and, likewise, at setting up ethnicity against womanhood.'

The identification of feminist ideas with westernization is revealed in the representation of the past in *Jasmine*. Since the distance in time between past and present lives also represents a distance between two cultures, remembering functions as translation in Mukherjee's novel. But the translations of the past life privilege the language of the present life and, therefore, become an example of what Gayatri Spivak calls 'translation-as-violation' ('Imperialism and Sexual Difference' 234). So we find Jyoti's mother – whom we know only as a quiet, traditional Indian woman – declaring to her daughter (after having been beaten the previous night by her husband for encouraging her daughter to study): 'They've come around. Just make sure you ace your exams' (52). The presence of American slang in the speech of an Indian village woman seems to be an attempt to translate her character by representing proto-feminist sentiments as an Americanism of attitude or value. This speech is particularly conspicuous given that her other utterances do not carry distinctively American linguistic markers and that most of the other Punjabi characters (except Prakash, another 'modern' Indian) speak Indian English.

The assimilation of a prior self into hegemonic constructions is embodied at another level through the self-exoticization that grants Jasmine mobility and opportunity: when the darkness of the Indian subcontinent is reconstituted as the darkness of the Indian woman's body, a liability is transformed into an asset for the immigrant. Exotic beauty becomes the passport to assimilation. While many of Mukherjee's female characters, like Jasmine, are acutely conscious of the way their beauty is read by Americans, they are themselves engaged in the process of writing their American experience as a narrative of sexual awakening and material promise, a narrative enabled by their exotic beauty. Therefore, they collaborate in the perpetuation of their own exoticism. As a result, the process of Americanization or assimilation is for these characters also a process of recreating their 'Indianness' – of othering themselves. Since this re-creation is directed toward assimilation, the possibilities for self-making are determined by the terms of the dominant culture.

Moreover, the celebration of Jasmine's singularity is dependent on flattening out the subjectivities of other nonwhite women whom she encounters and identifies with, but from whom she is carefully distinguished. The representation of nonwhite women in *Jasmine* inscribes them as emblematic collectivities. The women she lives with in Hasnapur are indistinguishable, except as gradations on a scale of rebelliousness and courage that confirms Jyoti's exceptionality. Their life histories can be summarized as a litany of disasters, which allow no room for will: 'All over our district, bad luck dogged dowryless wives, rebellious wives, barren wives. They fell into wells, they got run over by trains, they burned to death heating milk on kerosene stoves' (41). This discourse constructs a monolithically oppressive society where repression is absolute and resistance impossible, and where Jyoti (as the only example of a woman who 'escapes') can survive only as an anomaly. Mukherjee becomes, in a sense, trapped within the formulations of her own discourse – there is no escape for Hasnapuri women, but Jyoti is a woman who escapes. Rescue can, therefore, only be brought about through extraordinary means, hence the incredible scheme of the 'mission' as a bizarre ritual that subsumes Jyoti's agency within ritual imperative (Sati).

By a curious tautology that recurs throughout the novel, Jasmine's success is both proof and mark of her difference or distinctness. She is the one who is destined for success in America by a trick of fate, but she is also the brightest, the most educated, the bravest, the most 'modern' of the village women. She is an American before the fact. Therefore, Jasmine can simultaneously attest to the oppressiveness of India and the liberatory potential of America.

Once she arrives in America, Jasmine is readily distinguishable from other nonwhite women. Her benefactress, Linda Gordon, testifies to Jasmine's distinctness from the other undocumented women she helps: 'Jazzy, you don't strike me as a picker or a domestic. . . . You're different from these others' (134). Jasmine is being differentiated from the other women by a white woman who helps women in such situations and, therefore, evidently 'knows' them well enough. The context of this judgment is an informal conversation among a group of women who try to plan some work for Jasmine. The judgment is strategically framed in Jasmine's narration at the end of a climactic scene, so that although she may not speak it, she certainly gives it emphasis; the other women signal a collective endorsement: 'the Kanjobal women looked at her intently, nodding their heads as if they understood' (134). The Kanjobal women form the ground for a claim of Jasmine's exceptionality; thus, they are simultaneously central to the formulation of her difference and entirely peripheral to it.

This difference is never located in any specific qualities, but is part of Jasmine's mystique, an aura she communicates. Built loosely into these references is the suggestion that it is not just a matter of difference but also of superiority. Jasmine's inherent aristocracy sets her apart and destines her for assimilation in mainstream America. Mukherjee reveals early on in the story that even though Jasmine has grown up as a poor village girl, her family had aristocratic connections in their pre-Partition Lahore days. In this instance, difference is being used as a signifier to disguise and naturalize class distinctions.

It is also worth noting that in every instance this difference in Jasmine is something that the white characters draw attention to and commend with the term 'special' or 'heroic'. The movement of the novel, in which Jasmine is rewarded with love and happiness, seems to affirm the validity of these judgments. As the only example of a nonwhite woman who 'makes it' in a novel that celebrates 'making it', Jasmine is set apart from the others (the Kanjobal women, the migrant workers, the other 'day-mommies') who disappear into oblivion. By the same move she is also cast as superior to them. Jasmine's success (financial independence, romance, mobility) is linked to her ability to exoticize some elements of her ethnicity while shedding others, at will. The implication is that self-hood and fulfillment lie outside ethnicity.

Furthermore, Mukherjee is able to draw on the myth of Asian Americans as a model minority in her celebration of America. The solidarity between Jasmine and her Vietnamese-American adopted son Du (an element that is rather weakly incorporated into the text), both 'quick studies' in acculturation, seems to derive from and reenact this stereotype of Asian Americans. In one instance, Jasmine describes her identification with Asians during her visit to a hospital in Iowa: 'Kwang, Liu, Patel, I've met them all. Poke around in a major medical facility and suddenly you're back in Asia, which I find very reassuring. I trust only Asian doctors, Asian professionals. What we've gone through must count for something' (32). Certainly Kwang, Liu, and Patel constitute a political identity available to Jasmine as an Indian in America, but to ground this identity in terms of 'what we've gone through' is highly dubious. It erases crucial differences between the passages of refugees like Du, illegal entrants like Jasmine, and the post-1965 wave of middle-class, highly educated professionals from Asia. It is worth noting, however, that Jasmine's identification is directed toward an elite group of Asians. The Vadheras and the other Flushing Indians are bracketed outside this grouping.

The upward mobility that Jasmine aspires to is not simply a matter of money, although it would not be possible without money. This distinction can be substantiated by examining the ways in which the classic American story of upward mobility (Horatio Alger) is displaced in *Jasmine*. The displacement is effected through the rhetoric of romantic love and by grafting the narrative of upward mobility onto another classic American story – the narrative of outward mobility, or the pioneer tale. The language of romantic love, as it is used by Jasmine, provides a vocabulary of idealism, liberation, and rapture. It holds the promise of transcendence and transformation, powerfully seductive possibilities for an immigrant whose material realities are so circumscribed. Each of Jasmine's incarnations unfolds as a love story, Kali excepted. The allure that surrounds her first American lover, Taylor, is a sublimation of privilege and power as Jasmine explicitly acknowledges when she describes her attraction to him: 'The love I felt for Taylor that first day had nothing to do with sex. I fell in love with his world, its ease, its careless confidence and graceful self-absorption' (171). The conclusion of the novel also displaces the story of the heroine's progress. Jasmine's last incarnation transposes her into the tradition of American pioneers as she heads out West. Only now, the frontier signifies not land or gold, but the space where America is being remade in the collision and fusion of ethnicities. The novel hints that Jasmine's identity will be reconfigured here again. No longer the guarded self-representation required by her Anglicization as Jane in the Midwest but the possibility, still uncertain, of greater freedom and reunion with Du, himself now metamorphosed as a confidently hyphenated American. Both forms of displacement allow for the representation of Jasmine's mobility through the idiom of the heroic.

Mukherjee's representations of the Third World inscribe a space that suppresses female subjectivity. Thus, despite Mukherjee's claim that Jasmine provides a bold refutation of V.S. Naipaul's thesis (cited in the epigraph to this essay), her work offers only a sophisticated paraphrasing of his alleged racial and cultural determinism. Mukherjee makes it quite clear that Jasmine has to travel to America to 'make something of her life'; in the Third World she is fated to despair and hardship.

The opposition between ethnicity and womanhood obscrures rather than illuminates the cultural and historical variations in terms like 'subjectivity' and 'agency' because the reliance on the western bourgeois subject as an implicity standard inscribes a corresponding lack in other cultures. As a result, in *Jasmine*, becoming charts a particular geography that 'reproduce[s] the structural inequalities that exist between the "metropoles" and the "peripheries" ... in the form of inappropriate polarizations between the "First" and the "Third World", developed/ underdeveloped or advanced/backward' (Carby 223).[13] On the other hand, Mukherjee's earlier fictions, like *Wife* and *Darkness*, constantly undercut and ironize the fulfillments of the American Dream and foreground the splitting of identities as a sign of the incommensurability of migrant subjectivities and hegemonic cultural narratives. In her later fiction, however, self-making in the New World recasts prior histories in other worlds rather simplistically as the pre-texts for a subjectivity that can only be fully realized in America. The constrastive juxtaposition of an Indian past against an American present, Old World against New World, creates a continual slippage through which America comes to represent the space of modernity. By conceiving of ethnicity as the sign of the prior, of what must be used and then left behind in order to become fully American, the narrative of assimilation reinforces this slippage. But geographies of female subjectivity that seek to engage the postcolonial and the postmodern will have to imagine in more complex ways the heterogeneous spaces of modernity.

Notes

I am grateful to King-Kok Cheung and Ketu Katrak for constructive suggestions on earlier drafts of this essay. Khachig Tölölyan's comments helped me clarify my arguments, and George Koshy's advice helped me substantiate them.

1. Sant-Wade and Radell examine the situation of Mukherjee's immigrant women as an *existential* dilemma and consequently neglect to place their acts of self-fashioning in a larger and more specifically cultural context. Consequently, their article does not get beyond pointing to the 'heroism' of the women in 'rejecting the past and moving energetically toward an unknown future' (11).

2. Omi and Winant contend that assimilation theories have historically been based on the experiences of European immigrant groups and have not, therefore, addressed adequately the situation of 'third world' minorities; by subsuming race in the 'broader category' of ethnicity, these theories have failed to understand the force of racial stratification. Mukherjee's appropriation of assimilation without engaging its historic inadequacy in addressing the role of racial differences creates contradictions that I will address in my discussion of *Jasmine*.

3. In India, customs marks a highly charged field where the government attempts to regulate the flow of luxury goods through an elaborate,

inefficient, and corrupt bureaucracy. Some overseas travelers, for their part, have devised highly ingenious ways of evading customs surveillance, including several well-known cases that involved attempts to smuggle gold into the country in corpses. Mukherjee's choice of a customs official as Shaila's antagonist secures Shaila's victory even before the confrontation, since Mukherjee draws on the force of widespread popular antipathy to this group of bureaucrats – certainly the caricaturing of his physical appearance plays on these sentiments.

4. This is Raban's comment on *The Middleman and Other Stories*, but it also captures very effectively the tone of *Jasmine*.

5. Mukherjee returns to this theme again in 'Hindus' (*Darkness*). She offers a penetrating exploration of the production and consumption of Indian identity in the American publishing business and within the immigrant community of New York. Leela Lahiri's story is produced in the third-person narrative of gossip and scandal within the Indian community because of her failed marriage to an American. Leela's story allows the community to narrate its own identity within a discourse of purity figured by and reproduced through the behavior of women. Mukherjee takes as the subject of her story Leela's marginality to the authoritative narratives of cultural identity, whether produced by the immigrant community or by mainstream America (the soon-to-be-published memoirs of the maharaja).

6. Romila Thapar explains that the theory of the Aryan origins of the subcontinental people was first adumbrated in the work of late eighteenth- and early nineteenth-century Orientalists, who used linguistic evidence to support their claims. This theory was later extrapolated to provide a racial explanation for the evolution of the Hindu caste system by equating upper caste status with Aryan origins (qtd. in Mazumdar 28). Mazumdar adds that despite powerful evidence to the contrary, the theory of Aryan origins has persisted, making its appearance in nationalist discourse and in history textbooks in post-Independence India (29). Many of the claims for American citizenship filed by Indians in the early 1900s were grounded in their being of 'pure-blood Aryan stock' (30).

7. See Takaki for a detailed historical account of this debate (445–8) and an analysis of the larger context of Asian immigration to America.

8. Mazumdar explains that although many South Asians may classify themselves as Caucasian, they are viewed by other groups as being racially separate, either as 'black' or 'brown'. She cites the growing violence against South Asians in the United States as evidence of such racialized perception. She goes on to argue that with median income levels beginning to drop, statistics indicating patterns of downward mobility, and growing numbers of working-class immigrants within the group, South Asians may increasingly turn to other racial minority groups to forge alliances and redefine their identities. I differ with Mazumdar, however, in her view that these factors should force South Asians to recognize that they are indeed, contrary to their present views, 'black'. While such a political identification is compelling and viable within the British context, where immigration patterns, racism, and union organization have defined common struggles, the history of slavery in America and the formation of a black underclass require that other groups not appropriate this political identity to articulate their positions. The specificity of the South Asian American identity is just beginning to be

151

spoken and needs to be defined so as to allow connections with other oppositional movements; but it cannot be addressed by claiming blackness.

9. This ambiguous location is foregrounded in Mira Nair's *Mississippi Masala* but recuperated differently than in Mukherjee's fiction. In the film, the heroine's relationship with a young black man highlights affinities between the Ugandan Indian immigrants and the local black community. This commonality is evoked variously as a common origin in Africa, forced displacement, and minority status in America.

10. The problem of cultural identity has been addressed by asserting an 'Indian' identity; active mainstreaming; or, in limited cases, by establishing alliances with other oppositional groups. None of these practices is necessarily separate or opposed to the others; they overlap, intersect, or complicate each other. In fact, in most cases they coexist or are compartmentalized: for instance, 'Indian' in the home and 'American' at work. In a community that is still very new in America, the formulations of ethnicity are unstable, especially when the populations are dispersed and have not often formed around ethnic enclaves.

11. Speaking of social scientific theoretical paradigms, Omi and Winant explain that scholars who focus on ethnicity rather than race 'fail to grasp the extent to which US society is racially structured from top to bottom' (54). This leads them to formulate 'evolutionary models which optimistically predict the gradual absorption of distinct groups into the mainstream of American political, economic and cultural life' (11).

12. Trinh's comments are part of a theoretical argument and do not refer to Mukherjee, although they are very illuminating in relation to Mukherjee's writing.

13. Carby casts this statement as a warning against the colonizing moves within feminist theory.

Works cited

ALARCÓN, NORMA. 'The Theoretical Subject(s) of *This Bridge Called My Back* and Anglo-American Feminism'. *Making Face, Making Soul: Haciendo Caras*. Ed. Gloria Anzaldua. San Francisco: Aunt Lute, 1990. 356–69.

CARBY, HAZEL, V. 'White woman listen! Black feminism and the boundaries of sisterhood'. *The Empire Strikes Back: Race and Racism in 70s Britain*. Centre for Contemporary Cultural Studies. London: Hutchinson, 1982. 212–35.

CHUA, C.L. 'Passages from India: Migrating to America in the Fiction of V.S. Naipaul and Bharati Mukherjee'. *Reworlding: The Literature of the Indian Diaspora*. Ed. Emmanuel S. Nelson. Westport, CT: Greenwood, 1992. 51–61.

CONNELL, MICHAEL, JESSIE GREARSON, and TOM GRIMES. 'An Interview with Bharati Mukherjee'. *Iowa Review* 20.3 (1990): 7–32.

MAZUMDAR, SUCHETA. 'Race and Racism: South Asians in the United States'. *Asian Americans: Comparative and Global Perspectives*. Ed. Shirley Hune et al. Pullman, WA: Washington State UP, 1991. 25–38.

MOHANTY, CHANDRA TALPADE. 'Under Western Eyes: Feminist Scholarship and Colonial Discourses'. *Boundary 2* 12.3/13.1 (1984): 333–58. (Rpt. in *Third World Women and the Politics of Feminism*. Ed. Chandra Talpade Mohanty, Ann Russo, and Lourdes Torres. Bloomington: Indiana UP, 1991. 51–80.)

MUKHERJEE, BHARATI. *Darkness*. 1985. New Delhi: Penguin, 1990.

——. 'An Invisible Woman'. *Saturday Night* (March 1981): 36–40.

——. *Jasmine*. New York: Grove, 1989.

——. *The Middleman and Other Stories*. 1988. New York: Random, 1989.

——. *The Tiger's Daughter*. Boston: Houghton, 1971.

——. *Wife*. 1975. New Delhi: Penguin, 1990.

OMI, MICHAEL, and HOWARD WINANT. *Racial Formation in the United States: From the 1960s to the 1980s*. New York: Routledge, 1986.

RABAN, JONATHAN. Rev. of *The Middleman and Other Stories*, by Bharati Mukherjee. *New York Times Book Review* 19 June 1988: 1–3.

SANGARI, KUMKUM, and SUDESH VAID, eds. *Recasting Women: Essays in Colonial History*. New Delhi: Kali, 1989.

SANT-WADE, ARVINDRA, and KAREN MARGUERITE RADELL. 'Refashioning the Self: Immigrant Women in Bharati Mukherjee's New World'. *Studies in Short Fiction* 29.1 (1992): 11–18.

SOLLORS, WERNER. *Beyond Ethnicity: Consent and Descent in American Culture*. New York: Oxford UP, 1986.

SPIVAK, GAYATRI CHAKRAVORTY. 'Imperialism and Sexual Difference'. *Oxford Literary Review* 8.1 (1986): 225–40.

——. 'Three Women's Texts and a Critique of Imperialism.' *Critical Inquiry* 12 (1985): 243–61.

TAKAKI, RONALD. *Strangers from a Different Shore: A History of Asiani Americans*. New York: Penguin, 1989.

TRINH, T. MINH-HA. *Women, Native, Other*. Bloomington: Indiana UP, 1989.

Related critical essays that arrive at conclusions quite different from Susan Koshy's are CARMEN WICKRAMAGAMAGE, 'Relocation as Positive Act: The Immigrant Experience in Bharati Mukherjee's Novels', *Diaspora: A Journal of Transnational Studies* 2, 2 (1992): 171–97; JANET M. POWERS, 'Sociopolitical Critique as Indices and Narrative Codes in Bharati Mukherjee's *Wife* and *Jasmine*', in *Bharati Mukherjee: Critical Perspectives*, ed. Emmanuel S. Nelson (New York: Garland, 1993), pp. 89–108. See also 'An Interview with Bharati Mukherjee', *Iowa Review* 20, 3 (1990): 7–32.

10 History, Memory and Language in Toni Morrison's *Beloved**

Rebecca Ferguson

This essay, like those that follow, treats storytelling as a political act. Stories are taken to be the vehicle that allows colonized peoples access to their history, and thus their communal identity. Rebecca Ferguson describes the process of 'rememory' in Toni Morrison's *Beloved* in these terms, linking storytelling to the physical embodiment of a shared but 'disremembered' history. Ferguson's understanding of the process is phenomenological as well as historiographic, because 'rememory' involves the body of the teller. Meaning is produced by the inextricable interactions of subjects and objects; stories are the embodied teller's expression of his/her felt history – an understanding of experience that eschews the Western separation of mind from body. Thus, pain, hallucination, and madness will condition the storyteller's art, as will myths, legends, and the available facts of recorded history. Ferguson's discussion of 'rememory' is related to the Bakhtinian conception of 'voice', but it is less concerned with individual self-expression than with cultural construction. Morrison's premise, which Ferguson reflects, is this: if a usable past can be created, the single self will have a place to enter and reside.

In an interview with *City Limits* magazine in March 1988, a few months after *Beloved* was published, Toni Morrison restated with special urgency a point which has often been made about America and its history:

> We live in a land where the past is always erased and America is the innocent future in which immigrants can come and start over, where the slate is clean. The past is absent or it's romanticised. This culture doesn't encourage dwelling on, let alone coming to terms with, the

---

* REBECCA FERGUSON, *Feminist Criticism: Theory and Practice* (Toronto: University of Toronto Press, 1991), pp. 109–27.

truth about the past. That memory is much more in danger now than it was 30 years ago.[1]

These observations point to a crucial concern of many Afro-American novelists; to an unusual degree, they place memory at the forefront of their writing, in full awareness that their own history has been (to take a phrase from the closing passages of *Beloved*) 'disremembered and unaccounted for'.[2] Similarly, the act of writing – writing from and about that past – has special significance for authors who are conscious of belonging to a race once legally proscribed from attaining literacy or having access to education. So on both fronts, black writers find themselves in a complex position; theirs is a history of oppression, but one that must be remembered and accounted for, and while the language of the dominant culture and the written word itself have all too often been potent instruments in that oppression, not to have mastery of them is to be rendered impotent in ways that matter greatly. An awareness of both points is evident in much recent writing by black women:[3] in Alice Walker's *The Color Purple* with its emphasis on the liberating act of letter-writing, in certain of her short stories, and in the merging of both documented and mythic history in Walker's *Meridian* or Morrison's *Song of Solomon*, which moves backwards historically and southwards geographically to rediscover a heritage where oppression and liberation are paradoxically drawn together.

It is understandable too that the response of these writers to such contemporary concerns as the tenuous nature of our conceptions of history and identity and the instability of the language system itself is especially problematic. Michael Cooke has remarked that, notwithstanding the ludic experimentation of a text like Ishmael Reed's *Mumbo Jumbo* (1972) and the formal boldness of Ellison's *Invisible Man* (1952), 'the fabulator's sense of life as unreal and mad, though this might seem highly germane to black experience, has not really taken hold in black writing'.[4] Yet it is the term 'fabulation' as used by Robert Scholes to denote 'a return to a more verbal kind of fiction . . . a less realistic and more artistic kind of narrative' which Bernard Bell finds particularly appropriate to describe the work of black American postmodernists. Bell points to a crucial difference in what they are doing, however: 'unlike their white contemporaries, [these writers] are not merely rejecting the arrogance and anachronism of Western forms and conventions, but also rediscovering and reaffirming the power and wisdom of their own folk tradition: Afro-American ways of seeing, knowing, and expressing reality.' Thus, to leave behind the constraints of realism and naturalism does not mean abandoning 'such traditional narrative modes as myth and legend', nor does it have to entail the neglect of history.[5]

In this context, Toni Morrison's own comments on the question of modernism and postmodernism in the arts are especially interesting, since she too is concerned with essential distinctions between what this has meant for white culture and what it has meant within black culture and experience. She locates the inception of modernism, as she locates so many of her novels, in a time of radical *transition*, observing that it began in the West with writers and painters who registered the impact of industrialisation and 'the great transformation from the old world to the new', while at the same time Africa was being put through a parallel and extreme experience of severe dislocation:

> Modern life begins with slavery. . . . in terms of confronting the problems of where the world is now, black women had to deal with 'post-modern' problems in the nineteenth century and earlier. These things had to be addressed by black people a long time ago. Certain kinds of dissolution, the loss of and the need to reconstruct certain kinds of stability. Certain kinds of madness, deliberately going mad in order, as one of the characters says in the book, 'not to lose your mind'.[6]

Slavery, she contends, must be called more than an ideology or an economy; it was also a *pathology*, the effects of which are with us still. Whites 'have had to reconstruct everything in order to make that system appear true', and this in itself is a form of madness.

Though I would be wary of dwelling too much on the precise import of words which were after all delivered orally, 'reconstruct' none the less seems an important term in the way it is applied by Morrison to two subjects; to blacks, who were forced to reconstruct *themselves* as an act of survival, and to whites who (then as now) found themselves reconstructing the very order of things to sustain their supremacy. Reconstruction is also that time of attempted, though inadequate, transition between the Civil War and the new order of America which followed it, when – nominally at least – the institutions of slavery were ended. It is the era in which a significant proportion of *Beloved* is set; although it is most obvious to regard it as a novel 'about slavery', and although the use of narrative tenses and the interactions of past with present are so fluid, it is still apparent that Reconstruction constitutes the predominating 'present tense' of the novel, the point where it begins and ends, and the point to which we are constantly being returned.

Of the remarks quoted above, one of the most interesting – concerning pathology – is made again and expanded in a recent article by Morrison.[7] Discussing the suggestion that the white whale in Melville's *Moby Dick* represents the ideology of race,[8] she writes that, if it is understood in these terms,

156

what Ahad has lost to it is personal dismemberment and family and society and his own place as a human in the world. The trauma of racism is, for the racist and the victim, the severe fragmentation of the self, and has always seemed to me a cause (not a symptom) of psychosis.

It is significant that she focuses on the idea of that fragmentation being bodied forth as a literal dismemberment, especially as this emerges as such an important figure in *Beloved*.

My concern in this essay is to examine how these perceptions on madness, dissolution and pathology are expressed by Morrison in *Beloved*, a work which is formally very demanding – in ways that can sometimes evoke the 'postmodernist'[9] – but which is at the same time very exact in its reference to recorded history, a history which Morrison had carefully researched.[10] In handling this material, she is aware of dealing with what can best be described as a repression; but, as she has remarked, for blacks themselves 'the struggle to forget which was important in order to survive is fruitless', and this is a novel about living *with* the memory and surviving it. It is not only concerned with the claims the past may make upon the present, but with how far those claims may conceivably be met and on what terms. Behind the writing of the novel lay Morrison's conviction that (despite the published slave narratives) the records on that subject are still only an outline, and that the experience of slavery had never been adequately described on the imaginative level. Perhaps the most notable gap in the history is the beginning, and the absence of any but the barest records of the 'middle passage' on the slave ships – the most traumatic of the horrors a first-generation slave would have undergone.[11]

Along with this central concern with history and memory, there is also a compelling emphasis in the novel upon the survival of women within and beyond the structures of slavery – on their struggle to establish continuity through the protection of their children, their men and the community – and upon the possibilities for the shaping of the self within these changing structures.[12] It is striking that the dynamics and rivalries of the family should have such force within this novel where the orthodox conception of the 'nuclear family' is so tenuously formed and so conspicuously (sometimes comically) crowded out.[13] By the very nature of Sethe's drastic choice – to kill her baby daughter rather than let her be returned into slavery – the bonds of mother and daughter and the responsibilities they entail are probed with particular depth. In this sphere, as well as in the sphere of a 'disremembered' history, Morrison is attempting to express the inexpressible, to speak the 'unspeakable' partly by exploring domestic space and the space and language of the pre-Oedipal. The house, 124, is occupied by three women (daughter, mother and grandmother), plus the spirit of a fourth, after the two male children have departed and before Paul D appears; when he does, he is run off by Beloved and the household of women is re-established before it finally disintegrates. This is not to say that the place of the male is marginal within the novel, however; on the contrary, Paul D's story and his interactions with Sethe and her household are crucial to its development.[14] Morrison does not privilege mother–child over adult bonds, female over male, or 'the things behind things' over the future that is 'becoming', but she does demand that we give due weight to all of these as a part of survival.[15]

Beloved is dense with 'unspeakable thoughts, unspoken' (*Beloved*, p. 199). While those parts of the narrative that deal with the Reconstruction era set up a linear, progressive chronology, the text is fragmented – shattered, one might say – by what is termed 'rememory': the continual entry and re-entry of past into present.[16] From the beginning, with the abrupt entry into the house, the reader is confronted with a network of allusions from which full meaning is withheld, with constant intimations that sinister, even traumatic referents lie beyond them. 'Rememory' is ambivalently merged with individual acts of remembering, sometimes triggered by Proustian catalysts (notably when Sethe smells hair burning in the fire, and is suddenly rocked with repressed memories concerning her mother's death). But through individual memory – as well as in a host of other ways – there is the growing, insistent sense that a larger memory is pressing itself upon our attention. This deeper memory is expressed above all in a constant emphasis on the recurrent and on synchrony; the text dwells on images, sensory impressions, phrases and metaphors which connect and repeat themselves so often that it has the force of an obsession, a highly poetic haunting. As in Morrison's other novels, 'the psychological, like the sensual and sexual, is also historical'.[17] History is never over and done with; it exists always in the realms of the mind and senses as well as in specified places, and as I will show, in Morrison's writing it is constantly being called up by metaphor and analogy. In all these respects, *Beloved* is a deeply imagined historical novel, in which what is commonly called the supernatural is also the manifestation of history. When Paul D first touches the scars left on Sethe's back from her beating, the house explodes with the baby ghost's disturbance, and we witness the force of Beloved's jealousy, her will to obstruct any living person from appropriating Sethe's past, her guilt or her 'responsibility'.

Like Freud's 'uncanny', Beloved's disturbance manifests itself precisely within what is most intimately known and domestic (not only in her presence as poltergeist but later as occupant of 124). She is, in Freud's words, 'something repressed which *recurs*', something supposedly 'dead' returning painfully to life, through the supernatural at work in the 'world of common reality', yet 'in reality nothing new or alien, but ... familiar and old-established in the mind'.[18] 124 is thus a space which is both empty and full, intimate and strange. Denoted by a 'mere number', one which opens each section of the book, like all haunted houses it becomes 'personalised by its own activity'.[19] Through it, our attention is also fixed on the *differences* that have marked out the choices made by Sethe and Paul D, who share a large measure of the same past on the plantation Sweet Home; the focus is displaced from the potential questing male hero, the 'long gone ramblin' man' of black myth and fiction, to Sethe's choice of staying put and living with the worst of her own history, of piecing together – within very definite, cautious limits – an existence in the same place where she killed her child.[20] In this respect their stories become very different; it is not until much later that Paul D is able to 'put his story next to hers', and then this is only possible in so far as he has stayed long enough to hear and understand it.

Through Beloved's presence, which guards the very threshold, 124 is invested with an immense, disremembered suffering peopled by all the ghosts of those who died through slavery. Like many of Sethe's own memories, this is latent though potent until Paul D arrives; then Beloved makes herself known, insists upon her claim and interposes herself in the world of the living, demanding to be seen, heard and understood. And as Amy Denver says as she rubs Sethe's numbed feet back into feeling, ' "anything dead coming back to life hurts" '. Parts of the narrative treat Beloved's physical rebirth and the unsettling evidence of her identity through the conventions of the ghost story (her specific uncanny knowledge of her mother's song, her earrings and so on), yet despite this clear evidence of past links it is especially significant that the second daughter Denver – who should, after all, know least about it – is the first to establish a close and sympathetic bond with her. Her mother represses the knowledge for as long as possible – even though it is registered at once in her body – until she is ready to handle it; but Denver instantly recognises, in her isolation and loneliness, that Beloved is her sister, and she knows too that she is 'more than that'. Paul D acknowledges in a confused way that ' "she reminds me of something; something, look like, I'm supposed to remember" ',[21] while the grandmother Baby Suggs sees more wisely that there is nothing so exceptional about her as a ghost, that there can be no house in the district that is not 'packed to its rafters with some dead Negro's grief'. Since Beloved brings the whole traumatic experience of slavery with her, she not only knows more than she could otherwise have known in her previous short life, but she also contains the *effects* that slavery had, its profound fragmentation of the self and of the connections the self might have with others.[22] The dependency she shows towards Sethe is in the face of this fragility, and her confusion is profound; she is dislocated in herself as well as dislocated in time, full of grief and need, love and resentment. For Sethe, Beloved is above all a connection, the reconnection with and restoring of all that was lost when she was driven to kill her; even so, what appears to be an end, a closure in a healing restoration, is really only the beginning. Beloved yearns to make connections, but those she does make grow without restraint to become destructive, to break down rather than 'reconstruct'. While she strives to re-enter and lay hold on the world to which her lived history connects her, she is also strenuously holding herself together, defending herself from being engulfed or exploding in the space between the two worlds where she simultaneously exists.

This last point is vividly illustrated when Beloved comes close to a ghostly disappearing, 'eaten alive by the dark', in the shed where she was originally killed and where Denver was almost killed too. Returning, she tells Denver, ' "I don't want that place. This the place I am" ' (p. 123), willing herself into a single place and a present tense, but she is also able to point to herself as she exists in the other place, crouching and rocking in a foetal position. The physical posture suggests a regression, and what is especially striking is that Beloved's double presence, for all its potency, suggests equally powerfully a kind of absence. Being in both realms, she seems to exist fully in neither. Likewise, although being swallowed and exploding appear perhaps as opposite figures, both express the same physical instability, the potential for fragmentation and dissolution that the text so often invokes. Denver is herself overwhelmed by it as she faces the ultimate loss defined by her sister-companion's vanishing:

> If she stumbles, she is not aware of it because she does not know where her body stops, which part of it is an arm, a foot or a knee. She feels like an ice cake torn away from the solid surface of the stream, floating on darkness, thick and crashing against the edges of things around it. Breakable, meltable and cold. . . . Now she is crying because she has no self. Death is a skipped meal compared to this. She can feel her thickness thinning, dissolving into nothing. She grabs the hair at her temples to get enough to uproot it and halt the melting for a while. (p. 123)

The melting away of both body and self is experienced by Denver as the accumulation of all the losses she has sustained, death and leaving understood in terms of one another. Even within the microcosm of 124, where she and Sethe are given a wide berth by the local community, the only interactive relationships she has known (with her brothers, her grandmother, her mother) are seen as leading inexorably to this loss. On the very threshold of adulthood, Denver both chooses and is pushed back into a lost childhood, which is part of what Beloved represents for her. Her own dependency on her mother is very evident, and she jealously guards that relationship against the male interloper – she is waiting instead for an idealised father, an 'angel man' who is definitely not, for this time, Paul D – but what may come as more of a shock to the reader is the later revelation of her aggression and of her self-protective fears concerning Sethe. Through her suppressed knowledge of Beloved's fate she has been taught that, quite literally, 'mother love is a killer', and having only a limited sense of why this became so in the specific context of slavery, she has no way of knowing whether 'the thing that happened that made it all right for my mother to kill my sister could happen again' (p. 205).[23] The fantasy she has about being decapitated by Sethe ambivalently merges both responses, as it is both a murderous and a loving act, carried out 'carefully' with the same necessary pain as combing tangled hair. Hence, her own disappearance is one of the deaths that Denver anticipates, while Beloved's return from the other side seems to affirm that this fear could be exorcised. To possess Beloved is partly to protect her from Sethe, and partly to repossess a part of herself that has not been realised. It could be viewed as both regression *and* growth, and her first response to Beloved is jealously to mother her.

The episode within the shed is one of a number where the sense of both connection and disconnection is very strong; as I will show in discussing two more of these episodes, they also incorporate certain passages which demand to be read in a specific *historical* context which functions as both an analogy and an integral part of their meaning. Those I will refer to are, first, the set of passages late in the novel which deal with the 'unspeakable thoughts, unspoken' of the three women alone in the house, and, secondly, the earlier passage which tells of Beloved's first physical appearance on the tree stump outside 124.

Morrison's placing of the passages on the women's thoughts is arresting in its narrative context, which strongly marks the distinction between the exterior and the interior through the boundaries of 124. Stamp Paid, coming as he hopes to make his peace with Sethe, is unable to get any further than the door of the house, since all around it are the 'roaring' voices of the dead and dispossessed. Within, the scene is correspondingly peaceful and excluding; all he sees, as he peers through the window, is the backs of Denver and Beloved, preoccupied only with each other.[24] Morrison's rendering of the women's interior 'voices' (in which speech and thought are indistinguishable) powerfully conveys that absorption. Indeed, the phrase with which they are introduced – 'unspeakable thoughts, unspoken' – is resonant with complexity. All that is here presented is implicitly not speakable, nor writable, yet it articulates the deepest level of self expression and dialogue between Sethe, Beloved and Denver. What they say is for themselves alone, interactive yet intensely private, inexpressible yet 'overheard' by narrator and reader. Throughout, the narrator's intimacy has helped to direct us towards this, but now that mediation is withdrawn. Sethe's outpouring of memories (pp. 200–4) is addressed both to Beloved and to herself, as if the two were one. All the incidentals and details of memory – as urgently meaningful as they are – come down to the central affirmation that Beloved is her daughter, as Sethe would have been a daughter to her own destroyed mother, who 'left' her. This restoration is thus not only the return of her own child, but the restoration of herself *as* a child; she projects Beloved in a maternal and filial fantasy as a perfectly dutiful daughter who 'came right on back like a good girl' (p. 203) and 'understands everything already', effectively denying Beloved the expression of *her* anger at the savage separation.[25] Here, memory is above all a path to explanation, and explanation a plea for forgiveness; ironically, all of it is framed by the declaration that 'I don't have to explain a thing', capturing the ambivalent innocence and guilt in Sethe's moving, involved narrative.[26]

Beloved's first stream of ideas, impressions, recollections is still more complex in its shifting of pronouns, identities, and bodily parts; hers is an open, seeking, concentrated language of elision, approaching most nearly Julia Kristeva's concept of the pre-Oedipal 'semiotic'.[27] In the spaces between words, as much as in the words themselves, the traces of desire – and loss – are strongly felt. Within its poetry (a poetry of recurrent themes, images and statements), Beloved refers above all to the place where she 'crouched' in the dark among others who were dying, and how Sethe went into the sea and left her. For her, it is an eternal present, 'All of it is now', and a large part of the experience being described is recognisably that of the slave ships, where the men 'without skin' – white men – bring less than is necessary to keep their cargo alive:

> I am always crouching   the man on my face is dead   his face is not mine   his mouth smells sweet but his eyes are locked   some who eat nasty themselves   I do not eat   the men without skin bring us their morning water to drink   we have none . . . someone is thrashing but there is no room to do it in   if we had more to drink we could make tears   we cannot make sweat or morning water so the men without skin bring us theirs
> one time they bring us sweet rocks to suck   we are all trying to leave our bodies behind. (p. 210)

Throughout the passage there persist ambiguous impressions of separation and connection, but Beloved is clear that the face of the man dying on top of her is not her own face, while the woman who has her face, and whose face she wants, is Sethe. Again, the self exists both subjectively and objectively, but never integrally, since the sea is the place where all connections are lost. In this narrative of suffocation, starvation and death merging with the struggle to join and survive, Morrison has placed Beloved directly within a historical experience which (as the baby daughter of a second-generation slave) she could not actually have undergone; the displacement here is backwards in time, appropriately to the time when the fragmentation began, and Sethe is a part of it too with the iron collar about her neck which Beloved wishes to bite off. The salve ship represents the very worst time of transition, and the dispossession of which Beloved speaks is having '"no one to want me to say me my name"'. The closing of this section is in a willed union with 'the face that left me' so that 'now we can join' (p. 213).

A major aspect of this semiotic discourse, intimately bound in with the impressions of the slave ships and Beloved's earliest memories of her mother picking leaves, is the struggle to represent the infant's still fluid sense of 'identity', 'self' and 'body'. It is a process in which apperception and mirroring are active, so that there is no settled distinction between nor unification of images, and images cannot be pressed into language. Beloved's very existence is merged in the face and responding smile of her mother, corresponding closely to what Winnicott has described as 'the mother's role of giving back to the baby the baby's own self':[28]

> I AM BELOVED and she is mine . . . how can I say things that are pictures   I am not separate from her   there is no place where I stop   her face is my own and I want to be there in the place where her face is and be looking at it too   a hot thing[29]

While the overriding impression in this passage is of the depth of that pre-Oedipal bond, there is also a sad irony in that the nearest Beloved comes to seeing herself as 'separate' is when she is lost into death. Dissolution is forced on her at the very point when a fragile process of individuation might begin, in the midst of becoming, and Beloved finds that she is 'going to be in pieces'[30] just when she was striving to join: '"I see me swim away   a hot thing   I see the bottoms of my feet   I am alone   I want to be the two of us   I want the join"' (p. 213). Beloved's will to return again is to *exist*, to 'find a place to be', to identify 'the face that left me' so that finally when this is achieved, 'Sethe sees me see her and I see the smile' (p. 213). Hence, the second section representing Beloved's consciousness begins as a more articulate, clarifying version of the first, establishing that recognition and union; it soon shifts into dialogue between Sethe and Beloved, sometimes returning to the ambiguous separation and merging of identities through complex use of pronouns ('will we smile at me?'), while Denver's voice begins to enter as a more wary consciousness warning against too much love. Where the previous section had been made up of statements, this becomes a series of questions, answers, pleas and reproaches – active, responsive and troubled.

While the rediscovery of possession and belonging here is deeply moving, none the less the troubled aspects lie within the very framework of the language, and arguably they are a prelude to a process which becomes progressively more destructive than constructive in the reuniting of Beloved with Sethe. That destructiveness resides partly in Sethe's desire to lose herself in her daughter – a feeling which she first equates with sleeping and dying (p. 204) – and even more in what Beloved herself cannot rationalise, articulate or understand. Even her rebirth is into a repetition of babyhood and early childhood, in her long exhausted sleeps, her incontinence, her craving for sweet things, her demands and tantrums as well as in her devotion. There is always that aspect of the child and of the dislocated being in Beloved which cannot be mediated, even though it so powerfully communicates with Sethe and Denver.

The same sense of disconnectedness is once more conveyed through historical reference when Beloved first appears at 124. As mystifying as she is, Paul D relates her bewildered state of mind and the slow and painful spelling of her name to his recollections of the crowds of stunned, exhausted Negroes wandering the roads after the Civil War had ended. Seeking their relatives against all the odds, they are only capable of spelling out their names or bearing them on scraps of paper for others to decipher (p. 52). As we are told, 'the War had been over four or five years then, but nobody white or black seemed to know it'; the wandering groups, 'dazed but insistent', are chiefly made up of women and children, while the adult men have either been killed or driven off, living by stealth on the run. The code they adopt for survival is also a mute, cautious one; partly as a defensive necessity (too much information only spells danger), partly because the stories of their fugitive lives are too charged with trauma:

> chased by debts and filthy 'talking sheets', they followed secondary routes, scanned the horizon for signs and counted heavily on each other. Silent, except for social courtesies, when they met one another they neither described nor asked about the sorrow that drove them from one place to another. The whites didn't bear speaking on. Everybody knew. (p. 53)

Again, Morrison has linked Beloved with a critical *transitional* point in black history, with the exhaustion (like her physical exhaustion) of the passage over from one era to another, the notional freedom from slavery still dissipated by the lack of any established framework within which freedom could be realised. What is stressed once more is the experience of dislocation, inarticulacy (whether through the pointlessness or the sheer danger of speech), and the near-impossibility of risking or achieving connections. What Paul D first supposes about Beloved, then, is by no means wide of the mark. She grasps, yet can barely understand, the depth of one of Morrison's 'three-woman utopian households',[34] we later see that (like the parallel household of *Song of Solomon*) it cannot sustain itself indefinitely.[35] Eventually, Denver's and Sethe's physical and spiritual starvation develops to a crisis. The paradox we have to face is that Beloved's claim on them (on Sethe especially) is both just *and* excessive, a literally wasting claim to which there would be 'no end'. The starvation is both the outcome and opposite to an abiding theme within the novel: the linking of memory with food and the preparation of food.[36] The point at which Denver decides that she must break the boundary of the house and seek help in contact with others also has to be understood in its connection (through analogy and through textual metaphors) with the only other time she experienced a brief period of community. This was when she tentatively crept over to peer in from a side window on the classes where Lady Jones was teaching other illiterate black children to write. At that time Denver is forthrightly invited in, and for the first time becomes part of a group, engaged in a shared, constructive exercise. It is a personal unfolding, a liberation in the 'magic' of the chalk: 'the little i, the sentences rolling out like pie dough'[37] (here it is *language* that is linked to food). What throws her back into immediate and literal deafness is the question put by her classmate Nelson Lord about her mother's past; she cannot bear to hear her mother's answer because she has latent memories of her own (prison and rats) that tell her the story is true.

The significance of this network is that Denver's enclosure in the prison, her self-enclosure in silence and deafness, and the now closed world of 124 begin to share common ground, even though Denver herself associates her fear of the prison and the trauma that closed her in silence with the *outside* world (p. 243). The reader may also be reminded of those passages in which Sweet Home is revealed as a delusory cradle where, despite Garner's comparative liberality, his slaves remain illiterate and powerless. Ironically, in so far as they have any choices, they choose (all but Halle) to remain in that state; as Paul D later reflects, they imagined themselves free and whole men because they were permitted: 'to buy a mother, choose a horse or a wife, handle guns, even learn reading if they wanted to – but they didn't want to since nothing important to them could be put down on paper' (p. 125). Garner, like any other slave master, appropriates them in giving them names, and the system of slavery itself dictates their real impotence: 'One step off that ground and they were trespassers among the human race. Watchdogs without teeth; steer bulls without horns; gelded workhorses whose neigh and whinny could not be translated into a language responsible humans spoke.'[38]

Within the context of slavery, language and all its written definitions may well appear no more than the instrument of the oppressor – Schoolteacher with his books and his coachbox full of paper arriving to

connection she is trying to make, and where she came from, all is
confused, she knows no names. In the time and place that Paul D
is thinking of, little is happening that could really be described as
Reconstruction;[31] it is only now that he is trying to make a tentative
homecoming, a settling down, just as Beloved is. This is one of the
reasons why, as far as she is concerned, he is in the way; each of them
is jealously convinced that there is only room for *one* to come home,
while for both of them, Sethe is the centre.

As to this homecoming, despite the vital differences which Morrison
has pointed to as distinguishing 124 from the plantation Sweet Home,[32]
there are also certain analogies. Both are places overcharged with meaning
which is intimately related to personal experience (meaning in which
some are included while others appear to be excluded), and both can and
do become places of enclosure. Denver's heartfelt dislike of stories about
Sweet Home is understandable, because it marks out the difference
between her own and Sethe's relationships to the past. Sethe was born
into slavery, Denver was born (at another significant transitional point)
in the waters of the Ohio River which formed the boundary between
slavery and a vulnerable freedom. She has been protected from the
worst of that experience, but still – for all her resentment of Sethe's
anecdotes – she knows that she is being kept from something. Sethe
is both unconsciously and consciously guarding the territory of her
memory, not only because it is a responsibility and a site of bottomless
terror for her, but because everything in it exists as 'rememory' and will
never cease to be a threat to her children:

> 'Someday you be walking down the road and you hear something or
> see something going on. . . . It's when you bump into a rememory that
> belongs to somebody else. Where I was before I came here, that place
> is real. It's never going away. Even if the whole farm – every tree and
> grass blade of it dies. The picture is still there and what's more, if you
> go there – you who never was there – if you go there and stand in the
> place where it was, it will happen again; it will be there for you,
> waiting for you. So, Denver, you can't never go there. Never.' (p. 36)

Because Denver knows what it is to be excluded from the past which
is such a deep link between Sethe and Paul D, and because she knows
what it is to be closed away from others in 124, she has an intuitive
recognition of what the baby ghost feels: 'lonely and rebuked'. Just as
Beloved feels rage at her exclusion from the living, so Denver feels
dispossessed of her father's memory when her mother and her lover
speak of him so that even 'her own father's absence was not hers' (p. 13).
Even as a ghost, Beloved's presence fills that gap for her, supplying 'the
downright pleasure of enchantment, of not suspecting but *knowing* the

things behind things' (p. 37). When her mother does tell stories about the past, Denver prefers to hear only the one that relates to her, the story of her own birth; and when this is recounted in the text (pp. 28–35), Morrison introduces two significantly different narrative patterns. The first begins with Denver, playing in her secret boxwood bower, then looking in at 124 from the outside and seeing her mother praying with the mysterious white dress holding her waist. In her mind, she connects the approach to the story of her birth (which begins 'way back') with the approach to 124, whose single front door can only be reached by a circuitous route from the back. It is as if all her history was invested in the house, yet this does not prevent her from feeling in some respects isolated from it. By contrast, the other narrative pattern takes the story well beyond Denver's exclusive concerns and conceptions of things. It moves us instead much further back, from the white dress which reminds Denver of the white girl (Amy) who helped at her birth, to the detailed account of the circumstances of Sethe's escape, to Sethe's childhood memories of trying to identify her own mother among the slave workers. Unobtrusively, Morrison has allowed the reader to connect the line of mothers, a genealogical link which serves to make us aware of what Denver does *not* know (and what Sethe barely recalls), because the links between families were ruptured by slavery.[33] For her own part, Denver can only draw her history from Sethe in fragments, which may be cut short at any moment of the telling.

The intensity that characterises the relationship between Denver and Beloved, then, lies in a shared need and a *mutual* feeding – in Denver's desire to know about the place Beloved came from, and of course to have a companion, and in Beloved's desire to find out from Denver about the shape of things in the world and the history of the living. It is important to recognise that the people living have their own present 'history' – that is, one which is understood in terms of shared experience and kin relationships – and in so far as Denver knows something about these, she has something valuable to offer Beloved. Even so, Beloved's deepest needs are always for Sethe; in her she is seeking the strongest of her connections. She says as much to her sister, brutally: ' "She is the one I need. You can go but she is the one I have to have" ' (p. 76).

The double isolation of Denver, her existence in a limbo somewhere between a lost past and a lonely present, is of great importance to the closing sections of the novel. The process begins with Sethe and Paul D cautiously opening the Pandora's box of their shared memories, and continues with Beloved herself as the chest of hidden treasure which her mother cannot bear to lose again. Once Paul D has left, the pattern becomes one of dangerous obsession, with Sethe feeding only on her guilt, and Beloved, like an over-demanding child or a succubus, growing fat on it. If at first we are enfolded in the self-sufficient warmth and break Garner's slaves, measure Sethe's head and inscribe her (with the ink she herself has made) as 'animal'. Or the newspaper cutting which reports Sethe's crime, in black marks which neither she nor Paul D can decipher and which Sethe knows will say all about the what and nothing of the reasons why. From the slave's and the ex-slave's point of view, nothing could seem more hostile and less relevant than this controlling word.[39] Yet historically, the first movements towards a degree of constitutional freedom and the first concerted attempts to teach literacy to blacks were taking place in the Reconstruction years.[40] For Denver, living in that time, the outside world still appears fearful, but communication is even so the keyword in her course of action at the novel's end. She rightly recognises that in order to survive she is going to have to reconnect, and that nothing the past can offer will make up for the loss of a future. Initially, she is passing on to a second 'mother' in her second encounter with Lady Jones, who reads her face with complete familiarity as if it were her child's and addresses her with maternal sympathy; yet Morrison also describes her inauguration into the world 'as a woman' in terms of a place which she reaches following 'a trail . . . made up of paper scraps containing the handwritten names of others' (p. 248). Gifts of food from others appear on the very tree stump where Beloved had formerly materialised, and Denver's personal connection with the donors begins through her deciphering the names they leave, or alternatively through identifying their plates, pie dishes and so on. From that halting beginning, she proceeds to risk conversations and the social encounters that conversations entail. She finally shares in the wider history that the community is able to fill in for her, but only on the condition that she in turn tells *them* everything. Thus, when Nelson Lord next speaks to her, 'she heard it as though it were what language was made for. The last time he spoke to her his words blocked up her ears. Now they opened her mind' (p. 252).

The period in which Denver opens up again to wider verbal communication and interaction is bound in with the renewal of her formal education, first through Lady Jones and later through the (white) Bodwins. Throughout this part of the narrative, we are never allowed to forget how Denver is bridging a world which is full of terror, even though she has only heard about the terror that lies beyond the confines of her house; but she finds that at this stage and in this place, it no longer need be quite so terrifying.[41] Likewise, Morrison seems concerned to show that, as history can be outlived, so language can be enabling, not only as an instrument of power but because it is one of the crucial means by which we express and communicate.[42] However compelling the claims of the past may be – and this novel never ceases to make them so – it cannot interpret itself for us; we can only develop that understanding. Beloved's final disappearance, the fading of her traces, is gradual but necessary; it happens quite simply as others progressively forget her. In part it is a willed forgetting, since 'remembering seemed unwise'; thus, 'although she has claim, she is not claimed'. Morrison's final statement, that 'it was not a story to pass on', none the less sustains a paradox in its double reference, voicing the concern with both connection and disconnection which is expressed throughout the text. Within the frame of the narrative, the black community has chosen to close the door on this particular claim, and we have been shown the reasons why. The narrator, on the other hand, *is* passing the story on, and to do so is unquestionably to acknowledge its claim, at the very time when the traces seem to be vanishing.

Notes

1. 'Living memory', *City Limits* (31 March–7 April 1988), 10–11.

2. James Baldwin also observes that 'in the context of the Negro problem neither whites nor blacks, for excellent reasons of their own, have the faintest desire to look back', but maintains that the past will 'remain horrible' for as long as it is not honestly assessed. Furthermore, 'This horror has so welded past and present that it is virtually impossible and certainly meaningless to speak of it as occurring, as it were, in time' (*Notes of A Native Son*, 1995; London and Sydney: Pluto Press, 1985, p. 6, xii).

3. Margaret Homans examines the question of language and its adequacy in the work of contemporary women writers, white and black; see ' "Her very own howl": The ambiguities of representation in recent women's fiction', *Signs* 9, 2 (1983), 186–205, and VALERIE BABB, '*The Color Purple*: Writing to undo what writing has done', *Phylon* 47, 2 (June, 1986), 107–16.

4. MICHAEL G. COOKE, *Afro-American Literature in the Twentieth Century: The achievement of intimacy* (New Haven and London: Yale University Press, 1984), p. 4; see also his general remarks on p. 14.

5. BERNARD W. BELL, *The Afro-American Novel and Its Tradition* (Amherst, Mass.: Massachusetts University Press, 1987), pp. 283–4; ROBERT SCHOLES, *The Fabulators* (New York: Oxford University Press, 1967), p. 12. Bell rightly points out that while many black modernist and postmodernist writers 'are definitely influenced by the traditions of Western literature and committed to the freedom of hybrid narrative forms', none the less their experience of racial oppression and their sense of responsibility means that most 'are not inclined to neglect moral and social issues in their narratives' (p. 284). See also ROBERT ELLIOT FOX, *Conscientious Sorcerers: The black postmodernist fiction of LeRoi Jones/Amiri Baraka, Ishmael Reed, and Samuel R. Delany* (New York and London: Greenwood Press, 1987).

6. 'Living memory', p. 11.

7. 'Unspeakable things unspoken: the Afro-American presence in American literature', *Michigan Quarterly Review* 28, 1 (1989), 1–34; 15–16.

8. See MICHAEL P. ROGIN, *Subversive Genealogy: The politics and art of Herman Melville* (New York, 1979; California: University of California Press, 1985).

9. ELLIOTT BUTLER-EVANS in *Race, Gender and Desire: Narrative strategies in the fiction of Toni Cade Bambara, Toni Morrison and Alice Walker* (Philadelphia: Temple University Press, 1989) follows Fredric Jameson in characterising postmodern discourse as entailing among other features 'the emergence of a schizophrenic textual structure; a displacement of history by "historicism", in which the past is reread and reconstructed in the present' (p. 152), and also cites Jean-François Lyotard's definition of the postmodern as 'that which searches for new presentations . . . in order to impart a stronger sense of the unpresentable' (pp. 152–3).

10. Extracts from a range of source material are reproduced in *Black Women in White America: A documentary history*, ed. Gerda Lerner (New York: Random House, Pantheon Books, 1972), including passages concerning the case of Margaret Garner on which Sethe's story is based (pp. 60–3). Despite the notoriety of the case, such acts of infanticide by slave mothers were not in fact uncommon.

11. Henry Louis Gates has observed that for the slaves themselves, the general absence of written records to mark out their lives and their past history, together with the fact of their illiteracy, amounted to a radical undermining of their sense of time and of self. 'Slavery's time was delineated by memory and memory alone. . . . the slave had lived at no time past the point of recollection' (*Figures in Black: Words, signs, and the 'racial' self* (Oxford: Oxford University Press, 1987), pp. 100–1).

12. These aspects of *Beloved* (New York: Plume, p.b. edition, 1988; first published New York: Alfred A. Knopf, 1987) are briefly but brilliantly explored by MARIANNE HIRSCH in *The Mother/Daughter Plot: Narrative, psychoanalysis, feminism* (Bloomington: Indiana University Press, 1989); see especially pp. 5–8. As she observes, the novel begins with the mother and allows her a voice to express her rage at the loss of a child, while it also considers deeply 'the hierarchy of motherhood over selfhood' (p. 7). It owes as much to the 'woman-centered' myth of Demeter and Persephone, with its emphasis on the cyclical plot of loss and rebirth, as it does to the linear and fatal Oedipus plot, although Sethe is 'neither the silent Jocasta nor the powerful Demeter' (p. 6).

13. Hirsch notes that 'Familial structures in this novel are profoundly distorted by the institution of slavery', and that whenever a nuclear family group begins to frame itself, it is 'repeatedly broken up as a *fourth* term either supplements or replaces the third' (p. 6).

14. Paul D has a special place in relation to women from the first, when Morrison emphasises their sense of frank intimacy with him (p. 17); they 'told him things they only told each other'. At the novel's end, Sethe carries over this same intimacy with him to express her particular sorrow as mother and as daughter and as a self (p. 272). Similarly, he thinks of her as a woman who can leave his humanity and manhood intact in the midst of slavery's humiliations, and piece together his fragmented self (pp. 272–3).

15. Morrison acknowledges that black women 'are of compelling interest to me' (see *Black Women Writers at Work*, ed. Claudia Tate (New York, 1983, Oldcastle Books: Harpenden, 1985, p. 119), but she repeatedly stresses in interviews the necessity for interaction between men and women and for an inclusive vision

encompassing both ('Living memory', p. 11, and 'Rootedness: the ancestor as foundation', in *Black Women Writers 1950–1980*, ed. Mari Evans, New York: Doubleday, Anchor Books, 1984, pp. 339–45). As she observes, in the circumstances in which Sethe is placed, she is her children, and also the community. However, Elliott Butler-Evans (*Race, Gender and Desire*, pp. 3–9) sees a tension between the discourses of race and gender in Morrison's work and in that of Alice Walker and Toni Cade Bambara.

16.   This model of 'rememory' is akin to Freud's model of the psyche, which moved away from the notion of linearity and 'stages of development' towards 'a theory of imbrication, parallels, simultaneity, and diachronology. . . . a complex "time" of space, not a simple "time" of place' (JULIET MITCHELL, *Psychoanalysis and Feminism*, Harmondsworth: Penguin, 1974, p. 22).

17.   SUSAN WILLIS, *Specifying: Black women writing the American experience* (Madison: University of Wisconsin Press, 1987), p. 102.

18.   SIGMUND FREUD, 'The "uncanny"' (1919), in *The Standard Edition of the Complete Psychological Works of Sigmund Freud*, trans., ed. and rev. James Strachey (1955; London: Hogarth Press, 1971), XVII. Reprinted in *New Literary History* 7 (1976), 619–45. See pp. 634, 641. Freud takes his hint from Schelling, that ' "*Unheimlich*" is the name for everything that ought to have remained . . . secret and hidden but has come to light' (p. 623), and dwells at length on the connotations of the word 'heimlich' as 'belonging to the house', 'intimate', 'not strange', and yet also (conversely) 'concealed, kept from sight . . . withheld from others'. The apparent contradictions in the use of the word are, he proposes, an expression of an overlapping meaning, a common ground within apparent difference; this is suggestive with regard to the qualities of 124 in *Beloved*.

19.   Morrison, 'Unspeakable things unspoken', p. 31.

20.   Morrison comments that black women 'seem able to combine the nest and the adventure', to be 'both inn and trail' (Tate, *Black Women Writers at Work*, p. 122); this encompasses the distinction between the 'male' and 'female' plot, and helps to point up the fact that what takes place in Sethe's house makes it *both* a haven and a trail.

21.   Morrison, *Beloved*, p. 35. The point at which Paul D is forced to remember is presented as Beloved's seduction of him, with the ambivalently sexual injunction to ' "touch me on the inside part and call me my name" '. To be made to *speak* her name is to enact a kind of 'performative', that is to declare and seal a bond which he has striven to suppress; it is followed by his intercourse with her, which opens up the sealed tobacco-tin of his memory and touches the 'red heart' in its place (p. 117).

22.   In another sense, Beloved could be described as the symptom of what the trauma of slavery entailed, so that the story unfolds as a case history would unfold, backwards from the phenomenon which confronts us and through the intricacies of how it came to be. See Mitchell, *Psychoanalysis and Feminism*, pp. 14, 20, 27.

23.   Beyond this specific context, there is a recognition here of the child's 'active wishes' towards the mother, expressed in the desire both to mother her and to kill her. 'There is a fear in both sexes of being killed by the mother and so there is a shift to activity in an aggressive death-wish against her' (Mitchell, *Psychoanalysis and Feminism*, p. 58).

24. Roberta Rubenstein, in *Boundaries of the Self: Gender, culture, fiction* (Urbana and Chicago: University of Illinois Press, 1987), refers to Gaston Bachelard's analysis of 'the values of inhabited space, of the non-I that protects the I' as an important one for women writers especially. Houses may appear 'other' yet intimate in this sense, or may themselves represent bodily boundaries (pp. 4–5). See also Frances Bartkowski, *Feminist Utopias* (Lincoln and London: University of Nebraska Press, 1989), chapter 4.

25. Beloved's repeated reproach at this primal deprivation, ' "You left me" '; is echoed by Sethe's sad declaration, ' "She left me" ', at the novel's end.

26. Innocence is much more clearly the keynote in Sethe's final recognition of Beloved's identity (p. 176), where the colour white is emphasised in the domestic scene of the pan of milk, the snow, the 'lily-white stairs' which Sethe ascends 'like a bride'. Again, Stamp Paid is outside, fingering the red ribbon of the lynched girl.

27. Kristeva writes of 'a divided subject, even a pluralised subject, that occupies, not a place of enunciation, but permutable, multiple, and mobile places' (*Desire in Language*, Oxford: Basil Blackwell, 1986, p. 111).

28. D.W. Winnicott, *Playing and Reality* (Harmondsworth: Penguin, 1971); acknowledging 'the delicacy of what is preverbal, unverbalized, and unverbalizable except perhaps in poetry', Winnicott goes on to ask:

    'What does the baby see when he or she looks at the mother's face? . . . what the baby sees is himself or herself. In other words the mother is looking at the baby and *what she looks like is related to what she sees there.* (p. 131)

    See also Mitchell, *Psychoanalysis and Feminism*, pp. 39–40. Ronnie Scharfman challenges the idea of the self-alienation or splitting of the subject entailed in the mirroring process as propounded by Jacques Lacan and Jean Paul Sartre, arguing that because of identification with the mother the process may be different for girl children ('Mirroring and mothering in Simone Schwarz-Bart's *Pluie et vent sur Télumée miracle*, Paris: Editions de Seuil, 1972; and Jean Rhys, *Wide Sargasso Sea*, Yale French Studies 62, 1981, 88–106).

29. See also Steven Marcus, 'The psychoanalytic self', *Southern Review* 22 (1986), 308–25.

30. The way in which the body is figured in Beloved's passage and in some other parts of the novel can be related to Lacan's representation of the *pre*-mirror stage, 'a period in which an infant experiences its body as fragmented parts and images', figured in images of 'dismemberment . . . devouring, bursting open of the body' (Ellie Ragland-Sullivan, *Jacques Lacan and the Philosophy of Psychoanalysis*, London and Canberra: Croom Helm, 1986, pp. 18–19).

31. Eric Foner takes issue with Morrison's representation of the Reconstruction years as 'a time of unrelieved sordidness and corruption', arguing that this echoes a long-standing misrepresentation of the positive accomplishments of that period ('The canon and American history', *Michigan Quarterly Review* 28.1, 1989, 44–9). However, Morrison has previously spoken of the unusual split in Ohio, between the northern part representing freedom and the southern part, 'as much Kentucky as there is, complete with cross burnings' (Tate, *Black Women Writers at Work*, p. 119).

32. 'Unspeakable things unspoken', p. 31; the difference lies in the absence of adjectives or connotations applied to 124, while Sweet Home is marked by

the postures of 'arrivistes and estate builders . . . laying claim to instant history and legend'.

33. This disruption of the family, and the need to survive that rupturing, still presents an important issue for black women and black feminists; see ANGELA Y. DAVIS, *Women, Race and Class* (New York: Random House 1981; New York: Vintage Books, 1983), pp. 14–15, DEBORAH A. KING, 'Multiple jeopardy, multiple consciousness: the context of a black feminist ideology', *Signs* 14.1 (1988), 42–72, and ALICE WALKER's *In Search of Our Mothers' Gardens* (New York: Harcourt Brace Jovanovitch, 1983; London: The Women's Press, 1984).

34. Willis, *Specifying*, p. 106.

35. Morrison comments on this in *Black Women Writers*, ed. Evans, p. 344.

36. *Beloved*, pp. 16–17, 73.

37. It is significant that the letter 'i' is the one singled out here, representing Denver's fragile sense of an unfolding self, her sense of herself as a subject and of 'becoming' through the command of language symbolised by writing.

38. Denver also remembers her father's attitude to these issues as recounted by Baby Suggs; Sixo declared that it would

    make him forget things he shouldn't and memorise things he shouldn't and he didn't want his mind messed up. But my daddy said, If you can't count they can cheat you. If you can't read they can beat you. They thought that was funny. (p. 208)

39. Morrison stresses a fundamental difference between this coercive use of the word (where 'definitions belonged to the definers') and the Word which is 'given' to Baby Suggs, a suasive Call rather than a directive sermon. Compare the sermon of Mr Pike in HARRIET JACOBS' *Incidents in the Life of a Slave Girl*, Section XIII (in *The Classic Slave Narratives*, ed. Henry Louis Gates, New York: New American Library, 1987, pp. 397–8).

40. See note 31 above, and *Black Women in White America*, ed. Lerner, pp. 92–113. Henry L. Gates also observes, 'In literacy was power . . . the correlation of freedom with literacy not only became a central trope of the salve narratives, but it also formed a mythical matrix out of which subsequent black narrative forms developed' (*Figures in Black*, p. 108; see pp. 104–8 generally).

41. Denver's fear is partly offset by the intervention of her grandmother's voice, telling her not that the world is safe but that she must go on anyway. The importance of the link with Baby Suggs strongly resembles that of grandmother and granddaughter in Schwarz-Bart's *Télumée* (see Scharfman, note 28 above). Scharfman argues that 'through her grandmother's eyes, Télumée comes to know the world', including its political reality. She also prepares Télumée for connection with the community in which she will again be mirrored (pp. 91–6).

42. Julia Kristeva's assertion in *About Chinese Women* that we can only gain entry to social experience and to the 'temporal scene' of political affairs at the cost of 'identifying with the values considered to be masculine (dominance, superego, *the endorsed communicative word* that institutes stable social exchange)' is castigated by Gayatri Chakravorty Spivak as a directive for 'class- and race-privileged literary women . . . identifying the political with the temporal and linguistic'. See the extract from *About Chinese Women*

reprinted in *The Kristeva Reader*, ed. Toril Moi (Oxford: Basil Blackwell, 1986), pp. 138–59, and Spivak, 'French feminism in an international frame', *Yale French Studies* 62 (1981), 154–84; p. 158.

ANDREA NYE ('Woman clothed with the sun: Julia Kristeva and the escape from/to language' *Signs* 12, 4, 1987, 664–86) makes a case for acknowledging 'interpersonality' in language in the face of Kristeva's 'idealism', which (following Lacan) 'reduces all to the "I" and "me"; "you's" and "they's" are seen only as projections of an otherness first discovered within the subject' (pp. 682–3). Interpersonality, argues Nye, is 'not missing from language but only from Kristeva's representation of it', and it can be presented as 'the obvious reality of linguistic communication' (p. 683).

Further critical attention to Morrison's historicism is to be found in MAE G. HENDERSON, 'Toni Morrison's *Beloved*: Re-membering the Body as Historical Text', in *Comparative American Identities: Race, Sex and Nationality in the Modern Text*, ed. Hortense J. Spillers (New York: Routledge, 1991), pp. 62–86; ROBERTA RUBENSTEIN, 'Pariahs and Community', in *Toni Morrison: Critical Perspectives Past and Present*, ed. Henry Louis Gates, Jr., and K.A. Appiah (New York: Amistad Press, 1993), pp. 126–58. See also, by Toni Morrison, 'Unspeakable Things Unspoken', *Michigan Quarterly Review* 28, 1 (1989): 1–34, and 'Rootedness: The Ancestor as Foundation', in *Black Women Writers (1950–1980): A Critical Evaluation*, ed. Mari Evans (Garden City, NY: Anchor Press, 1984), pp. 339–45.

11 History, Postmodernism, and Louise Erdrich's *Tracks**

NANCY J. PETERSON

Nancy J. Peterson discusses Louise Erdrich's *Tracks*, a novel that dramatizes a familiar scenario in American history: the losing battle of a group of Native Americans to maintain their land and tribal culture against the incursions of homesteaders of European origin. *Tracks* dramatizes the late nineteenth- and early twentieth-century experience of the Turtle Mountain Chippewa in the northern plains of the United States. Peterson's critical approach is less anthropological than historiographic. She begins by invoking the poststructuralist conflation of history and narrative, citing Barthes, Derrida, Hayden White and others on the 'textuality of history'. Weighing this conflation against what Erdrich's novel demonstrates – that writing their history 'has become one way for marginalized peoples to counter their invisibility' – Peterson refuses this poststructuralist position. Instead, she cites Linda Hutcheon's distinction in *The Politics of Postmodernism* between ontology and epistemology – that is, between the past (events) and history (narrative). She demonstrates how Erdrich embodies Hutcheon's assertion that '[p]ast events are given *meaning*, not *existence*, by their representation in history'. Peterson concludes that Erdrich creates a 'new historicity' to deal with the 'crisis of history surrounding Native Americans'.

In a 1986 review of Louise Erdrich's second novel, *The Beet Queen*, Leslie Marmon Silko argues that Erdrich is more interested in the dazzling language and self-referentiality associated with postmodernism than in representing Native American oral traditions, communal experiences, or history. In Silko's view, the 'self-referential writing' that Erdrich practices 'has an ethereal clarity and shimmering beauty because no history or politics intrudes to muddy the well of pure necessity contained within language itself' (179). Whether or not one agrees with Silko's characterization

* Reprinted from *PMLA* 109, 5 (October 1994): 982–94.

of postmodernism, with her criticism of *The Beet Queen* as apolitical and ahistorical, or with the implicit agenda that she proposes for Erdrich, it is true that reviewers of *Love Medicine* and *The Beet Queen*, the first two novels of Erdrich's recently completed tetralogy, tend to praise Erdrich's lyrical prose style and to applaud her subtle treatment of Native American issues.[1] Erdrich's novel *Tracks*, published in 1988, almost seems to answer Silko's criticisms of *The Beet Queen* by overtly engaging political and historical issues.[2] But writing such a novel did not come easily to Erdrich: she put the original 400-page manuscript for *Tracks* aside for ten years, and only after she had worked backward in time from *Love Medicine* to *The Beet Queen* did she take it up again and begin to link it to her already completed novels about contemporary generations of Chippewa and immigrant settlers in North Dakota.

Erdrich's difficulty in fleshing out this historical saga is symptomatic of a crisis: the impossibility of writing traditional history in a postmodern, postrepresentational era.[3] It seems epistemologically naive today to believe in the existence of a past to which a historian or novelist has unmediated access. Radicalized in the poststructuralist movement, language and linguistics have not only led to skepticism concerning access to the past but also instigated a debate about whether historical narratives can be objective representations or are (merely) subjective constructions of a researcher's and a culture's ideologies. Following Lacan, Saussure, and Althusser, prominent poststructuralists have without regret or nostalgia asserted the textuality of history – that there is no direct access to the past, only recourse to texts about the past. Even the facts of history are constructed in language, as Barthes observes: 'It turns out that the only feature which distinguishes historical discourse from other kinds is a paradox: the "fact" can only exist linguistically, as a term in a discourse, yet we behave as if it were a simple reproduction of something on another plane of existence altogether, some extra-structural "reality"' (153). Similarly deconstructing the linkage of history and the real, Derrida demonstrates in *Of Grammatology* the degree to which historicity is linked to writing: 'Before being the object of a history – of an historical science – writing opens the field of history – of historical becoming' (27). And elsewhere in *Of Grammatology*, Derrida makes the now famous pronouncement 'there is nothing beyond the text' (158), which indicates to some readers a radical ontological and epistemological skepticism that makes history pure fiction, with no referential link to events of the past.[4] In the light of this cultural-intellectual trajectory, which radically destabilizes history, it is no wonder that Erdrich grappled with the difficulties and possibilities of telling a historical tale.

The crisis Erdrich confronts may also be viewed as an outgrowth of the Nietzschean view of history as a disease, an affliction, a burden. In

The Use and Abuse of History, Nietzsche argues that historicizing is abusive when it overdetermines the present and future or when it leads to paralysis rather than action. Indeed, Erdrich's lengthy hiatus from working on *Tracks* might be read as a symptom of this Nietzschean paralysis; certainly Erdrich's comments about *Tracks* echo a Nietzschean anxiety regarding the weight of history: 'I always felt this was a great burden, this novel' (qtd. in Stead). Extending Nietzsche's concerns about 'an excess of history', Hayden White asserts in a chapter titled 'The Burden of History' that 'it is only by disenthralling human intelligence from the sense of history that *men* will be able to confront creatively the problems of the present' (*Tropics* 40; emphasis added). Thus, as White suggests elsewhere, many historians and theorists have become interested in 'getting out of history' ('Getting' 2).

Getting out of history, however, is a strategy not available to those who have never been in it, as Diana Fuss observes. Fuss challenges White's position by arguing that '[s]ince women as historical subjects are rarely included in "History" to begin with, the strong feminist interest in forging a new historicity that moves across and against "his story" is not surprising' (95). The same claim can be made on behalf of other groups that have been marginalized in traditional historical accounts – Native Americans, Asian Americans, African Americans, Latinos and Latinas, and so forth. Indeed, the burden of history is markedly different for writers from such groups since a lack of historical representations can be as burdensome as an excess. For writers such as Erdrich, a part-Chippewa woman, the history of America has often been exclusionary – a monologic narrative of male Anglo-American progress that constructs others as people without history. Writing history (as historical novels and in other forms) has thus become one way for marginalized peoples to counter their invisibility. And yet at the very moment when they are writing their own accounts of the past, the possibility of writing history seems to have become passé.[5]

In *The Politics of Postmodernism*, Linda Hutcheon offers a way to rework and renegotiate these contradictions. She argues that postmodern culture does not renounce historical representation altogether but questions its status:

> To say that the past is only *known* to us through textual traces is not . . . the same as saying that the past is only textual, as the semiotic idealism of some forms of poststructuralism seems to assert. This ontological reduction is not the point of postmodernism: past events existed empirically, but in epistemological terms we can only know them today through texts. Past events are given *meaning*, not *existence*, by their representation in history. (81–2)

The distinction Hutcheon makes here between ontology and epistemology, between the past (event) and history (narrative), is crucial. To participate in the 'ontological reduction' that Hutcheon speaks of is to question or even to deny that the Holocaust occurred – or the massacre at Wounded Knee or slavery or the internment of Japanese Americans during World War II and so on. To use poststructuralism to question the occurrence of these horrific events is to inflict further violence on the victims and survivors.[6] And yet a historical position in postmodern culture necessitates the recognition that history is a text composed of competing and conflicting representations and meanings – a recognition that precludes any return to a naive belief in transparent historical representation or even in realism.

Writers like Erdrich thus face a vexing set of issues: unrepresented or misrepresented in traditional historical narratives, they write their own stories of the past only to discover that they must find a new way of making history, a way of 'forging a new historicity', in Fuss's terms. Erdrich works toward a new historicity through the novel. Analyzing the need for literature to intervene in 'the consequent, ongoing, as yet unresolved *crisis of history*' surrounding the Holocaust, Shoshana Felman and Dori Laub argue that 'literature becomes a witness, and perhaps the only witness, to the crisis within history which precisely cannot be articulated, witnessed in the given categories of history itself' (xviii). Similarly, Erdrich's historical novel, *Tracks*, enables readers to think through the issues and the stakes involved in the crisis of history surrounding Native Americans.

The past as reference point

Tracks poignantly portrays the history of the Turtle Mountain Chippewa's struggle to keep their land in the late nineteenth and early twentieth centuries.[7] Throughout the novel, a tribal elder, Nanapush, tries to change the course of events so that the contestation over land tenure between the tribe and white settlers, which culminates in the battle over Fleur Pillager's land, will not destroy the tribe. Fleur, one of the few unassimilated full-bloods among the Anishinabeg (Chippewa), has been allotted a valuable tract of timber-filled land adjoining Matchimanito Lake.[8] Although Nanapush does his best to retain Fleur's claim to the land, white lumber interests turn United States government policy to their advantage, and in the end, Fleur's land is lost.

Tracks opens with an elegiac description of the plight of the Chippewa at the turn of the century. Nanapush, one of the novel's first-person narrators, tells Lulu, Fleur's daughter, the history of their people. I quote and analyze the passage at length because it serves as a microcosm of Erdrich's method throughout the novel.

> We started dying before the snow, and like the snow, we continued to fall. It was surprising there were so many of us left to die. For those who survived the spotted sickness from the south, our long fight west to Nadouissioux land where we signed the treaty, and then a wind from the east, bringing exile in a storm of government papers, what descended from the north in 1912 seemed impossible.
>
> By then, we thought disaster must surely have spent its force, that disease must have claimed all of the Anishinabe that the earth could hold and bury.
>
> But the earth is limitless and so is luck and so were our people once. Granddaughter, you are the child of the invisible, the ones who disappeared when, along with the first bitter punishments of early winter, a new sickness swept down. The consumption, it was called by young Father Damien, who came in that year to replace the priest who succumbed to the same devastation as his flock. This disease was different from the pox and fever, for it came on slow. The outcome, however, was just as certain. Whole families of your relatives lay ill and helpless in its breath. On the reservation, where we were forced close together, the clans dwindled. Our tribe unraveled like a coarse rope, frayed at either end as the old and new among us were taken. My own family was wiped out one by one, leaving only Nanapush. And after, although I had lived no more than fifty winters, I was considered an old man. I'd seen enough to be one. In the years I'd passed, I saw more change than in a hundred upon a hundred before.
>
> My girl, I saw the passing of times you will never know.
>
> I guided the last buffalo hunt. I saw the last bear shot. I trapped the last beaver with a pelt of more than two years' growth. I spoke aloud the words of the government treaty, and refused to sign the settlement papers that would take away our woods and lake. I axed the last birch that was older than I, and I saved the last Pillager. (1–2)

Erdrich's writing lays tracks here for a revisionist history and a new historicity. Nanapush's speech is revisionist because it defamiliarizes the popular narrative of American history as progress by showing the costs of that 'progress' to native peoples.[9] His speech to Lulu presents an alternative narrative of certain past events – epidemics ('the spotted sickness', 'consumption') and 'government papers' (various federal treaties and legislative acts) – that led to hardship and death for members of the tribe. Indeed, academic history 'documents' the 'fact' that Nanapush's historical account corresponds to past events: academic accounts report that North Dakota was afflicted with outbreaks of smallpox from 1869 to

1870 and of tuberculosis from 1891 to 1901. In fact, European diseases such as smallpox, measles, and tuberculosis are said to have been more deadly to native populations across the country than Indian–white warfare was.[10]

But Erdrich's work moves beyond documentation. Such historical 'facts' do not fully acknowledge the horror of depopulation and genocide, a horror that is marked in the opening passage by the shift from 'we' (the people) in the first paragraph to 'I' (the only surviving witness) in the last. The problem of relating the past in the form of history is further addressed in that passage when Nanapush instructs Lulu on the limits of his own narrative: 'My girl, I saw the passing of times you will never know.' Without denying the referentiality or importance of his historical narrative, Nanapush acknowledges that the real (or 'what really happened') is that which Lulu 'will never know' – in other words, the complexity of the past exceeds his (and anyone else's) ability to re-present it fully.[11] Nonetheless, Nanapush insists on telling this history to Lulu, for only by creating his own narrative can he empower her.

The question of power and empowerment is central: Erdrich's novel focuses not only on the limits of documentary history but also on its politics. 'Documents originate among the powerful ones, the conquerors', writes Simone Weil, a French Jew exiled to London during World War II. 'History, therefore, is nothing but a compilation of the depositions made by assassins with respect to their victims and themselves' (224–5). Indeed, a documentary history of Native America would necessarily be based on treaties, legislative acts, and other documents written or commissioned in the name of the United States government and subsequently (ab)used to take land from indigenous peoples.[12] The history of treaty making and treaty breaking with Native Americans demonstrates that such documents are not autonomous, objective, or transparent statements but texts open to interpretation by whoever is in power.

Since traditional written history, based on documents, is another kind of violence inflicted on oppressed peoples, *Tracks* features oral history. The opening of the novel uses oral storytelling markers: the narrator does not name himself, as he would not in a traditional face-to-face storytelling situation, nor is the addressee named except to designate her relationship to the narrator ('Granddaughter'); the last two paragraphs quoted above contain a rhetorical pattern typically associated with orality, repetition with variations ('I guided', 'I saw', 'I trapped'). Other oral markers signify Erdrich's rejection of the language of documents: Nanapush refers to 'the spotted sickness', not to smallpox or measles; he uses traditional oral tribal names (Nadouissioux, Anishinabe) rather than anglicized textual ones (Sioux, Chippewa); he speaks of 'a storm of government papers' instead of naming specific documents affecting the tribe. The turn to oral history in *Tracks* signals the need for indigenous peoples to tell their own stories and their own histories.

But the evocation of the oral in a written text implicates this counterhistory in the historical narrative that it seeks to displace. *Tracks* renders a history of Anishinabe dispossession that moves within and against an academic account of this history. Indeed, the need to know history as it is constructed both orally and textually is indicated by the contextual phrases that begin each chapter: first a date, including the designation of season(s) and year(s), then a phrase in Anishinabe followed by an English translation. This information establishes two competing and contradictory frames of reference: one associated with orality, a seasonal or cyclic approach to history, a precontact culture; the other linked with textuality, a linear or progressive approach to history, a postcontact culture. Erdrich creates a history of dispossession that moves between these frames, that is enmeshed in the academic narrative of dates and of causes and effects concerning the loss of land. Indeed, only by knowing this narrative can the reader attach any significance to the fact that chapter 1 begins in 1912.

The academic historical narrative that Erdrich uses and resists typically begins with the reservation period: the United States government initially disrupted tribal ways of life by establishing reservations so that the tribes were confined within strict boundaries while white settlers claimed more territory.[13] Then the Dawes Allotment Act of 1887 codified a turn in government policy, making it relatively easy to divide up land formerly held communally on reservations and to allot it to individual Indians.[14] The point of allotment was to convert tribes such as the Chippewa from a communal hunting and gathering organization to a capitalistic, individualistic agricultural economy. The allotted tracts were to be held in trust for twenty-five years (according to the original plan), during which time the owners would be encouraged to profit from the lands (by farming, selling timber rights, and so on) but would not be required to pay property taxes. The goal was to use the trust period to assimilate the Indians into the 'white man's' way of life so that they would become productive capitalists, capable of assuming the responsibilities of landholding – such as paying taxes – without further governmental intervention. But in 1906 Congress passed the Burke Act, which allowed the commissioner of Indian affairs to shorten the twenty-five-year trust period for 'competent' Indians. Under this act, those deemed competent were issued a fee patent rather than a trust patent; they could therefore sell or lease – or lose – their allotments. Then in a 1917 'Declaration of Policy', Commissioner of Indian Affairs Cato Sells announced that all Indians with more than one-half white blood would be defined as competent and thus would be made United States citizens and that they would be granted fee patents for their allotments. Although the professed original intent of allotment was to maintain Indian land ownership, the policy had the opposite effect: 'before allotment 139 million acres were held in trust for Indians. In 1934 when allotment was officially repealed, only 48 million acres of land were left and many Indians were without land' (Schneider 85). Some Indians lost their allotments because they could not pay the taxes after the trust period ended; others were conned into selling their allotments at prices well below the land's value; still others used their allotments as security to buy goods on credit or to get loans and then lost the land after failing to repay the debts.[15]

By opening in 1912 and proceeding through the disastrous consequences of Sells's 1917 declaration, *Tracks* dramatizes the tenuousness of land tenure for Native Americans. Although Nanapush tells Father Damien, 'I know about law. I know that "trust" means they can't tax our parcels' (174), the map Father Damien brings along – with its seemingly innocuous little squares of pink, green, yellow – shows that the agent's office is busy calculating who will be unable to pay. As Fleur, Nanapush, Eli, Nector, and Margaret work to raise money to pay their taxes, native traditions are forced into a new economic context: the Pillager-Kashpaw family gathers and sells cranberry bark, just as Turtle Mountain women sold herbs and roots to raise money, while Eli traps and sells hides, activities that Turtle Mountain men had to engage in (Murray 16, 29). These efforts raise just enough money. But when Margaret and Nector go to pay the taxes, they are told that they have enough only to pay the taxes on their own tract. No doubt Fleur's land is too valuable to be left to Indian ownership; the lumber is worth too much for the encroaching capitalists to leave it unharvested. As Nanapush recognizes, the late-payment fine levied by the agent is probably illegal, yet greed and desire divide the Anishinabeg, turning some, such as Bernadette Morrissey and Edgar Pukwan Junior, into 'government Indians', while prompting others – Margaret and Nector – to look out for themselves at the expense of communal values.

Erdrich's novel takes up (corresponds to) a turning point in the history of Anglo-Indian land conflicts. But the absence of names for the dates, acts, and other specifics attached to this kind of history displaces this narrative, even as it is invoked. That is, the tension and conflict at the heart of *Tracks* come into focus only when readers have some knowledge of the Dawes Allotment Act of 1887, but the text does not refer to the act directly.[16] The documentary history of dispossession that the novel uses and resists functions as an absent presence; the text acknowledges the way in which this historical script has impinged on the Anishinabeg but opposes allowing this history to function as the only story that can be told.

Moreover, by refusing to participate in such documentation, Erdrich's novel refocuses attention on the emotional and cultural repercussions that the loss of land entails. In one of the final events of the novel, the trees on Fleur's tract are razed. Fleur does not communicate the trauma of this event; she is not a narrator in the novel, though she is a central character (perhaps *the* central character). Instead, the razing of the trees accrues import through its link to two earlier episodes: Fleur's rape by the butchermen of Argus, North Dakota, after her victory at poker and Margaret's 'rape' by Clarence Morrissey and Boy Lazarre, who shave her head out of vengeance. In all three incidents, a nexus of forces – capitalism, sexism, violence – causes irreparable loss. Fleur has ways to redress these wrongs: she causes the tornado in Argus that maims and kills the butchermen, she reduces Boy Lazarre's speech to babbling because of his voyeurism, and she asks the manitou of Matchimanito Lake to drown men who cross her. But her powers cannot ward off the whites and government Indians greedy for land, money, and power. The novel portrays Fleur's loss in this sociocultural war as tragic: it is because traditional Anishinabeg like Fleur and Nanapush are dispossessed and because Native American clans and tribes are consequently fragmented that the tracks of Native American history and culture are so difficult to discern. At the end of the novel Fleur is said to walk 'without leaving tracks', a foreboding development since she is described by Pauline as 'the hinge' between the Chippewa people and their manitous and by Nanapush as 'the funnel of our history' (215, 139, 178). And yet, Fleur's disappearance and tracklessness at the end of the novel function as a present absence – her absence becomes a haunting presence in the narrative,[17] signifying the need for a reconceptualization of history, for a new historicity that both refers to the past and makes a space for what can never be known of it.

History as story

Tracks dramatizes the problematic nature of historical narrative, which cannot give voice to the (precontact) past directly – a notion figured in the character of Fleur – but which mediates that past in language and narrative. The novel works toward an understanding of history not as an objective narrative but as a story constructed of personal and ideological interests. Arising from this insight is a vexing theoretical issue: if history is just a story, how is it possible (or is it possible at all) to discriminate between one account of the past and other accounts?

The postmodern novel, which Hutcheon terms 'historiographic metafiction', characteristically foregrounds the fictionality of history. E.L. Doctorow exemplifies this position in his essay 'False Documents', where he argues that there is no difference between history and fiction, that both are narratives constructing the only world that can be known.[18]

Erdrich's work resists absolute groundlessness or relativity by contrasting the two narrators who construct the story of *Tracks*.

The second narrator – in addition to Nanapush – is Pauline, an orphaned young woman who is trying to make sense of the beginnings of sexual desire and her alienation from both the tribe and Anglo society. She eventually resolves this psychic tension by becoming a nun, but only after becoming pregnant, trying to force a miscarriage, and then forgetting about the illegitimate baby after it is delivered. Ignoring her part-Chippewa ancestry, she declares herself to be 'wholly white' in order to become a nun (137).[19] Pauline's narrative voice reproduces a phenomenon bell hooks describes in *Black Looks*: 'Too many red and black people live in a state of forgetfulness, embracing a colonized mind so that they can better assimilate into the white world' (191). Indeed, Pauline embraces Catholicism to repress her sexual desire and her connection to tribal culture; but the perverseness of this repression becomes apparent when she begins masochistically punishing herself for being unworthy.

Because of different identities and allegiances, Nanapush and Pauline narrate contrasting interpretations of the historical moment that unfolds in *Tracks*. Nanapush's elegiac historical saga runs contrapuntally with Pauline's assimilationist version, which interprets the Anglo settling of America as progress. Whereas Nanapush sees the allotment policy and the concomitant conversion of the Anishinabeg from hunters and trappers to farmers as the cause of starvation, poverty, and land loss, Pauline suggests that 'many old Chippewa did not know how to keep' – that is, to farm – their allotments and therefore deserved to lose them. In addition, while Nanapush views the destruction of Anishinabe society and culture as tragic, Pauline sees it in terms of Christian millennialism:

> [A] surveyor's crew arrived at the turnoff to Matchimanito in a rattling truck, and set to measuring. Surely that was the work of Christ's hand. I see farther, anticipate more than I've heard. The land will be sold and divided. Fleur's cabin will tumble into the ground and be covered by leaves. The place will be haunted I suppose, but no one will have ears sharp enough to hear the Pillagers' low voices, or the vision clear to see their still shadows. The trembling old fools with their conjuring tricks will die off and the young, like Lulu and Nector, return from the government schools blinded and deafened. (204–5)

Although part Chippewa, Pauline justifies the maneuvers of Christian and governmental authorities to dispossess the people of their land and culture. By teaching at Saint Catherine's, Pauline becomes one of the agents that blind and deafen children to their native culture and language. In contrast, Nanapush rescues Lulu from boarding school and its inevitable racism. This difference in perspective is also reflected in Pauline's eagerness to be renamed and reborn as Leopolda – a name given to her by white Christian authorities – in contrast to Nanapush's refusal to reveal his name to those authorities. Pauline recognizes that indoctrination into white culture is a kind of mutilation – her students will be 'blinded' and 'deafened' as she herself has been – but she sees this development as inevitable. The white Christian capitalists will win the cultural-epistemological war, in Pauline's view, and she will side with the victor.

Erdrich's novel holds Nanapush's and Pauline's antithetical views in tension, showing point of view to be inherent to any historical narrative. Moreover, these conflicting stories and visions reflect a tribal vision of the world that allows for competing truths and, according to Paula Gunn Allen, for gender balance rather than gender oppression.[20] Because historical events caused intact tribes and bands like the Turtle Mountain Chippewa to become split at the root, Nanapush's and Pauline's points of view are both necessary to provide an 'indigenous' account of what happens in *Tracks*.

Pauline's and Nanapush's narratives also correspond to the need to comprehend both textual and oral history. Nanapush tells the story to Lulu, but Pauline addresses no one in particular and thus implicitly addresses a reader, not a listener. The lack of an immediate audience also signifies Pauline's distance from oral tribal culture. But Nanapush himself cannot maintain an exclusively oral perspective. At one level he participates in the construction of a binary opposition that measures the distance between his narrative and Pauline's: oral 'tribal' values in contrast to textual 'Anglo' values. In the novel, an Anglo-American worldview is figured in terms of money and writing, systems that historically have been alien to the Anishinabeg and that Nanapush believes pose a threat to the tribe:

> I've seen too much go by – unturned grass below my feet, and overhead, the great white cranes flung south forever. I know this. Land is the only thing that lasts life to life. Money burns like tinder, flows off like water. And as for government promises, the wind is steadier. (33)

Nanapush sees that money is an unstable system of value: for white capitalists, it is the measure of progress, but for his people, '[d]ollar bills cause the memory to vanish' (174). Moreover, the white settlers prefer documents, written words, to fix their meaning, whereas the Anishinabeg rely on spoken words, oral promises, to wield power. Nanapush alone foresees that the white man's written promises are texts that are open to endless interpretation and reinterpretation:

[O]nce the bureaucrats sink their barbed pens into the lives of Indians, the paper starts flying, a blizzard of legal forms, a waste of ink by the gallon, a correspondence to which there is no end or reason. That's when I began to see what we were becoming, and the years have borne me out: a tribe of file cabinets and triplicates, a tribe of single-space documents, directives, policy. A tribe of pressed trees. A tribe of chicken-scratch that can be scattered by a wind, diminished to ashes by one struck match. (225)

Nanapush deconstructs the West's reverence for the written word as the stabilizer of meaning and tradition.

And yet Erdrich's novel points out that conserving Anishinabe history and worldview is not by itself a successful political strategy for withstanding the threat of colonialism. Nanapush recognizes that paper must be fought with paper, in contrast to Fleur, who trusts in tradition to prevent her land from being taken – 'She said the paper had no bearing or sense, as no one would be reckless enough to try collecting for land where Pillagers were buried' (174). Paradoxically, Nanapush's ability to adapt to these new conditions comes in part from his traditional namesake: the Chippewa trickster Naanabozho.[21] In fact, episodes in the story of Naanabozho parallel episodes in Nanapush's story. Both share the ability to come back to life after death or near death; both are noted for their keen ability to track people; both avenge wrongs committed on family members; both are powerful storytellers.[22]

Most significant, perhaps, is that both Nanapush and Naanabozho are tricksters who are sometimes tricked by others. Once duped, however, both adopt the techniques of the oppressor to even the score and to balance the distribution of power. For instance, when underwater spirits (manitous) kill his nephew, Naanabozho finds and wounds them, but they escape. He tracks them, however, and tricks the old woman who is doctoring them into divulging not only where the manitous are but also how to get past the guards and kill the manitous. He then kills the woman and skins her; putting on her skin, he disguises himself as the oppressor. His tactics succeed, and he avenges his nephew's death. Like Naanabozho, Nanapush assumes the guise of the oppressor to defuse the oppressor's power. For example, Nanapush allows Father Damien to write a letter recommending Nanapush as a tribal leader. In making this concession, Nanapush does not leave behind his earlier (traditional) skepticism concerning the written word; rather, he increasingly realizes that it is politically necessary for him not to stay outside the system of written discourse but to use the technology against itself. In fact, he becomes a bureaucrat and uses the 'authority' of the written word to save Lulu from exile at boarding school. Producing the birth certificate filed by Father Damien, which names Nanapush as Lulu's father,

Nanapush gains the power to call Lulu home. Ironically, Lulu's birth certificate – recognized as an authentic document by white authorities – is a lie, for Nanapush is not her biological father. And yet in a tribal view Nanapush is certainly Lulu's spiritual father, the one who mentors her and teaches her the old ways.[23] Thus, the piece of paper – both fiction and fact – becomes a clever tool for saving Lulu from assimilation.

The final paragraph of *Tracks*, describing Lulu's return from school, thus strikes a note of cautious optimism. As Lulu emerges from 'the rattling green [government] vehicle', she bears the marks of her encounter with Anglo-American authority: hair shorn, knees scarred from attempts to make her docile, attired in the shameful 'smouldering orange' of a runaway, Lulu at first seems alien to Nanapush and Margaret. As they watch, however, Lulu's prim, school-taught walk becomes a leap, and her face is electrified with Fleur's bold grin and white-hot anger. Marked by her encounter with the shapers of mainstream American history, Lulu is only 'half-doused' and will carry forward a trace of Anishinabe history and myth (226).

Nanapush's negotiation between the old ways and the exigencies of the present is the significant legacy he leaves to Lulu. He recognizes that it is no longer possible to rely solely on the oral tradition to pass down narratives of the past. To do so would be to end up like Fleur, the funnel of oral history silenced by white encroachment and by writing itself. As pure Indian, Fleur is a near-mythic figure – a source of inspiration for Lulu, but one that seems beyond emulation. (And this is perhaps why Fleur does not have a direct voice in the narrative.) Pauline, Fleur's opposite, does not offer Lulu a model either, for Pauline's assimilation into the dominant culture results in a voice that echoes hegemonic history. Moreover, by forgetting the past and radically rewriting her own identity and experience, Pauline signifies history as pure fiction with no referential value whatsoever – a position that Erdrich's work ultimately rejects.[24] By contrast, the link between Lulu and Nanapush, which the novel affirms, signifies a kind of history writing and history telling that neither relinquishes nor oversimplifies its referential debt to the past, that is grounded in tradition and ready to adapt to (post)modern conditions.[25]

Both Nanapush's and Pauline's narratives suggest that history is not objective and impartial, as traditional documentary historians assert. It is always constructed in the interests of a particular party or ideology. In his critique of documentary history, Dominick LaCapra asks historians to acknowledge that they are in 'dialogic interchange with the past', that is, that they rewrite the past in part out of presentist interests (139). What interests, then, resonate in Erdrich's late-twentieth-century reconstruction of Native American history? In part, Erdrich's work seems to be a reaction to the excesses of poststructuralism and postmodernism, which attempt to reject the referential function of language and narrative. Thomas M. Kavanagh suggests in *The Limits of Theory* that the unrecognized need for theory to 'master' its object means that 'the real itself' has become 'at best irrelevant' – because of its complexity and unpredictability (15). Similarly, Susan Stanford Friedman argues for a complex reactivation of certain terms poststructuralism has rendered 'taboo', such as *the author, agency, identity,* and *reference* (472–6). Erdrich participates in this revisionary project by renegotiating the postmodern crisis of history. The new historicity that *Tracks* inscribes is neither a simple return to historical realism nor a passive acceptance of postmodern historical fictionality.[26] *Tracks* takes up the crucial issue of the referentiality of historical narrative in a postmodern epoch and creates the possibility for a new historicity by and for Native Americans to emerge.[27]

Notes

1. Susan Pérez Castillo analyzes the Silko-Erdrich controversy at greater length than I do here. Unlike Silko, Julie Maristuen-Rodakowski argues that Chippewa history is significant in Erdrich's first two novels.

2. *Tracks* has prompted at least one other critic to consider some of the problems of writing American Indian history. See James D. Stripes, who questions whether Erdrich's novels can effectively 'challenge the conventions of "objective" history' (26).

3. In other words, the writing of history is at an impasse. Many academic historians continue to practice history using a scientific model that has been deconstructed in various ways. Writing history in such a documentary, objective mode is impossible today if the insights of poststructuralism are taken seriously. Of course it is much easier to theorize the need for a new history or historicity than actually to practice or to write one. See, for example, the essays in *Post-structuralism and the Question of History* (Attridge, Bennington, and Young), whose contributors ably theorize the need to rejoin Marxism and poststructuralism but do not articulate how to put into practice such a negotiation.

4. American philosophers of history have reacted to what they perceive as an extreme rejection of the referentiality of history by the French poststructuralists. Hayden White's work, for example, deconstructs the binary oppositions – fact and fiction, history and myth, history as art and history as science – on which history as an academic discipline has been constructed. Yet White has also called poststructuralism 'the absurdist moment in contemporary literary theory' (*Tropics* 261). Like the French poststructuralists, White is willing to acknowledge that, at the level of language, history is indistinguishable from literature, that neither one is more real than the other, but unlike the poststructuralists, White asserts the importance of historical meaning making as a human activity. White's

followers in America, among them Dominick LaCapra and Hans Kellner, have also tried to theorize a negotiation between poststructuralist analysis and referentiality.

5. In her essay 'The Re-imagining of History in Contemporary Women's Fiction', Linda Anderson acknowledges this concern on behalf of women but sets it aside by invoking its opposition, the return of naive bourgeois realism: 'The fear that post-structuralist theory could be disabling for women, making history disappear even before we have had a chance to write ourselves into it, needs to be set against another danger: the constant danger that by using categories and genres which are implicated in patriarchal ideology we are simply re-writing our own oppression' (134).

6. See Jean-François Lyotard's analysis of the possibility of representing the Holocaust in 'The *Différend*, the Referent, and the Proper Name'; in this essay he works against the excesses (and idealism) of his vision in *The Postmodern Condition* of locally produced and circulated *petits récits*, none of which is more authentic or valid than the others.

7. In examining Erdrich's sense of history, I refer to the history of the Turtle Mountain Chippewa because Erdrich belongs to the band and learned its history as she was growing up – as the acknowledgments sections of both *Tracks* and *Love Medicine*, as well as her comments in various interviews, attest; because it is the only band of Chippewa that was allotted land in North Dakota, the setting for Erdrich's novels; and because the dating of the novels corresponds loosely to historical events involving this band.

8. I have followed Gerald Vizenor's distinction between the terms *Chippewa* and *Anishinabe*: he points out that *Chippewa* is an appellation that white Americans gave to the tribes and used in treaties, whereas *Anishinabe* (plural *Anishinabeg*) is the older, oral, tribal-derived name (*People* 13–21). This distinction is important in Erdrich's novels; in *Tracks* only Nanapush uses the term *Anishinabe*.

9. Stephen Janus, the superintendent of the Turtle Mountain Chippewa in 1912 – the year in which *Tracks* opens – used words such as 'able-bodied' and 'expert' to describe the people and their transition to agricultural capitalism (Camp 31–2). His inflated, romantic view of Turtle Mountain Chippewa life is in sharp contrast to the opening of *Tracks*.

10. Carl Waldman reports that disease wiped out 25 to 50 percent of Native Americans, in contrast to Indian-white warfare, which killed an estimated 10 percent (166). The threat of tribal extinction from disease is exemplified by the Mandans, a Dakota tribe that 'declined from 1,600 to 131 during the smallpox epidemic of 1837' (166). This comparison raises the question why popular representations of Native American history dwell on warfare rather than on disease.

11. See David Lowenthal: 'No historical account can recover the totality of any past events, because their content is virtually infinite. The most detailed historical narrative incorporates only a minute fraction of even the relevant past; the sheer pastness of the past precludes its total reconstruction' (214–15).

12. The issue of (re)constructing American history from an Indian perspective as it relates to this politics of documentation is discussed in several essays in *The American Indian and the Problem of History* (Martin); see, in particular, the essays by Michael Dorris and Haunani-Kay Trask.

13. For a detailed documentary discussion of the United States government's mishandling of negotiations with the Turtle Mountain band, see Stanley N. Murray; Gregory S. Camp. I want to recount briefly part of this history here for my own purposes: motivated by the search for unsettled land and by a developing interest in fur trapping as a means of economic subsistence, the Turtle Mountain band of Chippewa came to what is now northern North Dakota in the late eighteenth and early nineteenth centuries as part of the Ojibwa migration from the East. The Turtle Mountain reservation was not established until 1882 (after treaties establishing reservations for other Indian nations and bands were drawn up), however, because the United States government wanted to relocate the band to Minnesota or Montana so that white settlers could have the land, while the band wanted to remain in North Dakota. Further exacerbating the Chippewa's difficulties, the United States government refused to count all persons in the band as tribal members; thus, despite the 1882 agreement to set aside 72,000 acres for the Turtle Mountain Chippewa, the government reduced the tract to 34,000 acres in 1884. This action led directly to the impoverishment of the Chippewa that continues today and that Erdrich poignantly depicts in *Love Medicine*. These historical events suggest a postmodern insight: an originally migratory (fluid) people is reduced by a conceptual framework to a fixed plot of land, a reserve situated on the United States–Canadian border; because tribal members cross the border freely, they are denied representation in the United States government's accounting.

14. Not all reservation lands throughout the United States were allotted. The stated motive of allotment – to open up 'surplus' land to settlement by whites – was a determining factor only where reservation lands were arable. Thus, 'most of the land cessions in this period occurred in the areas of greatest White interest: the Chippewa areas of Wisconsin and Minnesota, the Sioux country of North and South Dakota, and the Indian lands in central and western Oklahoma Territory' (Washburn 66). This kind of documentary information exposes a Foucauldian irony: regulations drawn up ostensibly to assist with land tenure for the Chippewa actually effected the loss of land. Perhaps the history of allotment as a regulating mechanism is figured in the postmodern ironies that almost always haunt Erdrich's characters, who are afflicted by a homelessness and rootlessness not shared by Silko's Laguna Pueblo characters, who occupy lands historically held by the tribe.

15. I am grateful to Donald Parman for his assistance with these historical details. Any errors are my own.

16. See Catherine Rainwater for an analysis of how conflicting narratives and cultural codes in Erdrich's novels produce a kind of alienation for the reader that can lead to 'epistemological insight' (422).

17. I have extended Robert Silberman's description of June in *Love Medicine* to characterize Fleur here (104). Two of Erdrich's other novels also revolve around the disappearance of a key mother figure: June dies in a blizzard at the beginning of *Love Medicine*, and Adelaide abandons her children by flying off in a plane at the beginning of *The Beet Queen*. Erdrich seems particularly sensitive to the social dislocations that these mothers experience and that fracture their families (see Wong). Moreover, the absence of these women – Fleur, in addition to June and Adelaide – is analogous to the omission of women from history.

18. '[H]istory is a kind of fiction in which we live and hope to survive, and fiction is a kind of speculative history . . .'; 'there is no fiction or nonfiction as we commonly understand the distinction: there is only narrative' (Doctorow 25, 26).

19. Pauline's desire to be 'wholly white' is understandable in the light of the discrimination that the Catholic Church practiced in nineteenth-century North Dakota. Valerie Sherer Mathes points out that Native American women were not allowed to join religious orders until the latter part of the century, when separate sisterhoods for Native American women were founded (22). One of the religious figures important in this movement was Francis Craft, a part-Mohawk priest who established a community of Native American sisters on the Fort Berthold reservation. Unfortunately, he forbade the women to eat meat, and 'because this was the mainstay of the Plains tribes' diets, their health slowly began to deteriorate' (24). By 1894 only five sisters remained, the others having died of tuberculosis or having left the order.

20. In fact, Erdrich has said that while writing *Tracks* she agonized over point of view until Michael Dorris, her husband and collaborator, remarked on the difference in self-conception between native and white peoples: 'Michael started talking about the Athapaskin Indians who live around Tyonek, Alaska, where he once hunted. In their language, there is no word for "I" – only "we"' (qtd. in Stead). See Allen's *The Sacred Hoop* for a valuable (and controversial) analysis of Native American women's empowerment in intact tribal communities.

21. Despite differing orthography, these names are consonant. The name *Naanabozho* has been transcribed in various ways: 'Manabozho', 'Nanabush', 'Wenebojo', and 'Nehnehbush', to cite a few. See Vizenor's 'Trickster Discourse' for an analysis of the trickster as a postmodern figure.

22. Although his analysis suffers from ethnocentrism, see Victor Barnouw for a transcription of Wenebojo stories ordered to compose a full narrative of Wenebojo's attributes and actions.

23. Hertha Wong argues that Nanapush is in fact the character 'who "mothers" most consistently throughout the novel' (185).

24. Erdrich's characterization of Pauline as afflicted by 'increasing madness' corroborates this argument (Stead).

25. The revised and expanded edition of *Love Medicine* makes clear even more than the original does that Lulu learns Nanapush's lesson well. A new story, 'The Island', reveals that Moses Pillager is the father of Lulu's first son, Gerry Nanapush, who – as his surname suggests – is a contemporary trickster. See also *The Bingo Palace*, where Lulu uses the media to create a politically effective image of herself in traditional dress, handcuffed by federal authorities.

26. My argument here runs parallel to Arnold Krupat's critique of the politics of postmodernism (see especially 8–25). My position differs from his, however, in that I carry out this critique *within* a postmodern framework.

27. I am grateful to Susan Stanford Friedman, Fiona Barnes, Geraldine Friedman, Patrick O'Donnell, and Aparajita Sagar for their willingness to read and discuss previous drafts of this essay.

Works cited

ALLEN, PAULA GUNN. *The Sacred Hoop: Recovering the Feminine in American Indian Traditions*. Boston: Beacon, 1986.

ANDERSON, LINDA. 'The Re-imagining of History in Contemporary Women's Fiction'. *Plotting Change: Contemporary Women's Fiction*. Ed. Anderson. London: Arnold, 1990. 129–41.

ATTRIDGE, DEREK, GEOFF BENNINGTON, and ROBERT YOUNG, eds. *Post-structuralism and the Question of History*. Cambridge: Cambridge UP, 1987.

BARNOUW, VICTOR. *Wisconsin Chippewa Myths and Tales*. Madison: U of Wisconsin P, 1977.

BARTHES, ROLAND. 'Historical Discourse'. *Introduction to Structuralism*. Ed. Michael Lane. New York: Basic, 1970. 145–55.

CAMP, GREGORY S. 'Working Out Their Own Salvation: The Allotment of Land in Severalty and the Turtle Mountain Chippewa Band, 1870–1920'. *American Indian Culture and Research Journal* 14.2 (1990): 19–38.

CASTILLO, SUSAN PÉREZ. 'Postmodernism, Native American Literature, and the Real: The Silko-Erdrich Controversy'. *Massachusetts Review* 32 (1991): 285–94.

DERRIDA, JACQUES. *Of Grammatology*. Trans. G.C. Spivak. Baltimore: Johns Hopkins UP, 1976.

DOCTOROW, E.L. 'False Documents'. *E.L. Doctorow: Essays and Conversations*. Ed. Richard Trenner. Princeton: Ontario Review, 1983. 16–27.

DORRIS, MICHAEL. 'Indians on the Shelf'. Martin 98–105.

ERDRICH, LOUISE. *The Beet Queen*. New York: Henry Holt, 1986.

——. *The Bingo Palace*. New York: Henry Holt, 1994.

——. *Love Medicine*. 1984. Rev. edn. New York: Harper, 1993.

——. *Tracks*. New York: Henry Holt, 1988.

FELMAN, SHOSHANA, and DORI LAUB. *Testimony: Crises of Witnessing in Literature, Psychoanalysis, and History*. New York: Routledge, 1992.

FRIEDMAN, SUSAN STANFORD. 'Post/Poststructuralist Feminist Criticism: The Politics of Recuperation and Negotiation'. *New Literary History* 22 (1991): 465–90.

FUSS, DIANA. 'Getting into History'. *Arizona Quarterly* 45.4 (1989): 95–108.

HOOKS, BELL. *Black Looks: Race and Representation*. Boston: South End, 1992.

HUTCHEON, LINDA. *The Politics of Postmodernism*. London: Routledge, 1989.

KAVANAGH, THOMAS M. Introduction. *The Limits of Theory*. Stanford: Stanford UP, 1989. 1–22.

KELLNER, HANS. *Language and Historical Representation: Getting the Story Crooked*. Madison: U of Wisconsin P, 1989.

KRUPAT, ARNOLD. *Ethnocriticism: Ethnography, History, Literature*. Berkeley: U of California P, 1992.

LaCAPRA, Dominick. *History and Criticism*. Ithaca: Cornell UP, 1985.

LOWENTHAL, DAVID. *The Past Is a Foreign Country*. Cambridge: Cambridge UP, 1985.

LYOTARD, JEAN-FRANÇOIS. 'The *Différend*, the Referent, and the Proper Name'. Trans. Georges Van Den Abbeele. *Diacritics* 14.3 (1984): 4–14.

——. *The Postmodern Condition: A Report on Knowledge*. Trans. Geoff Bennington and Brian Massumi. Minneapolis: U of Minnesota P, 1984.

MARISTUEN-RODAKOWSKI, JULIE. 'The Turtle Mountain Reservation in North Dakota: Its History As Depicted in Louise Erdrich's *Love Medicine* and *Beet Queen'. American Indian Culture and Research Journal* 12.3 (1988): 33–48.

MARTIN, CALVIN, ed. *The American Indian and the Problem of History*. New York: Oxford UP, 1987.

MATHES, VALERIE SHERER. 'American Indian Women and the Catholic Church'. *North Dakota History* 47.4 (1980): 20–5.

MURRAY, STANLEY N. 'The Turtle Mountain Chippewa, 1882–1905'. *North Dakota History* 51.1 (1984): 14–37.

NIETZSCHE, FRIEDRICH. *The Use and Abuse of History*. Trans. Adrian Collins. Rev. edn. Indianapolis: Liberal Arts, 1957. Trans. of *Vom Nutzen und Nachteil der Historie für das Leben*, 1874.

RAINWATER, CATHERINE. 'Reading between Worlds: Narrativity in the Fiction of Louise Erdrich'. *American Literature* 62 (1990): 405–22.

SCHNEIDER, MARY JANE. *North Dakota Indians: An Introduction*. Dubuque: Kendall, 1986.

SILBERMAN, ROBERT. 'Opening the Text: *Love Medicine* and the Return of the Native American Woman'. *Narrative Chance: Postmodern Discourse on Native American Indian Literatures*. Ed. Gerald Vizenor. Albuquerque: U of New Mexico P, 1989. 101–20.

SILKO, LESLIE MARMON. 'Here's an Odd Artifact for the Fairy-Tale Shelf'. Rev. of *The Beet Queen*, by Louise Erdrich. *Impact/Albuquerque Journal* 17 Oct. 1986: 10–11. Rpt. in *Studies in American Indian Literatures* 10.4 (1986): 177–84.

STEAD, DEBORAH. 'Unlocking the Tale'. *New York Times Book Review* 2 Oct. 1988: 41.

STRIPES, JAMES D. 'The Problem(s) of (Anishinaabe) History in the Fiction of Louise Erdrich: Voices and Contexts'. *Wicazo Sa Review* 7.2 (1991): 26–33.

TRASK, HAUNANI-KAY. 'From a Native Daughter'. Martin 171–9.

VIZENOR, GERALD. *The People Named the Chippewa: Narrative Histories*. Minneapolis: U of Minnesota P, 1984.

——. 'Trickster Discourse: Comic Holotropes and Language Games'. *Narrative Chance: Postmodern Discourse on Native American Indian Literatures*. Ed. Vizenor. Albuquerque: U of New Mexico P, 1989. 187–211.

WALDMAN, CARL. *Atlas of the North American Indian*. New York: Facts on File, 1985.

WASHBURN, WILCOMB E., ed. *History of Indian-White Relations*. Ed. William C. Sturtevant. Washington: Smithsonian, 1988. Vol. 4 of *Handbook of North American Indians*.

WEIL, SIMONE. *The Need for Roots: Prelude to a Declaration of Duties toward Mankind*. New York: Putnam's, 1952.

WHITE, HAYDEN. 'Getting out of History'. *Diacritics* 12.3 (1982): 2–13.

——. *Tropics of Discourse: Essays in Cultural Criticism*. Baltimore: Johns Hopkins UP, 1978.

WONG, HERTHA D. 'Adoptive Mothers and Thrown-Away Children in the Novels of Louise Erdrich'. *Narrating Mothers: Theorizing Maternal Subjectivities*. Ed. Brenda O. Daly and Maureen T. Reddy. Knoxville: U of Tennessee P, 1991. 174–92.

See also by JUDITH RAISKIN, 'The Art of History: An Interview with Michelle Cliff', *The Kenyon Review* 15, 1 (1993): 57–71.

12 Literary Foremothers and Writers' Silences: Tillie Olsen's Autobiographical Fiction*

Rose Kamel

In her discussion of Tillie Olsen's autobiographical fiction, Rose Kamel stresses the necessity of a shared history for women writers, and more specifically the necessity of a shared literary tradition. Her term 'literary foremothers' signals the need of women writers to know that other women have also written, and have also done so in spite of family responsibilities and economic obstacles. Reversing Harold Bloom's construction of male writers' anxiety of influence, Kamel shows how women writers seek literary precursors who can empower them to overcome their silence. Women's anxiety is caused not by excessive influence but by its absence.

Kamel's critical approach is biographical. She shares Toni Flores's phenomenological understanding of the 'authority of experience' of her subject, recounting Olsen's personal history and placing several of her books in the context of that history. Focusing on women's roles as dictated by social class and ethnic origin, she shows how Olsen was affected not only by the poverty of her lower-class Jewish immigrant origins but also by her eventual situation as a middle-class housewife and mother of four. Olsen may be compared to Virginia Woolf in her early exposition of the need for 'a room of one's own', but she adds to Woolf's feminist critique a strong feeling for social class and its consequences – for women, men and children.

Ellen Moers observes the consistent and fervent penchant for women writers, themselves rendered invisible by patriarchy, to read other women's writings, even those from whom they were geographically and culturally distanced:

---

* Reprinted from *MELUS* 12, 3 (Fall 1985): 55–72. This essay is now part of Kamel's *Aggravating the Conscience: Jewish American Literary Foremothers in the Promised Land* (New York: Peter Lang, 1998).

Not loyalty but confidence was the resource that women writers drew from possession of their own tradition. And it was confidence that until very recently could have come from no other source. . . . The personal give-take of the literary life was closed to them. Without it, they studied with a special closeness the works written by their own sex, and developed a sense of easy, almost rude familiarity with the women who wrote them.[1]

Moers supports this observation with extensive examples of nineteenth-century women writers reading their counterparts' lives and texts. She also notes that despite changes for the better in the lives of twentieth-century writers, women persist in reading and writing about other women:

In the case of most women writers, women's traditions have been fringe benefits superadded upon the literary associations of period, nation, and class that they shared with their male contemporaries.

In spite of the advent of coeducation, which by rights should have ended this phenomenon, twentieth-century women appear to benefit still from their membership in the wide-spreading family of women writers.[2]

Tillie Olsen's well-known apologia, *Silences*, a lamentation for her own sparse literary output, laments as well the waste of creative potential in working-class and women's lives. Indeed, mourning others' silences so exceeds mourning her lost opportunities, that the reader of *Silences* must diligently search Olsen's self-reference. Born in 1913 to East European Jews living in Nebraska, Olsen had no formal college education, but read voraciously. She became a longshoreman's wife raising four daughters in working-class San Francisco, taking low-paying jobs, becoming active in radical politics, and organizing unions. Only when the last of her children entered school could she concentrate on writing. A Ford grant apparently allotted Olsen the solitude she needed but 'time granted does not necessarily coincide with time that can be most fully used'.[3] Dishearteningly often, writer's paralysis diminished her productivity.

In 1954, when she was fifty, Olsen published the brilliant short story 'I Stand Here Ironing', having served a prolonged apprenticeship during which 'there was a conscious storing, snatched reading, beginnings of writing' and always 'the secret rootlets of reconnaisance' (p. 19). This reconnaisance involved not only obsessive reading but internalizing the lives of women writers, especially writers who were also mothers.

Their emergence is evidence of changing circumstances making possible for them what (with rarest exception) was not possible in the generations of women before. I hope and I fear for what will result. I hope (and believe) that complex new richness will come into literature; I fear because almost certainly their work will be impeded, lessened, partial. For the fundamental situation remains unchanged. Unlike men writers who marry, most will not have the societal equivalent of a wife – nor (in a society hostile to growing life) anyone but themselves to mother their children.[4]

Nowhere is Olsen's reading of another woman writer, her identification with this writer's concerns so elegaic, as in *Silences'* reprinting of Olsen's postscript to Rebecca Harding Davis's *Life in the Iron Mills*, a postscript longer than Harding's poignant novella. This postscript almost seamlessly blends critical analysis with self-scrutiny.

In particular, two patterns in Davis's life story parallel Olsen's. The first is an awareness of working-class hardship. Rebecca Harding Davis, daughter of an affluent businessman, moved to the raw industrial town of Wheeling, Pennsylvania, in 1936 when she was five, and spent most of her childhood observing the human misery trudging to factory and mine; she was separated from them by more than the pane of glass through which she watched them go by:

> It was in front of the Harding house that the long train of mules dragged their masses of pig iron and the slow stream of human life crept past, night and morning, year after year, to work their fourteen hour days six days a week. The little girl who observed it grew into young womanhood, into spinsterhood, still at the window in that house, and the black industrial smoke was her daily breath.[5]

The second was Davis's frustration as a woman. Of her father she later wrote: 'We were not intimate with him as with our mother.'[6] Secluded in his study with Shakespearian volumes, he refused to confront the give and take of domestic life and was cold to his wife and children:

> The household revolved around him. Her mother ('the most accurate historian I ever knew, with enough knowledge to outfit a dozen modern college educated women') was kept busy running the large household *noiselessly*. [my italics] (*LIM*, 71)

Consistently Olsen links Davis's sensitivity to both social/political issues and women's private misery. Graduating from a female seminary in Washington did not assuage Davis's 'hunger to know', and at seventeen she left Wheeling for Washington State College where she met Francis LeMoyne, a physician, radical reformer, and agnostic whose beliefs opposed those embodied by her family. LeMoyne's recognition of

197

' "the gulf of pain and wrong . . . the underlife of America" ' (*LIM*, 73) deepened Davis's perception of the twin injustices she would write of in *Margaret Howth* and *Life in the Iron Mills*.

First, however, the long literary apprenticeship. After graduation she returned to Wheeling, refusing the restrictions marriage would put on a Victorian wife, assuming, instead, the thankless role of eldest daughter:

> There was much help to be given her mother in the commonplace necessary tasks of caring for family needs, younger children; keeping the atmosphere pleasant especially for her father. The bonds of love were strong – she writes of the protection and peace of home – 'but they were not bonds of mutuality.' She had to keep her longings, questionings, insecurities secret. (*LIM*, 76)

Although Davis published minor works about problems of dutiful daughters, difficult fathers, and older women pariahs, articulating 'the vein of unused powers, thwarted energies, starved hopes; the hunger for a life more abundant than in women's sanctioned sphere . . .' (*LIM*, 79), it was thirteen years later that *The Atlantic Monthly* published *Life in the Iron Mills*, which brought her fame.

Painstakingly, Olsen follows the twists and turns of her literary foremother's life. Feted by the transcendentalist pundits at Concord, Massachusetts, Davis found their ideals false to reality.[7] Unmarried until the age of thirty-one, she was the object of pity, curiosity, sometimes scorn. When she finally married Richard Harding Davis (much to her father's dismay at losing his eldest daughter's unpaid services), Davis discovered that wife-motherhood drained her of time and energy to write, even though she continued to do so. From her husband and literary critics she received little encouragement or recognition. At the age of seventy-nine she died in relative obscurity (*LIM*, 152).

Davis's voice permeates at least two recurring themes in Olsen's autobiographical fiction: The tyranny of class struggle eroding the bodies and minds of workers and the children of workers; household drudgery and child care undermining a woman writer's creativity. But another still small voice, Olsen's own, is heard in her depiction of *Jewish* mothers and daughters struggling for selfhood in the promised land and of Jewish immigrant experience shored up in secular humanism. Characteristically, Olsen justifies her autobiographical focus by citing yet another woman writer, Ntozake Shange: 'When women do begin to write . . . we write autobiography. So autobiographically in fact that it's very hard to find any sense of any other reality.'[8]

When still a young writer in the 1930s, having assimilated Davis as foremother, and long before she ever heard of Shange, Tillie Olsen wrote *Yonnondio*, a clumsy yet powerful depiction of a working-class family driven from a rural village to a hog-slaughtering factory in the midwest where all succumb to grinding poverty and spiritual attrition.

Yonnondio's title is taken from Walt Whitman's poem. It undercuts the good grey poet's celebrating an America with limitless space, endless opportunity. Not that Olsen doesn't share Whitman's vision of collective human dignity; like Davis, Whitman's *contemporary*, She is outraged at an ideal being betrayed:

> When in 1861 industry was considered at all, it was as an invasion of pastoral harmony, a threat of materialism to the *spirit*. If working people existed – and nowhere were they material for serious attention, let alone central subject – they were 'clean-haired Yankee mill girls,' . . . or Whitman's 'workwomen and workmen of these states having your own divine and strong life.' (*LIM*, 88)

Anna and her daughter Maisie respond as intensely as Whitman did to nature. The nature images suggest an extension of women's bodies – 'the trees dipped and curtsied, the corn rippling like a girl's skirt'; the clouds are likened to Anna's belly big with child.[9] But nature aligned with ruthless capitalism blights their lives, becomes a domesticity yoked to industrial waste: 'Indeed they are in hell: indeed they are the damned, *steamed, boiled, broiled, fried, cooked*, geared, meshed' (*Yonnondio*, 180).

Olsen's compiling of passive verbs links two spaces inhabited by working women. The first renders the stifling August air of a slaughterhouse where at a temperature of 108° immigrant women swelter below in 'casings', their task to dismember hog carcasses because men working on the floor above cannot endure the stench of pigs' blood and entrails. The second is Anna's kitchen, where she rhythmically stirs jam, tends a sick child while other children tap her flagging energy. Anna also is 'geared and meshed'; she thinks of drowned children while softly singing a childhood song, 'I saw a ship a'sailing'. In this context the sea fantasy obliquely evokes the pivotal immigrant experience Olsen will return to in 'Tell Me a Riddle'.

In *Yonnondio*, the plaintive immigrant voice only faintly infuses Anna's American dream:

> School for the kids Maisie and Willie Jim her Protestant husband working near her, . . . lovely things to keep, brass lamps, bright tablecloths, vines over doors, and roses twining. A memory unasked plunged into her mind – her grandmother bending in such a twilight over lit candles chanting in an unknown tongue, whitebread on the table over a shining white tablecloth and red wine – and she broke into song to tell Jim of it. (*Yonnondio*, 88)

These occasional roses succumb to the struggle for bread. Linking factory and kitchen drudgery makes inevitable the reduction of iron-willed humans to scrap; in such an environment, analogous to Upton Sinclair's *The Jungle*, it is small wonder that Anna loses her baby, takes sick, and dies.

> Earth sucks you in, to spew out the coal, to make a few bellies fatter. Earth takes your dreams that a few may languidly lie on their couches and trill 'How exquisite' to be paid dreamers. (*Yonnondio*, 8).

Far more than her faint allusion to Jewish immigration, Anna suggests Davis's Korl Woman, the central metaphor in *Life in the Iron Mills*. Fashioned in pig iron by Hugh Wolfe, the wretched miner in Davis's story, this sculpture is 'a nude woman's form, muscular, grown coarse with labor, the powerful limbs instinct with some one poignant longing. One idea: there it was in the tense muscles, the clutching hands, the wild, eager face . . .' (*LIM*, 32). Hardly a Galatea, the Korl Woman symbolizes nearly all Olsen's narrator-personae, from Anna to Eva in 'Tell Me a Riddle', women of extraordinary potential wasted by capitalism and patriarchy. Whether pure or scrap, the iron image resonates throughout Olsen's texts.

'I Stand Here Ironing' depicts a nameless mother-narrator, who, having received a phone call from her daughter Emily's high-school guidance counselor that Emily is an underachiever, pushes an iron to and fro across the board on which Emily's dress lies shapeless and wrinkled. The narrator begins 'dredging the past and all that compounds a human being'. Her thoughts flow with the rhythm of the iron as she attempts to grasp the 'rootlet of reconnaisance' to explain why it was that her oldest child was one 'seldom smiled at'.[10] What would appear as understandable reasons – the Depression, the nineteen-year-old mother, who at her daughter's present age worked at menial jobs during the day and at household chores at night, the iron necessity that made her place Emily in a series of foster homes, the desertion of her first husband, bearing and rearing four other children of a second marriage, all clamoring for attention – should account for Emily's chronic sorrow; but somehow they do not. Necessity dominating the mother's life could have tempered Emily, but the reader soon perceives that there may be another reason why Emily and the mother-narrator are silenced counterparts. The mother has remarried, but material comforts, an emotionally secure middle-class existence, cannot assuage her loneliness. Never having experienced the celebratory rituals of working-class communality, middle-class anomie distances her from other women. Her entire adult life has been interrupted by child care described by Olsen quoting another women writer:

My work 'writing' is reduced to five or six hours a week, always
subject to interruptions and cancellations . . . I don't believe there is
a solution to the problem, or at least I don't believe there is one which
recognizes the emotional complexities involved. A life without children
is, I believe, an impoverished life for most women; yet life with
children imposes demands that consume energy and imagination at
the same time, cannot be delegated – even supposing there were a
delegate available.

Quoted from Sally Bingham in *Silences*, 210.

In 'I Stand Here Ironing', characteristic stylistic clues embedded in
the occasionally inverted syntax, run-on sentences interspersed with
fragments, repetitions, alliterative parallels, an incantatory rhythm evoke
the narrator's longing not only for a lost child but for a lost language
whereby she can order the chaotic dailiness of a working mother's
experience.

She was a beautiful baby. The first and only one of our five that was
beautiful at birth. You do not guess how new and uneasy her tenancy
in her now-loveliness. You did not know her all those years she was
thought homely, or see her pouring over her baby pictures, making
me tell her over and over how beautiful she had been – and would be,
I would tell her – and was now to the seeing eye. But the seeing eyes
were few or non-existent. Including mine.

. . .

Ronnie is calling. He is wet and I change him. It is rare there is such a
cry now. That time of motherhood is almost behind me when the ear is
not one's own but must always be racked and listening for the child to
cry, the child call. We sit for awhile and I hold him, looking out over
the city spread in charcoal with its soft aisles of light. 'Shoogily', he
breathes and curls closer. I carry him back to bed, asleep. *Shoogily*. A
funny word, a family word, inherited from Emily, invented by her to
say: *comfort*. (ISHI, 2 & 9)

Emily's word play appears rooted in Yiddish (*shoogily – meshugah*) and
there is something archetypically talmudic in her fascination with riddles
(for which a younger sibling gets recognition) 'that was *my* riddle, Mother,
I told it to Susan . . .' (p. 9), foreshadowing the leitmotif Olsen will
orchestrate in 'Tell Me a Riddle'. When language inventiveness fails to
mitigate against Emily's lack of achievement at school, when she tries and
fails to authenticate herself, she escapes into another's role. Desperate for
attention, identity, she responds to the mother's suggestion that she try

out for a high school play – 'not to have an audience is a kind of death' (*Silences*, 44) – and becomes a comic crowd pleaser to the sound of thunderous applause. Thus, Emily finally commands some attention and affection and to a limited extent a control of life's randomness. Nonetheless, only articulation through language can free her from oppression. Silenced at home she lacks and will probably continue to lack centrality.

The story ends with the mother still ironing out the wrinkles in Emily's dress; like Emily she is 'helpless before the iron', aware that this Sisyphus-like ritual cannot atone for the past, nor can she ultimately answer the riddle Emily poses within and without the family constellation.

. . .

Olsen has given the closest reading possible to silenced writers, demonstrating two basic premises underlying their writing. The first, an ongoing tension between an artist (worker, Black, woman, Jew) in need of a voice, and a silence societally imposed, psychically internalized. The second, an imperative to find an audience for that energy, that authentic voice, an audience unlike the wealthy dilettantes in *Life in the Iron Mills*, fascinated by the Korl Woman while they allow its sculptor to rot in prison. If *not* to find an audience is always a kind of death, discovering the responsive reader valorizes the obscured artists' suffering and strength, giving them the power to formulate riddles we have never addressed, let alone redressed. As Harold Bloom has explained, literary forefathers have always influenced their writing sons, often causing them the 'anxiety of "this" influence'. For Tillie Olsen, literary foremothers help engender and empower otherwise silenced women writers.

Notes

1. ELLEN MOERS, *Literary Women: The Great Writers* (New York: Anchor Books, 1977), p. 64.

2. Moers, pp. 67–8.

3. TILLIE OLSEN, *Silences* (New York: Delta Press: 1978), p. 21.

4. *Silences*, p. 19.

5. See Olsen's postscript, 'A Biographical Interpretation' in REBECCA HARDING DAVIS, *Life in the Iron Mills or The Korl Woman* (Old Westbury: The Feminist Press, 1972), p. 69.

6. Olsen learned this, having perused all of Davis's writings 'accessible to me for reading', from letters, official biographies and old issues of *The Atlantic*

Monthly. She writes that Davis (who said 'Literature can be made out of the lives of despised people' and 'you, too, the future reader, anonymous must write') absorbed this dictum increasingly over the years. See footnotes to *Life in the Iron Mills*, pp. 157–8.

7. Olsen devotes an entire paragraph to her literary foremothers. See *Silences*, p. 32. See also pp. 31, 196–212 and *passim*.

8. *Silences*, p. 242.

9. TILLIE OLSEN, *Yonnondio: From the Thirties*, (New York: Delacorte Press, 1974), pp. 43, 61. Hereafter cited in the text as *Yonnondio*.

10. TILLIE OLSEN, 'I Stand Here Ironing', in *Tell Me a Riddle*, (New York: Delta Books, 1961), p. 12. Subsequent references to 'O Yes' and 'Tell Me a Riddle' are to this edition and hereafter cited in the text.

Also relevant is ELAINE NEIL ORR, *Tillie Olsen, and a Feminist Spiritual Vision* (Jackson: University Press of Mississippi, 1987).

13 A Perfect Marginality: Public and Private Telling in the Stories of Grace Paley*

Victoria Aarons

In her essay on the short fiction of Grace Paley, Victoria Aarons follows several of the essays in this volume in emphasizing the importance of storytelling for Jewish women writers. She analyses the thematic and structural role that storytelling takes in their fiction, eventually combining this essay with another one, 'Talking Lives: Storytelling and Renewal in Grace Paley's Short Fictions', to comprise a chapter in her book-length study, *A Measure of Memory: Storytelling and Identity in American Jewish Fiction*.

Aarons balances the social and the psychological functions of storytelling. If, in previous essays, the emphasis has been on the creation of a collective history, here storytelling is also and equally a means of 'making selves', a relational process of self-discovery. Aarons relates the 'community of memory' created by storytelling to the responsibility of the individual teller to tell her stories, because individuals' stories bring people together. Aaron connects Paley's literary style to the oral style of storytelling, and finds it similar to the style of late nineteenth- and early twentieth-century Eastern European Yiddish writers such as Sholom Aleichem, and to contemporary Jewish writers such as Tillie Olsen and Isaac Bashevis Singer.

> It was possible that I did owe something to my own family and the families of my friends. That is, to tell their stories as simply as possible, in order, you might say, to save a few lives.[1]

So resolves Grace Paley's narrator in the short story 'Debts' as she – like so many of Paley's narrators – begins to make public, to reinvent, personal history. These lines, spoken by a narrator who is also a character dramatized in the story, suggest that Paley at once thematizes the act of telling stories in her fiction and employs storytelling as a fundamental

* Reprinted from *Studies in Short Fiction* 27, 1 (1990): 35–43.

narrative structural device. The resolve to 'tell' stories, as set forth by
Paley's narrator in 'Debts', illustrates by no means simply a classic
storytelling prelude, which frames a story within a story. More to the
point, Paley's narrators reflect an urgency to tell stories. For them,
recording the lives of their families and friends becomes a *necessity*
which can be heard in the immediacy in their individual and collective
voices; it is the 'debt' that Paley's narrator 'owes'.[2] One might well
claim that virtually all of Paley's stories call attention to *telling* in one
sense or another (many of the titles of the stories themselves reflect this
preoccupation: 'A Man Told Me the Story of His Life', 'The Story Hearer',
'Zagrowsky Tells', 'Listening', and the like). For Paley and her host of
character-narrators, telling becomes the collective experience of *bearing
witness*, the making public of personal mythologies, validating both self
and community. Through her skillful use of terse, simple language, Paley
creates a community of shared belief and experience. It is this communal
experience that is reinforced through the words of her narrators,
characters who tell their stories and the stories of their families and
friends. The dramatic unfolding of these narratives, derived from the
tension created by Paley's stark and unsparing use of language,
underscores, paradoxically, a source of hope and optimism for her
characters. For, in verbalizing and thus making real individual histories,
telling stories serves as a means of connecting, of creating a community
in which Paley's narrators and characters may indeed 'save a few lives'.
It is this saving power of storytelling, the merging of public and private
discourses, that moves Paley's short fiction and demonstrates the
life-affirming force of memory enlivened through community.

Paley's characters cry out to be heard, to connect with others, believing
that, in doing so, they will imbue their lives with meaning. In 'Listening',
for example, Faith (a reappearing character who governs the telling in
many of Paley's stories)[3] is confronted by her friend Cassie, who, angered
that she has been omitted from Faith's stories, feels that her identity has
been denied. In her characteristic mixture of irony and humor, Paley
constructs a character who steps into the narrative to demand
characterization, so to speak, to assert her place in the unfolding of the
story. In doing so, she demands a kind of public approbation from her
friend, the narrator of the story:

Listen, Faith, why don't you tell my story? You've told everybody's
story but mine. I don't even mean my whole story, that's my job. You
probably can't. But I mean you've just omitted me from the other
stories and I was there. In the restaurant and the train, right there.
Where is Cassie? Where is *my* life? . . . you even care about me at least
as much as you do Ruthy and Louise and Ann. You let them in all the
time; it's really strange, why have you left me out of everybody's life?[4]

On the one hand, as Cassie makes clear above, it is her responsibility to tell her *own* story, to take control over her own life. On the other hand, however, individuals do not live in isolation from each other in Paley's fictional universe. They have a responsibility to one another, to include one another in the telling of stories, in the making and reinforcing of reality. And they do so carefully, deliberately. In leaving her friend out of the stories she tells, Faith has essentially denied her a reality. Furthermore, in omitting Cassie from her story, Faith prevents her from participating in the community. Cassie's plaintive tone is very suggestive here; it calls attention to her *need* to be a part of 'everybody's life', an ongoing communal heritage. Cassie, of course, is the narrator's invention, just as Faith is Paley's fictive creation. Paley's self-conscious, reflexive narration here renders her own authorial position ironic. She, as writer, invents and thus gives life to her characters. Their utterances, however fictive, enliven them, make them real. And what makes this passage so compelling is the implied relation between self and others, and the reminder of the storyteller's responsibility to tell and, in so doing, to bring together the lives of her friends. In recognition is affirmation, is self-identity. Faith responds to her friend by acknowledging her outrage: 'It must feel for you like a great absence of yourself' (210).

Storytelling thus becomes a process of discovery, a *making of selves* for Paley's characters, but a making of selves *in relation to others*, to a community of belief, a community of shared values. I am reminded here of the 'community of memory' and the creative, enduring power of such 'communities' set forth by Robert N. Bellah, et al., in *Habits of the Heart:*

> Communities, in the sense in which we are using the term, have a history – in an important sense they are constituted by their past – and for this reason we can speak of a real community as a 'community of memory', one that does not forget its past. In order not to forget that past, a community is involved in retelling its story, its constitutive narrative, and in so doing, it offers examples of the men and women who have embodied and exemplified the meaning of the community. These stories of collective history and exemplary individuals are an important part of the tradition that is so central to a community of memory.[5]

The 'community of memory' for Grace Paley's characters depends upon a coming-to-terms with the past, which, by necessity, is comprised of the ethical choices and circumstances of others. These choices, of course, determine possibilities for the future. In 'The Immigrant Story', for instance, Jack tells the haunting story of his parents' past. Polish immigrants who have lost three sons to famine, they live out the remainder of their lives – sorrowfully, from Jack's point of view – in

America. Their story becomes the vehicle, the filter, through which Jack views the world: 'Isn't it a terrible thing to grow up in the shadow of another person's sorrow?'⁶ Jack can't let go of his parents' past because in it he views his own agency, his own participation and thus compliance. In describing their lives in America, he concludes his story:

> They are sitting at the edge of their chairs. He's leaning forward reading to her in that old bulb light. Sometimes she smiles just a little. Then he puts the paper down and takes both her hands in his as though they needed warmth. He continues to read. Just beyond the table and their heads, there is the darkness of the kitchen, the bedroom, the dining room, the shadowy darkness where as a child I ate my supper, did my homework and went to bed. (175)

The abrupt closure of Jack's story, the matter-of-fact, abbreviated rendition of the narration at large, suggests a combination of reluctance and urgency – an uneasy compulsion to tell. Jack's 'memory' of his parents' past is fictionalized in the *telling* of it, fictionalized in such a way that he can see it in the light of his own day, making their lives *real* in the telling. It is this connection between memory and stories, community and a shared past, that we find in Paley's unique voice and in the varied voices of her narrators.

It is, in no small part, this multi-layered narrative interplay of voices that enriches Paley's fiction so dramatically. Her short stories, characteristically related in first-person narration, are 'told' by characters in conversational style, a necessarily abbreviated form of address, because they speak a language that the other characters understand. Paley creates a linguistic community based on shared assumptions about how the world *works*: her characters speak the same language, as it were, and recognize that in talking – in conversations about people, living and dead, about experiences, about politics, love, children – they are giving meaning to the past and so create a 'community of memory' out of shared stories. In, for example, 'Friends', a small group of women, friends for a generation, sit at the bedside of their dying friend, another woman whose own child died. Their gathering is defined by storytelling – stories of their pasts, collective and individual, and of the lives of their children. In recollecting the past, in naming the dead child of their dying friend, the women bring her back to life: 'I wanted to say "Abby" the way I've said "Selena" – so those names can take thickness and strength and fall back into the world with their weight',⁷ affirms the narrator.

Individual tragedies are embraced by the community here, as they always are in Paley's stories. But the community is selective and, more often than not, gender-defined. In 'Listening', for example, Faith responds to Jack's question of why she doesn't tell stories 'told by women about women' by claiming, 'those are too private' (203). However, there is virtually no distinction between public and private for Paley. Faith's reluctance here to tell Jack stories about women speaks to the establishment of and belief in a community of women, which provides mutual strength and support. By its very nature, telling stories is a public act, but one which gives meaning to private sorrow, personal suffering, and tragedy. However, in the telling – and this is what makes words so powerful for Paley's characters – sorrow is mitigated. The act of telling provides hope; it suggests a future because the private is shared and preserved in the memory, in the language, of others. And this, finally, for Paley, defines community. Dena Mandel argues in 'Keeping Up with Faith: Grace Paley's Sturdy American Jewess' that Paley's Faith Darwin, in particular, functions as 'an emblem of hope in a hopeless world'.[8] I would go on to argue that hope exists not only in the ways in which Paley's narrators live in the world, but also in the ways in which they *talk about* living in that world. Talk enlivens the past for Paley's characters as well as ensures a future: 'You grab at roots of the littlest future', says the narrator in 'Friends', 'sometimes just stubs of conversation' (83) – as a stronghold on life. It is these 'stubs of conversation' with which Paley creates a community into which we too are drawn, since, as John Clayton contends in a very interesting essay, 'Grace Paley and Tillie Olsen: Radical Jewish Humanists', 'it is our common life, our common pain, that concerns her. . . . In the stories of how many modern writers do we hear of collective experience?'[9]

This 'collective experience' is achieved through the active telling voices of Paley's characters. And this community can only occur and remain intact if the stories are told. Paley's narrator in 'Debts' tells us: 'There is a long time in me between knowing and telling' (9). Such invention is a process of making knowledge, a process refined. In creating characters who tell their own stories and the stories of their friends, Paley is able to bring to her fiction a multiplicity of perspectives. This coming-together of diverse points of view enriches our reading experience and, perhaps even more to the point, provides us with a more complete worldview, suggesting to us – as it does to her characters – the possibilities for life. Paley as the implied author who invents characters, dramatic situations, and actions, remains behind the scenes, as it were, allowing her characters to speak for themselves. In this way, Paley is very much in the tradition of the late nineteenth-century/early twentieth-century Eastern European Yiddish writers such as Sholom Aleichem, who made a place for Yiddish fiction, who formed a written tradition of Jewish storytelling in which we can locate such contemporary Jewish writers as Issac Bashèvis Singer and Tillie Olsen. Sholom Aleichem, the great Yiddish realist and humorist, creates in his short fiction the qualities of oral storytelling – an orality, preserved in written prose, that has continued to be a fundamental characteristic of Jewish literature.[10]

The orality in Paley's fiction contributes to the fluidity of her prose and engages the reader in what often appears to be direct address with the character-narrators. In constructing characters who become narrators, the tellers of their own tales, Paley's characters resemble the monologists in Sholom Aleichem's early stories of ordinary *shtetl* Jews – Jews who relate their troubles, their complaints, to the writer Sholom Aleichem. In doing so, Sholom Aleichem's monologists seek vindication. The monologist in the short vignette 'Gitl Purishkevitch' is typical in beseeching the writer, Sholom Aleichem, to record the injustices of her life: 'do I deserve having people laugh at me and poke fun at me, having everyone's tongue wagging about me? . . . This town's made up of wags, numbskulls and loafers. . . . Write them up so that the whole world will know about them. Write it all down so that not a single one of them will escape being written up.'[11] Like Sholom Aleichem's narrator, Paley's characters believe, more often than not, that making public their personal inequities will give them control over their lives; through the telling they, in fact, secure a future. How like Sholom Aleichem's monologist is Paley's character-narrator Zagrowsky, in 'Zagrowsky Tells':

> since I already began to tell, I have to tell the whole story. I'm not
> a person who keeps things in. Tell! That opens up the congestion a
> little – the lungs are for breathing, not secrets. My wife never tells,
> she coughs, coughs. All night. Wakes up. Ai, Iz, open up the window,
> there's no air. You poor woman, if you want to breathe, you got to tell.
> So I said to this Faith, I'll tell you how Cissy is but you got to hear
> the whole story how we suffered.[12]

I emphasize the connection between such seemingly unrelated writers because both Sholom Aleichem and Grace Paley are masters of the construction of dialogue in the short-story form.[13] Both not only construct characters who, as I've said, are compelled with such urgency to tell their life-stories, but also write about them with a mixture of affection and irony. Their characters are ordinary people, *not* exemplary individuals noted for exceptional deeds. Or perhaps I should say, they are exemplary *because* they are ordinary – recognizable, identifiable people whose lives revolve around common occurrences. When asked to record the life of a stranger's grandfather, 'a famous innovator and dreamer of the Yiddish theatre', Paley's narrator in 'Debts' declines, saying, 'I owed nothing to the lady who'd called' (10). She opts to tell, rather, a story about the family of her friend Lucia. By no means, however, are we meant to believe that the quotidian is any less tragic than the extraordinary. The very stuff of ordinary dialogue is full of tragic possibilities, as 'Listening' demonstrates. In this story, the narrator overhears a conversation in which two men dispassionately discuss the timing and relative merits of suicide. Paley's characteristically understated tone underscores the pathos in the lives of her speakers. It is, indeed, *in* the ordinary that Paley's narrators uncover a rich and complex heritage.

Again I refer to Robert Bellah's description of a 'community of memory', a community constructed of the stories of ordinary people:

> The stories that make up a tradition contain conceptions of character, of what a good person is like, and of the virtues that define such character. But the stories are not all exemplary, not all about successes and achievements. A genuine community of memory will also tell painful stories of shared suffering that sometimes creates deeper identities than success. . . . And if the community is completely honest, it will remember stories not only of suffering received but of suffering inflicted – dangerous memories, for they call the community to alter ancient evils. The communities of memory that tie us to the past also turn us toward the future as communities. They carry a context of meaning. . . . (153)

It is this context of meaning that allows for identification and community. John Clayton, in defining the underlying Judaism in Paley's fiction, argues that Paley establishes a community based on a 'radical Jewish humanism' (41), a communal sense of Judaism as a recognition of suffering, of the role of the oppressed, as a kind of 'populist politics' (42) and, moreover, that the value in such a culture is preserved through her stories of ordinary people living out lives with which we can identify. While I agree with Clayton that Paley's fiction is grounded in Judaism – that her fiction indeed reflects and affirms a Jewish heritage, the heritage of the immigrant, the outsider – I think that her stories speak even more powerfully to a universal human experience, an experience defined by seeming antitheses: public and private, traditional role expectations and feminism, suffering and hope, life and death. It is in the resolution of these tensions that Paley's characters and narrators survive. And they survive through the telling, through the making of fictions, through the integration of their collective pasts, their communal experiences and beliefs.

Nowhere more poignantly do we find this relation between invention and reality than in the brilliantly constructed story 'A Conversation with My Father'. The dramatic situation of this story is, on the surface, relatively simple. The narrator, a writer, is at the bedside of her father, who makes of her a request: ' "I would like you to write a simple story just once more," he says, "the kind de Maupassant wrote, or Chekhov, the kind you used to write. Just recognizable people and then write down what happened to them next." '[14] The narrator agrees, despite the fact that it's the kind of writing she has 'always despised' (162), and the body of the narrative is governed by her invention and revision of a story constructed for her father. It is a story about a woman who joins her son and his friends in becoming junkies, only to find herself alone, abandoned by her son, who opts for health food and a clean life instead. It is a story, says the narrator, 'that had been happening for a couple of years right across the street' (162). Fiction, reinforced by reality becomes the governing metaphor for the frame story as well. The two 'stories' work together: the 'outer' story, the narrator's conversation with her father; and the 'inner' story, the story she constructs to please him.

Her story, however, does not please him. He wants motive, character development, plot – 'the absolute line between two points' (162). She can't give this to him because, in her estimation, such a story 'takes all hope away. Everyone, real or invented, deserves the open destiny of life' (162). What we come to discover, in the dramatic unfolding of the frame story, is that the narrator's insistence upon what she describes as 'the open destiny of life' is, beyond anything else, self-protective. After several drafts of her story, in which her protagonist's life ends in despair, she constructs a hopeful story of a woman who has options. Yet the narrator's father insists on a tragic ending to her story. In this moving dialogue between the narrator and her father, we come to appreciate the source of the story's tension:

> 'Yes,' he said, 'what a tragedy. The end of a person.'
> 'No, Pa,' I begged him. 'It doesn't have to be. She's only about forty. She could be a hundred different things in this world as time goes on. A teacher or a social worker. An ex-junkie! Sometimes it's better than having a master's in education.'
> 'Jokes,' he said. 'As a writer that's your main trouble. You don't want to recognize it. Tragedy! Plain tragedy! Historical tragedy! No hope. The end.'
> 'Oh, Pa,' I said. 'She could change.'
> 'In your own life, too, you have to look it in the face.' He took a couple of nitroglycerin. 'Turn to five,' he said, pointing to the dial on the oxygen tank. (166–7)

The narrator has constructed a story – a tragicomic story about a woman with options, with hope for the future – as a protective shield against reality. The fabricated story about hope, the story with 'the open destiny of life', functions as a way of denying the reality to her father's inevitable death. As the narrator revises her story about the heartbroken woman, she amends it in such a way that prevents closure. She believes that she has a responsibility not to let that woman die alone and miserable: 'She's my knowledge and my invention. I'm sorry for her. I'm not going to leave her there in that house crying'; 'She did change. Of course her son

211

never came home again. But right now, she's the receptionist in a
storefront community clinic in the East Village. Most of the customers are
young people, some old friends. The head doctor has said to her, "If we
only had three people in this clinic with your experiences ..."' (167).
And here the two stories merge in what becomes more and more a battle
for authorial control, since the narrator's father responds to her story's
conclusion by arguing, 'No. . . . Truth first. She will slide back. A person
must have character. She does not' (167).

Somewhat ironically and self-consciously, Paley's character has just
told the internal narrator-writer that her protagonist lacks character.
'Character' becomes the key in making stories real, because it creates
empathy and identification. This is the responsibility that Paley gives
her narrators and that she assumes herself. For 'A Conversation with
My Father' ends in mid-dialogue, ends with a question posed to the
narrator by her father: 'Tragedy! You too. When will you look it in the
face?' (167). Of course, what he wants her to look at is the inevitability
of his own death. Life, he implies, is indeed 'the absolute line between
two points' between living and dying. However, Paley's storytelling
defies such sharp delineation. In writing this story, Paley's narrator does
more than simply immortalize her father. He is not a static character any
more than her narrator is, but rather, an active participant in an ongoing
dialogue which gives him the last word.

Herein lies the 'perfect marginality'[15] of Grace Paley's prose: 'marginal'
because the line between fiction and reality is precarious and because,
for her characters, identity is a continual process; 'perfect' because both
self-identity and community are preserved in that precarious relation.
Through the telling of stories, the ongoing dialogues among her characters,
Paley creates a balance, which is, for her, a source of power. Dialogue
provides her characters with possibilities for the future because it prevents
resolution; it gives them the strength to insist on survival. Recording
personal histories, creating and reinventing interaction and events,
sustains her characters because it places them in the context of a wider
human history. It makes such stories public, part of the heritage from
which we all draw. The telling of stories becomes, in a very real sense,
the saving of lives.

Notes

1. 'Debts', in *Enormous Changes at the Last Minute* (New York: Farrar, Straus,
   Giroux, 1983), p. 10. Subsequent references are cited in the text.

2. Grace Paley herself refers to the transmission of stories as a kind of moral
   obligation: 'People ought to live in mutual aid and concern, listening to one

another's stories' ('A Symposium on Fiction', *Shenandoah*, 28 [Winter 1976], 31).

3. For a discussion of the evolving role of this character-narrator, see MINAKO BABA, 'Faith Darwin as Writer-Heroine: A Study of Grace Paley's Short Stories', *Studies in American Jewish Literature*, 7 (Spring 1988), 40–54.

4. 'Listening', in *Later the Same Day* (New York: Penguin, 1985), p. 210. Subsequent references are cited in the text.

5. *Habits of the Heart: Individualism and Commitment in American Life* (New York: Harper & Row, 1985), p. 153. Subsequent reference is cited in the text.

6. 'The Immigrant Story', in *Enormous Changes at the Last Minute*, p. 171. Subsequent references are cited in the text.

7. 'Friends', in *Later the Same Day*, p. 79. Subsequent references are cited in the text.

8. See *Studies in American Jewish Literature*, 3 (1983), 85–98.

9. 'Grace Paley and Tillie Olsen: Radical Jewish Humanists', *Response*, 46 (Spring 1984), 43. Subsequent references are cited in the text.

10. For a comprehensive account of the origins of Yiddish literature, see DAN MIRON, *A Traveler Disguised: A Study in the Rise of Modern Yiddish Fiction in the Nineteenth Century* (New York: Schocken Books, 1973), and my *Author As Character in the Works of Scholom Aleichem* (New York: Edwin Mellen Press, 1985).

11. SHOLOM ALEICHEM, 'Gitl Purishkevitch', in *Old Country Tales*, trans. Curt Leviant (New York: Paragon Books, 1966), p. 148.

12. 'Zagrowsky Tells', in *Later the Same Day*, p. 161.

13. I realize that the relation between Sholom Aleichem and Grace Paley, especially in terms of the function of Sholom Aleichem's monologists, is much too complex to address within the scope of this paper. Sholom Aleichem's monologists live in a very different world from that defined by Paley's playgrounds and neighborhoods of New York. I hope, however, that my much-abbreviated comparison is useful in placing Paley within the larger tradition of Jewish writers.

14. 'A Conversation with My Father', in *Enormous Changes*, p. 161. Subsequent references are cited in the text.

15. I have liberally borrowed this phrase from Cynthia Ozick's wonderful description of what it means to be 'a third-generation American Jew (though the first to have been native-born) perfectly at home and yet perfectly insecure, perfectly acculturated and yet perfectly marginal' ('Toward a New Yiddish: Note', in *Art & Ardor: Essays by Cynthia Ozick* [New York: Knopf, 1985], p. 152). For an analysis of the paradoxical position of contemporary Jewish-American women, see my 'The Outsider Within: Women in Contemporary Jewish-American Fiction', *Contemporary Literature*, 28 (Fall 1987), 378–93.

Selected Bibliography

Anthologies of critical essays

Anthologies of critical essays devoted exclusively to contemporary American women writers, or that include essays about contemporary American women writers, include:

BERG, TEMMA F., ANNA SHANNON ELFENBEIN, JEANNE LARSEN and ELISA KAY SPARKS, eds. *Engendering the Word: Feminist Essays in Psychosexual Poetics*. Urbana: University of Illinois Press, 1989.

BLACKSHIRE-BELAY, CAROL AISHA, ed. *Language and Literature in the African American Imagination*. Westport, CT: Greenwood Press, 1992.

CULLEY, MARGO, ed. *American Women's Autobiography: Fea(s)ts of Memory*. Madison: University of Wisconsin Press, 1992.

GEOK-LIN LIM, SHIRLEY and AMY LING, eds. *Reading the Literatures of Asian America*. Philadelphia: Temple University Press, 1992.

HERRERA-SOBEK, MARÍA and HELENA MARÍA VIRAMONTES, eds. *Chicana Creativity and Criticism: Charting New Frontiers in American Literature*. Houston, TX: Arte Público Press, 1988.

HORNO-DELGADO, ASUNCIÓN, NANCY S. STERNBACH, ELIANA ORTEGA and NINA M. SCOTT, eds. *Breaking Boundaries: Latina Writing and Critical Reading*. Amherst: University of Massachusetts Press, 1989.

SÀNCHEZ, ROSAURA and ROSA MARTÍNEZ CRUZ, eds. *Essays on La Mujer*. Los Angeles: Chicano Studies Center, 1977.

SINGH, AMRITJIT, JOSEPH T. SKERRETT, Jr. and ROBERT E. HOGAN, eds. *Memory, Narrative, and Identity: New Essays in Ethnic American Literature*. Boston, MA: Northeastern University Press, 1994.

SINGLEY, CAROL J. and SUSAN ELIZABETH SWEENEY, eds. *Anxious Power: Reading, Writing, and Ambivalence in Narrative by Women*. Albany, NY: SUNY Press, 1993.

WILLIS, SUSAN. *Specifying: Black Women Writing the American Experience*. Madison: University of Wisconsin Press, 1987.

ZINN, MAXINE BACA and BONNIE THORNTON DILL, eds. *Women of Color in U.S. Society*. Philadelphia: Temple University Press, 1994.

Monographs on contemporary American women's writing

BUTLER-EVANS, ELLIOTT. *Race, Gender and Desire: Narrative Strategies in the Fiction of Toni Cade Bambara, Toni Morrison and Alice Walker.* Philadelphia: Temple University Press, 1989.

CALLAHAN, JOHN F. *In the African-American Grain: The Pursuit of Voice in Twentieth-Century Black Fiction.* Urbana: University of Illinois Press, 1988.

CHEUNG, KING-KOK. *Articulate Silences: Hisaye Yamamoto, Maxine Hong Kingston, Joy Kogawa.* Ithaca, NY: Cornell University Press, 1993.

COSER, STELAMARIS. *Bridging the Americas: The Literature of Paule Marshall, Toni Morrison, and Gayl Jones.* Philadelphia: Temple University Press, 1994.

DAVIES, CAROLE BOYCE. *Black Women, Writing and Identity: Migrations of the Subject.* London: Routledge, 1994.

GHYMM, ESTHER MIKYUNG. *Images of Asian American Women by Asian American Women Writers.* New York: Peter Lang (Many Voices: Ethnic Literatures of the Americas Series), 1995.

GUTIÉRREZ-JONES, CARL. *Rethinking the Borderlands: Between Chicano Culture and Legal Discourse.* Berkeley: University of California Press, 1995.

HUMM, MAGGIE. *Border Traffic: Strategies of Contemporary Women Writers.* Manchester: Manchester University Press, 1991.

KRUPAT, ARNOLD. *The Voice in the Margin: Native American Literature and the Canon.* Berkeley: University of California Press, 1989.

MEESE, ELIZABETH A. *Crossing the Double-Cross: The Practice of Feminist Criticism.* Chapel Hill, NC: University of North Carolina Press, 1986.

PERREAULT, JEANNE. *Writing Selves: Contemporary Feminist Autobiography.* Minneapolis: University of Minnesota Press, 1995.

ROMINES, ANN. *The Home Plot: Women, Writing and Domestic Ritual.* Amherst: University of Massachusetts Press, 1992.

SOLLORS, WERNER, ed. *The Invention of Ethnicity.* New York: Oxford University Press, 1989.

WONG, SAU-LING CYNTHIA. *Reading Asian American Literature: From Necessity to Extravagance.* Princeton, NJ: Princeton University Press, 1993.

Anthologies of interviews with American women writers

JORDAN, SHIRLEY M., ed. *Broken Silences: Interviews with Black and White Women Writers.* New Brunswick, NJ: Rutgers University Press, 1993.

MAGLIN, NAN BAUER and DONNA PERRY, eds. *'Bad Girls'/'Good Girls': Women, Sex and Power in the Nineties.* New Brunswick, NJ: Rutgers University Press, 1996.

eighteenth-century literature, literature and the visual arts, and African American women writers. She is the author of *The Unbalanced Mind: Pope and the Rule of Passion* (Harvester Wheatsheaf, 1986), and is currently completing a book entitled *Transition and Exchange in the Novels of Toni Morrison*. The essay in this volume was originally published in *Feminist Criticism: Theory and Practice* (University of Toronto, 1991). Rebecca Ferguson lives in Wales with her husband and small son.

TONI FLORES was born of Spanish and Italian-American parents and grew up deeply connected to her Brooklynese immigrant extended families but living, incongruously, in Main Line and Chestnut Hill Philadelphia suburbs. She received her BA in anthropology from Bryn Mawr and her PhD in folklore from the University of Pennsylvania. She has taught since 1971 at Hobart and William Smith College, first in anthropology and then in American studies and women's studies. There she was co-founder of the Women's Studies Program, one of the earliest in the country, as well as co-founder of one of the earliest courses on Native American texts. She has done fieldwork in Mexico and Spain, focusing on women's work and creativity. She regards her work as the mother of five children and a teacher of young people as the main focus of her working life.

THOMAS FOSTER is Assistant Professor of English at Indiana University, where he teaches twentieth-century studies and is co-editor-in-chief of the journal *Genders*. He has published articles in *Signs, Genders, PMLA,* and *Comparative Literature,* as well as in such collections as *Feminist Theory in Practice and Process* (1989), *Engendering Men: The Question of Male Feminist Criticism* (1990), and *Centuries' Ends, Narrative Means* (1996). He is currently completing a book entitled *Homelessness at Home: Oppositional Practices and Modern Women's Writing*.

ROSE YALOW KAMEL is Professor of English at the Philadelphia College of Pharmacy and Sciences, where she teaches women's studies and autobiographical fiction. The essay included here was first published in *MELUS* 12, 3 (Fall 1985) and is also included in her book, *Aggravating the Conscience: Jewish American Literary Foremothers in the Promised Land* (New York: Peter Lang, 1988), which also includes chapters on Anzia Yezierska, Grace Paley, and E.M. Broner. She is completing a literary memoir, *Leah and Rosa: Wandering Jews in the Old World and the New,* which focuses on a mother–daughter relationship spanning the lives of working-class Jewish women from the turn of the century to the present.

SUSAN KOSHY is Assistant Professor of Asian American Studies at the University of California, Santa Barbara. Her articles on Asian American literature, transnationalism, feminism and South Asian racial identity have appeared in *The Yale Journal of Criticism, Transition, Diaspora* and in several anthologies. She is currently working on two books: one that theorizes Asian American literary production and another that deals with neocolonial discourses. She received her MA from Delhi University and her PhD from UCLA.

SIDNER LARSON is Assistant Professor of English at the University of Oregon. He was born on the Fort Belknap Indian Reservation and raised in the Gros Ventre Tribe. He has written introductions to *Indian Why Stories: Sparks from War Eagle's Lodge-Fire* (1996), *Indian Old Man Stories* (1996), and Walter McClintock's *The Old North Trail* (1992), all published by University of Nebraska Press. His autobiography, *Catch Colt,* was published by University of Nebraska Press in 1995. His articles have appeared in *MELUS, American Indian Culture and Research Journal, American Indian Quarterly,* and *Studies in American Indian Literature,* and his entry for James Welch is in the *Dictionary of Literary Biography, Native American Writers of the United States.*

MARY O'CONNOR is Associate Professor of English at McMaster University in Hamilton, Ontario, Canada, where she teaches American literature, feminist theory and African-American women writers. Her present research is a study of women's representations of domestic objects, and she is also working on the modernist photographer, Margaret Watkins. She has a PhD in English from the University of Toronto. Her publications include a book on John Davidson (Scottish Academic Press, 1987), as well as articles on Bakhtin and Kristeva (in *Bakhtin: Carnival and Other Subjects,* Rodopi, 1993), Alice Munro and Bharati Mukherjee, and Zora Neale Hurston.

DONNA PERRY is Professor of English at William Paterson University, in New Jersey, where she also teaches women's studies. Her interviews with Jamaica Kincaid and several other writers discussed in this collection appear in *Backtalk: Women Writers Speak Out* (Rutgers University Press, 1993). Her latest book, *'Bad Girls'/'Good Girls': Women, Sex, and Power in the Nineties* (Rutgers University Press, 1996), is a co-edited collection of essays on contemporary feminism.

NANCY J. PETERSON is Associate Professor of English and American Studies, and Assistant Editor of *Modern Fiction Studies* at Purdue University, Indiana, where she teaches women's literature and twentieth-century American literature with a particular interest in race and gender studies. She is the editor of *Toni Morrison: Critical and Theoretical Approaches* (Johns Hopkins University Press, 1997) and is finishing a book titled *Against Amnesia: Contemporary North American Women Writers and the Crisis in Historical Memory*, which also includes the essay on Erdrich reprinted in this collection.

MALINI JOHAR SCHUELLER is Associate Professor of English at the University of Florida, where she teaches courses on race theory, women of colour, postcoloniality and American literature. She is the author of a book on personal narratives, *The Politics of Voice: Liberalism and Social Criticism from Franklin to Kingston* (State University of New York Press, 1992), and another book, *U.S. Orientalism: Gender, Race, and Nation in Literature, 1790–1890* (University of Michigan Press, 1997). She has edited a special issue of *Prose Studies*, entitled *U.S. Personal Narratives and the Subject of Multiculturalism*, and has published essays in such journals as *American Literature, Genders, Criticism*, and *Modern Fiction Studies*.

YVONNE YARBRO-BEJARANO is Professor of Spanish, Portuguese and Chicana/o Studies at Stanford University, California. She is the author of *Feminism and the Honor Plays of Lope de Vega* (Purdue University Press, Indiana, 1994), co-editor of *Chicano Art: Resistance and Affirmation* (Wight Art Gallery, California, 1991), and has published numerous articles on Chicana/o literature. She has worked to develop a digital archive called 'Chicana Art', soon to be on the Internet, that features over 2,000 images by leading Chicana artists. She is now director of the Chicana/o Studies program in Stanford's Center for Comparative Studies in Race and Ethnicity. Her most recent book is *'The Right to Passion': Collected Essays on Cherríe Moraga*, forthcoming from the University of Texas Press.

LOIS PARKINSON ZAMORA is Professor of Comparative Literature and Dean of the College of Humanities, Fine Arts and Communication at the University of Houston, Texas. Her area of specialization is contemporary fiction in the Americas. Her books include: *Writing the Apocalypse: Historical Vision in Contemporary U.S. and Latin American Fiction* (Cambridge University Press, 1989); *Magical Realism: Theory, History, Community* (Duke University Press, 1995), co-edited with Wendy B. Faris; *The Usable Past: The Imagination of History in Recent Fiction of the Americas* (Cambridge University Press, 1997); and *Image and Memory: Photography from Latin American, 1866–1994* (University of Texas Press, 1998), co-edited with Wendy Watriss. She frequently writes about the visual arts and their relation to Latin American literature, and is preparing a book on that subject to be titled *The Inordinate Eye*.

Index

221